GUIDANCE FOR NAVIGATING
Your Spiritual Awakening

33 TRUE STORIES FROM
WISE WOMEN WORLDWIDE

divine flow
PUBLISHING CO.
Minneapolis, MN

Cover design: Jennifer Ann Birge

Published in the United States by Divine Flow Publishing Co.
Minneapolis, MN • www.divineflow.co

Hardcover Print ISBN: 979-8-9916794-5-9

Paperback Print ISBN: 979-8-9916794-4-2

eBook ISBN: 979-8-9916794-3-5

Audiobook ISBN: 979-8-9916794-6-6

Publisher's Cataloging-in-Publication Data

Title: Soul rising : guidance for navigating your spiritual awakening / Divine Flow Publishing Co.

Description: Minneapolis, MN : Divine Flow Publishing Co., 2025. | Summary: Anthology of 33 essays written by wise women worldwide, sharing their stories and guidance on navigating a spiritual awakening and how they have integrated their expanded awareness into their life and work. Provides reassurance for those developing their intuition and seeking a like-minded community to learn from.

Identifiers: LCCN: 2025905325 | ISBN 9798991679459 (hardback) | ISBN 9798991679442 (pbk.) | ISBN 9798991679435 (ebook) | ISBN 9798991679466 (audiobook)

Subjects: LCSH: Spiritual life. | Women – Religious aspects. | Intuition. | Self-actualization (Psychology). | Spirituality. | BISAC: RELIGION / Spirituality. | SELF-HELP / Personal Growth / General. | SELF-HELP / Spiritual.

Classification: LCC BL625.7 S68 2025 | DDC 291.4082--dc23

LC record available at https://lccn.loc.gov/2025905325

To all of the brave souls who are bold enough to speak up about their spiritual experiences so we can create a world where no one has to be afraid to be their true selves.

Table of Contents

Step into the Sacred Circle

By Natalie Walstein
Minneapolis, Minnesota, USA

I remember going through my first soul activation and feeling scared, crazy, and alone. I didn't know anyone I could talk to during a time when I desperately needed support the most. The urgent questions I had about my increasing intuitive abilities could not be answered by anyone I knew in my life, so I was forced to navigate them all on my own.

Have you started seeing signs, hearing voices, sensing hidden things that don't seem to be fully *here*? If you're reading this, you have awoken to the call of your soul's expansion, and now you are craving an entirely different and more spiritually driven type of life.

Perhaps your soul has begun stirring as you question the mundane, uncomfortable, or unfair reality you've been handed, and now you find yourself seeking something more meaningful and aligned. Maybe you've realized that you have unknowingly been choosing the path of suffering on this human plane, and now you are ready to rise above the noise of your ego mind (and other people's voices) and shine. These are all clues that your consciousness—your soul—is rising!

When you have a spiritual awakening, your entire perspective of the world changes. At the same time, whatever (or whomever) can no longer meet you at your heightened energetic frequency must fall away. This can be strangely uncomfortable or even earth-shattering.

When you are left with nothing, where do you turn? You will need a new community, a source of support to guide you back to yourself and your own inherent power, but many don't know where to find this. This is the purpose for which this book, *Soul Rising*, was created. Written by 33 wise women from all over the world, we have gathered together to share our stories, spread our soul guidance, and show you that you are not alone. Although "333" is the magical number for spirit guides, we seek to become your guides in human form.

We have been through the muck of transforming our fear into love while realizing there is more to this world than meets the third eye. Through our experiences, we have learned to rise above the grief, worry, frustration, and sadness that has been caused by our old, known world, shaking loose to claim our place as spiritual leaders in our own right. We've been in your shoes and know how it feels to question your reality, your sanity, and everything you've been taught was true about the world while simultaneously seeking to find your footing on a higher plane.

Our 33 authors live in different places, scattered like fireflies in the night that are lighting up across the globe, and write in different dialects to show you just how far and wide humanity's spiritual evolution has grown. While our awakening experiences may differ from your own—depending on our soul missions and unique life journeys—our sentiments are all the same: humanity is evolving, and we are certainly not the first (or the last) to walk this path.

Just as puberty has become a normal rite of passage into adulthood, it is highly likely that most of us will be discovering our multidimensional nature more and more over time. As humanity develops in conscious awareness, we are growing towards greater spiritual maturity, too.

With spiritual awakenings becoming the norm, we will need support, guidance, and reassurance that the breakdowns that lead to our breakthroughs are all part of the ride. We will need to know that what we are experiencing is a normal part of the new age that is already fast approaching—or the "now age" that many of us are already living in.

The stories in this book were brought together because it is more crucial than ever that we have raw, real, and open conversations about navigating our spiritual evolution. This way, we can harness our gifts for the highest good of ourselves and humanity instead of being afraid of our power. We cannot stomp out this sensitive, empathic, and intuitive side of ourselves; therefore, we need to learn to embrace it.

At this pivotal time of change on our planet, we must declare what is happening and own our truth. The Earth is rising in consciousness, and so are we. We are growing and expanding as souls. As our collective vibration rises, ancient knowledge is returning anew, and the lower, negative, and dark vibrations must be purged.

Don't you think this process will feel even messier and more complicated if we keep our experiences hidden underground?

As alone as I once felt while trying to integrate my spiritual side, I now know there are many other so-called "woo-woo weirdos" out there who have had similar experiences of trying to figure out what to do with their newfound spiritual gifts—not to mention navigating the fear, indecision, breakdowns, and breakthroughs that accompany them. The gaslighting and rejection of our spiritual beliefs by others certainly isn't helpful, either!

In my world, spirituality was once a *hush-hush* subject you made extra sure no one would overhear you discussing in restaurants and cafés. We all evolve at our own rate, and it seemed like others around me were not keeping up with my pace. Because of this, it was isolating and confusing trying to process my ever-changing perceptions of myself and this magical, mystical, new world without anyone around me to help validate, explain, or confirm what I was experiencing.

Everything began to change when I slowly started to share my spiritual awakening stories with others. By doing so, I eventually attracted a community of other spiritual friends who knew how I felt. By opening the door to these deeper conversations, many of them have gone on to share crazy stories similar to my own. This has helped me feel more accepted and safe in a world that once made me feel like a complete and utter alien. Can you relate?

My Awakening Story

Even though I've always felt I was a more sensitive child than others around me growing up, my spiritual superpowers didn't officially turn on until I was an adult.

Before then, I often felt pulled to a more mystical side of life, including Tarot cards, astrology, and dream interpretation; however, my involvement with the spiritual world was more like witnessing a spectator sport that I watched from the sidelines. I was eager to learn and gobble up everything I could on esoteric subjects, but I did so without a real visceral experience of what it truly meant to be "a soul having a human experience" (as the gurus preach), until my spiritual awakening eventually activated within me.

Deep down, I always knew there was something more to this world, but I couldn't yet see it in plain sight. Imagine my surprise when I began receiving prophetic dreams in which I saw visions of my future before it happened. Although this magical ability took its sweet time to kick in rather than being activated at birth, it arrived in perfect timing, just as all spiritual awakenings do.

In my mid-20s, I was beginning an amazing journey into the unknown, and I needed all the divine help I could get. Each prophetic dream I received showed me what would happen next, so I could keep the faith as I escaped my suburban upbringing and began exploring what else was out there for me in this big, wide world.

Born and raised in Minnesota, USA, my partner (at the time) and I were feeling called to re-wild ourselves and live a healthier lifestyle somewhere with nice warm weather all year round. Both hopeless dreamers and, some would say, "hippies", we flung ourselves into the unknown by selling everything we owned and moving across the ocean to an island we hoped to make our home—without ever even visiting beforehand. It was an adventure, and we were young, in love, and finally free. Yet, even with those prophetic dreams, I still remained mostly blissfully unaware of the extent of the intense experiences—and spiritual activation—that would soon be greeting me.

There we were, following our dreams and listening to our hearts, and then everything fell apart. Moving to rural Hawai'i was a big change. We certainly hadn't anticipated how insanely difficult it would be to find even just a temporary home in a remote region where very few rental opportunities were to be found. The "Great Hawaiian House Hunt" saw us hopping from a mold- and fire-ant-infested jungle bungalow to a lime green shack on a lava field with no running water, and then worst of all, to a mattress on someone's screened-in garage floor.

Ahead of time, I dreamed about each place we would rent while we continued looking for our home. When we finally arrived at each new rental after the previous stay had expired, I sighed with the relief of recognition. These weren't exactly five-star establishments (by any means), but I was glad to know I was at least following the right track, thanks to my dreams. I certainly didn't have time to question these psychic impressions, which were new realizations I was coming to find about myself, because I was so deep in survival mode.

We had great difficulty finding a house to buy that was within our dwindling budget. After more than six months, we were lucky to find a hidden treehouse down the road from our rental with a sign posted outside that simply offered a phone number and stated: "For Sale by Owner". We miraculously became its new homeowners and, as it turned out, Airbnb hosts, thanks to an extra studio unit it had in the back.

We thought we had finally reached the finish line on our quest to live our dreams, but over this time, my partner and I both became increasingly ill—the complete opposite reason for why we originally wanted to come to this island in the first place (we were initially drawn to the Big Island of Hawai'i, in particular, because of their ban on GMOs).

Within weeks of finally moving into our new treehouse, I woke up sicker than I ever had in my life. It was too painful to even lie down, so I slept sitting straight up on the couch. I couldn't eat, I couldn't sleep, and I kept passing out. I had no idea what was wrong with me. After hours in the emergency room, I was eventually diagnosed with cancer.

Note: I later found out that I did not actually have cancer—it was a total misdiagnosis, the kind that comes from being in a rural hospital with limited resources—and it was not until nearly ten years later that I finally discovered I had actually been experiencing complications from mold toxicity. Needless to say, it's a long story, but the "cancer" word sort of tends to scare people, so I wanted you to have the facts. Regardless of the misdiagnosis, the pain and weakness I was experiencing were real, and I nearly died.

I came home from the hospital in disbelief. The oncologist had said they wouldn't know *for sure* how to treat the so-called cancer unless they removed one of my organs. Unhappy with that so-called "solution", I decided I would ignore the doctors and try to heal myself. I tried juicing and a raw food diet, but I still sunk deeper and deeper into my illness.

At the same time, we had an unexpected guest visiting our newly opened vacation rental that week. When our guests—a normal-looking middle-aged man and his wife—arrived, I received a rather out-of-the-ordinary embrace. It was certainly not typical for us to hug our guests when they arrived, and it was even more unusual that I would leave the couch where I was camping out to come down and say hello. Although I was sick and not quite of sound mind to begin with, this hug seemed to bring a strange spiritual activation.

When I returned to the main house and looked out the window, I began noticing that the lawn was breathing. I marveled in awe as waves of energy moved through the grass. I heard the deafening sound of crickets, but when I asked my partner if he also heard them, he said, "No, why?"

It was as if the universe was rising up all around me as the veil between me and other realms dissolved and disappeared. I started seeing visions of my former lives—one day, remembering a time of fleeing Lemuria by transmogrifying into a sea creature and plunging myself into the ocean, and the next, believing I was a warrior princess as I tied small braids at the sides of my head and donned my longest, most colorful dress. When my partner left for work each day, he had no idea what—or whom—he was going to come back home to. I didn't know who I was either!

At night came the hauntings. I was being terrorized by ghosts. As I clutched my burning sage wand to dispel the most negative vibes I had ever experienced, I suddenly had a strange feeling about the guests who were visiting—especially the man who had hugged me. To my own surprise, I told my partner I strongly believed he was a shaman. I had never actually met a shaman, nor did I know what they looked like (or, really, what they even did).

It was the middle of the night, and I was ready to march down there to force him to leave so I could finally get some sleep, but in my crazed state, my partner tried to calm me down so I wouldn't make a scene. Can you imagine the review they would leave? *A crazed lady woke us up in the middle of the night and demanded for us to leave because she claimed I sent ghosts to haunt her!*

The final night of our guests' stay was the roughest. I heard voices all night and felt frozen with fear. I imagined it was the end of the world as apocalyptic scenes danced in my head. At the same time, I was incredibly weak, starving, and barely holding on for dear life. I was completely confused about what was real and what was contrived by my mind!

When morning eventually came, I was surprised to discover I was still alive. At first, I heard the sound of birds flapping their wings. Along with them came angels overhead. The angels asked me telepathically if I'd still like to stay and live out my life. I spoke my answer out loud: "Yes." And then, finally, I fell asleep.

Later that morning, our mysterious vacation rental guests departed, generously leaving me with a big meal to eat because they had heard I was sick. *And would you believe it?* They also left me a shaman necklace as a gift! It was a wire-wrapped crystal hanging from a buckskin string. As I held it in my hands, I was giddy with shock, knowing that I had been right all along while simultaneously realizing they may not have been quite as malicious as they seemed. As these strange guests drove further and further away, I seemed to come back to my senses while the all-encompassing visions I had been experiencing all week finally dissipated.

Although I was given the choice of whether or not to leave this life, I chose to stay. I was not ready to die with my magic still in me. You see, in the weeks before I dwindled into 80 pounds of nothingness, I had begun studying astrology. Living on an island where the stars and planets shone extra bright—the very same island where NASA takes pictures of space—the study of the stars had piqued my interest more than ever before in my life.

When we were still rental-hopping, prophetic dreams weren't the only thing lighting my way. I became obsessed with reading my horoscope to help me make sense of these confusing and challenging times. The astrologers who wrote them seemed to know exactly what I was going through and what I needed to hear each day to feel reassured. As I refreshed my horoscope app each day, their words gave me a magical feeling of calm amidst the chaos.

Inspired to learn more about astrology, I unexpectedly found that I could "see into" the symbols and feel their meanings deep in my soul. I had discovered not a new skill but, more likely, a long-forgotten one. While others complained about how complicated astrology was, I picked it up with ease within just a few weeks.

I had finally started to understand myself and the purpose of my life as an ultra-sensitive person. My astrology chart helped me see that I was meant to help people on a deeper, spiritual level. As a double Pisces, I was naturally intuitive and psychic, but these were sides of me I had kept hidden within me. I had spent my whole life up until this point trying to pretend I was the same as everyone else so I could fit in. As I dove deeper into astrology, I discovered that my unique abilities and sensitivities were a special gift.

Furthermore, I realized I could use this ancient modality of astrology to help others find their calling, and in doing so, I would be living in alignment with my own. Astrology was a safe, systematic, and structured way for me to explore my intuition and my newfound ability to receive clairvoyant visions. These abilities would blossom and develop even further in later years as I began channeling my higher self, angels, ancestors, ascended masters, galactic beings, and other spirit guides.

I still don't completely understand the purpose of the shaman's activation or the ghosts that terrorized me in the night, but it had a profound effect on me that changed me for the rest of my life. Whether it was the illness making me lose my mind so I could find my soul or, more likely, the universe conspiring to do everything in its power to "wake me up" and set me on my rightful path, it worked!

This chapter of my wild and winding story ends with me giving up my home on the Big Island so I could heal, painfully ending my 7.5-year soul contract with my then-fiancé (with 7.5 years being the length of a karmic Saturn cycle, as I would learn as I furthered my astrological studies), and moving back into my dad's house—and my old high school bedroom—in Minnesota, where I slowly struggled to regain my health.

As I made this transition, a massive volcano on the Big Island erupted, sending hot lava shooting only three blocks from my former jungle treehouse home. It turns out I had given up everything I thought I had cared about most (before my awakening) at the exact perfect time. Fate had stepped in, and I no longer questioned my urge to flee.

Back in my hometown, I started a business from my sick bed as a professional astrologer specializing in helping spiritual seekers discover their soul mission. It quickly became wildly successful on levels I had never anticipated! Eventually developing into a multiple six-figure business with a team of five people working under me, I created an entire empire from my spiritual gifts. Another 7.5 years later (and another Saturn cycle), I was called to evolve *beyond this* yet again... but this is how my initiation into spiritual entrepreneurship all began.

The Catalyst

When I finally became brave enough to share this awakening story, it became the top-played episode on my podcast, with well over ten thousand downloads. I was so scared to share it initially because I thought people wouldn't possibly be able to believe me (I barely believed it myself!). However, I wanted to share my story so that people would understand what a spiritual awakening is like in case they were wondering if they were having one of their own.

The number of people who contacted me, after listening, to tell me they had shared it with their friends showed me that others *definitely* wanted to hear more stories about spiritual awakenings. I saw there was a huge demand for these messages! I believe this is because we are all going through our own versions of spiritual awakenings in our own way, whether they come from changes in our health, relationships, or work, which result in a growing ability to see beyond the veil. Hearing about others' experiences helps us feel validated and comforted on our journey back home to ourselves and to Source.

Today, I have no problem talking loudly in public about the latest downloads from my spirit guides or bringing up Mercury Retrograde to the muggly post office clerk when techy things go awry. I constantly remind people to ask for help from the universe and follow how they feel, sharing openly about my synchronicities and telling people around me that everything in life is a sign from our guides.

By releasing my story instead of keeping it hidden and "safe", I have given myself permission to be fully me, unafraid to be seen as the mystical soul I was born to be. This metamorphosis occurred because, over time, I practiced telling my spiritual awakening stories so much that it no longer scared me. This opened the door for others to share their experiences as well. I hope that, after reading this book, you will not be as afraid anymore to share yours, too!

Soul Rising is your new spiritual community in a book—the one I know I wish I had when I was initiated into this wild, new, ethereal realm of otherworldly experiences without a physical human guide or mentor to light my way. Now, all 33 of us are here to help guide yours. Step into our sacred circle of women who have come together to share their spiritual awakening experiences. You will be cradled, held, and supported, and you will know that you are not alone. You are not crazy, psycho, or a total mess—you are on the cutting edge of spiritual advancement just like the rest of us.

Natalie Walstein is the founder of Divine Flow Publishing Co., where she and her team now help spiritual entrepreneurs publish beautifully designed books that are raising the vibration of the planet.

As a former astrologer and quantum hypnosis practitioner, dream oracle, artist, and angel medium, she is a lifelong spiritual seeker who is constantly drawn to explore our connection with our souls and other worlds that live behind the veil.

She is the author of Messages from the Higher Self *(2024) and* Find Your Cosmic Calling: A Guide to Discovering Your Life's Work with Astrology *(2022).*

Website: www.divineflow.co

Podcast: www.divineflow.co/podcast

Instagram: www.instagram.com/divineflow.co

02

Arriving Home

By Kerry Ferber
Lisbon, Portugal

So, here you are! Your journey has led you here. Here in this present moment to these words within this book. Here on this planet, during these dynamic times. Okay, okay, okay, I'm not sharing with you anything you don't already know. Yet these stories and insights from 33 unique, powerhouse women in one book?! You are receiving perspective, insight, and wisdom that will be new to you and may or may not resonate in varying degrees. This text can act as a tool to assist you in your own remembering journey if you are truly open to receiving it as such: an awakening, a divine activation of sorts to connect you back to your own stories and truth. Thank you for embarking on another phase of your expansion simply by cracking open this text.

The truth is, you are here on Earth for a reason, many actually. This incarnation can feel like a season—a sacred blip in your oversoul's journey throughout time and space. Yet you're here now—reading this and courageously choosing to explore the vastness of your soul while being in human form. So, thank you again for arriving here.

Of all the times to engage with such a tool on Earth, you're right on time. Welcome to the gathering of soul family! It might sound cheesy or cliché, but it's true. This book is simply one physical tool that acts as a divine thread to weave a beautiful tapestry of soulful connection on a planet that is ascending, a.k.a. remembering, alongside us.

You are holding this book on a particular location of the globe—whether this place is somewhere you live or are visiting. Regardless, the land you are physically on in the present moment is consciously and unconsciously connecting with you through nature, energetic sensations, synchronicities, animals, plants, other people, and this book—all at once.

As you continue to read these stories, you will be simultaneously connecting to the particular grid or area of land where you are. This creates an intricate web of light around our beloved planet—specific light frequencies from you, the land you are currently on, each of these authors, our soul families both on and off this planet, and the heart of Gaia. I call this grid working and it naturally happens simply by being present with yourself, nature, and what you are engaging with in that moment.

You are grid working right now by feeling and sensing the energies of the land where you currently are, how they interact with your innate frequencies, receiving and processing the words and energy within this book along with the loving energy from everyone else who has already read this and those who will in the future. It's a continuous creation of light precisely woven all over Earth by every person choosing to read this book. Powerful stuff! Alright, let's dive in.

This chapter is written from my heart to yours, casually yet sincerely, as if we are gathering around a fire together, witnessing the comforting glow of gentle sparks and flames. You may find yourself in these words or simply receive what I share as my truth to deepen your own knowing of truth within you.

My life has been a series of awakenings, creating one wild and adventurous human experience that only continues. My major awakening moments have been formed and shaped by the compilation of more subtle awakenings. It's hard to pinpoint the first spiritual awakening or the most impactful one, as I believe it has all miraculously unfolded in micro and macro ways since birth, whether I was consciously aware of it or not.

Life has offered me many opportunities to experience layers of fear, anxiety, grief, disassociation, victimhood, shame, confusion, and attachment—only to be given chances to realize that feeling these emotions over time evoked a deep yearning to experience something totally different. It propelled me to seriously consider that there had to be other ways of living, even thriving, on this planet.

This invited me to feel the enormity of my feelings and the stories in my mind and body before calling me up to something different. It propelled me to sprout through the density of the soil and come into my own knowing and power as a co-creator of my reality. It created spaciousness in my body to feel and open to the divinity in all beings in entirely new ways.

Essentially, I felt my higher self calling me up into new levels of curious devotion to explore living a heart-led life. A life and human experience rooted in freedom, sovereignty, and empowerment, trusting that I could do that by focusing my energy, opening my heart to the mystery of it all, and allowing life's intelligence to flow. I began to remember who I was without societal conditioning, complex family dynamics and relationship soul contracts, and deep programming of fear, doubt, self-deprecation, and lack.

Quite imperfectly, moment by moment, I chose to lean into opening myself to allow love, limitlessness, wonder, serendipity, compassion, grace, and expansion within my body, mind, heart, and spirit. After years of moving through life in excess of caution, playing small, and abandoning myself, I began to deepen my awareness and presence in the now moment. I began to feel worthy of receiving more of my own love, more of my own attention and care.

I've walked paths of fear to reroute and return to a newfound sense of devotion to harnessing the power of choice in every moment to walk and create paths of love, curiosity, openness, and empowerment instead. These pathways are created imperfectly, showing up to this human experience with trust in my own truth and a deep knowing of the innate wholeness and divinity within me, this planet, and all beings everywhere.

This remembrance of sorts came through various interesting experiences in my life. The nitty gritty version of my journey begins as a very anxious child who frequently disassociated from my body and found safety in fragmenting my energy in big and small ways. I experienced a phase of pulling out my eyelashes (unaware at the time that it was an anxious impulse control disorder). I was known as the "sorry girl" growing up, perpetually apologizing for seemingly anything and everything. I experienced panic attacks. My parents divorced when I was 16, right at the start of exploring my femininity and sense of self. I graduated college after a period of academic probation due to intense anxiety and an overall lack of focus. I began a career in management and worked a number of years in Human Resources before I found myself feeling utterly exhausted, overextended, confused, frustrated, and angry with myself and how this could be my life. I had unhealthy patterns of over-eating and extreme shopping—behaviors of attempting to self-soothe in order to receive a sense of love, nourishment, safety, and security.

Overall, I had been carrying a lot of shame and guilt—unaware of where it was actually coming from because some of it didn't even feel like mine. How could I have allowed all of this to compile itself like this? How was this my reality, and how had this become my current experience?

I became acutely aware of how I was consciously and unconsciously taking on other people's energy, fear, and confusion and making it my own. I also became aware of where I was doing this for our planet Gaia as well. All the while, I was losing touch with my own feelings and truest essence. I did not know who I was, what I valued and treasured in life, what my needs and boundaries were, and seriously wondered why I was even here.

In 2017, a friend of mine introduced me to Reiki, and it felt like a soulful sip of connecting to something true: energy... a spark of remembrance! While I had been intrigued by mediumship and astrology for years and explored a few sessions, Reiki became a doorway into a more energetic and spiritual experience in my journey. I became a Reiki master and kept the spiritual side of my life relatively low-key. Soon after, I decided to leave my 9-5 job, move to a new city, and embark on entrepreneurship.

Becoming an entrepreneur was a huge spiritual initiation for me. I still find that it's one of the most potent pathways for soul growth and evolution, as everything within you is mirrored in this creation that is your business. These awakenings have revealed my true calling, desires, and confidence to trust my inner voice, which has allowed my business to pivot and realign in beautiful ways.

Another layer of this time period was that I experienced many waves of grief. I had nine loved ones pass onto the other side within a span of eight years, one of which being my Dad. He passed away in January 2020, less than three weeks after my business launch party and just a few weeks before the global pandemic. I was appointed Executrix of his will and estate, which was simultaneously a true honor to close out his life on Earth and a total chaotic whirlwind that I navigated while living alone and not in a romantic relationship at the time.

Relationships have significantly shifted throughout these awakenings; some friendships have completed, and others have deepened and evolved. Family relationships and dynamics have felt amplified, yet my role within them has felt clearer and freer. Romantically, I was almost engaged twice to two different men who were not in full alignment. In a span of a year and a half, I experienced a karmic relationship, met my twin flame and began that uniquely intense journey, and then met a divine counterpart. The most significant shifts have been how I connect to myself and my own heart. Leading from that space with full confidence and trust in my choices and actions, along with speaking my truth from my heart, has been a true gift.

The spiritual space has shifted over the years, as has our collective consciousness and interpretation of spirituality on this planet. I have odd yet profound stories that have significantly strengthened my inner knowing while also activating new layers of discernment. I witnessed spiritual abuse during a spiritual retreat in Egypt, I met someone at Mount Shasta who claimed he was from the future, and I attended a spiritual retreat in Oregon that ended up being a very strange attempt at a cult initiation. All of which were doozies, destabilizing me in many ways. I look back at some of those instances now with humour and deep appreciation for how each instance has shaped and fortified my sense of self, along with a newfound connection to what true spirituality means to me.

As I became more conscious of my grid working missions, I was guided to many particular places to 'anchor in the drop' of light frequencies onto precise ley lines, sacred sites, cities, and rural areas around the world. I physically moved my life from place to place, ping-ponging across the United States, seeking a sense of resonance in ways that my life felt incomplete in: finding an aligned guy, creating a wonderful partnership and family, discovering an aligned community in which I felt I could contribute and receive from, and rooting down in an area where I felt I could nest into. It wasn't until I moved abroad to Portugal that I began feeling more embodied in all parts of my being, propelling another huge threshold of soul growth. I received a new astrological chart (different from my natal chart and not a soul walk-in) representing a new era of myself, acting as a map for this next expression of my evolution.

I share all of these brief and chunky nuances because of the context they provide. Awakenings are multi-layered and multi-faceted because we are multi-layered and multi-faceted beings. The story of awakening is found in the layers, pieces, and aspects that you allow yourself to see, feel, and experience. It's found in how open you allow your heart to be, and how available you are to trusting the natural intelligence that guides us when our mind doesn't get in the way.

A spiritual journey doesn't just "happen"; it only occurs when you are truly open to embark on this level of awareness and remembrance.

This is when your human self looks at your life and knows in the depths of your being that it's meant to experience more than a humdrum, auto-pilot existence. It unlocks a wellspring of inner wisdom and courage to empower yourself to feel your emotions in order for a new story to emerge. A self-liberation of sorts. Trusting your unique knowing, bravely claiming the sense of home that is within you, and having the courage to integrate and embody it as such is key.

Navigating the various awakenings forges a level of grace, trust, and inner strength, yet integrating it sometimes requires the most courage. It's an act of bravery to sit and be truly present with all that is changing, unfolding, and revealing itself to you and within you. Yet this is the invitation of our individual and collective human experience!

What I've realized is that Earth is not just a planet of density that we are forced to adjust to and helplessly navigate. We are not meant to slog through this human experience to complete karmic contracts and free ourselves from societal constructs, agendas, and boxes just to reach the other side where we feel free and light again. We are meant to experience that joyful freedom, creation, and divine expression here. Gaia and nature remind us of that. Seeing her as so much more than the perceived density projected upon her and more than the Mother archetype she's been bestowed with. Witnessing her truth as an empowered divine feminine energy propelled by love, joy, wonder, intelligence, and awe has been huge in my awakening journey. It's a sacred remembering to know that my soul is a facilitator of unifying the spiritual realms and the earthly world. An aspect of my spiritual responsibility is to keep the channels of light between heaven and earth not only open but healthy, vibrant, and stable.

You navigate spiritual awakenings through your relationship with trust. Through active courage and bravery towards the unknown, to see a path of fear that you could walk, but instead, choose to walk the path of love through your grounded actions and choices.

Your spiritual awakening journey can offer many wild moments that illuminate and reveal more of your innate wholeness and divinity. After years of disassociation from my body—from childhood, my early and mid-twenties, 15 years of taking hormonal birth control pills, and varying degrees of trauma—seeking safety and a sense of validation from outside of myself, I'm choosing to focus my life force energy towards becoming more embodied. To choose the home that is my body. My heart. This expression of my oversoul in this time and space while on this planet.

This human experience is a series of many, many awakening moments that allow your truest essence to blossom into your fullest expression. May you remember the innate home within yourself. May you let your heart be light. May you open to life's natural intelligence to move you and move through you. May you authentically reveal yourself to this planet. May you remember your creative power with every step you take, simply by walking your own path of love, surrender, and trust. Welcome to the journey of remembering that your soul is always rising.

As you devote yourself to this voyage, navigating the unknown and unfamiliar becomes more empowering. Your curiosity expands as you remember your own distinct expression of love, joy, excitement, grace, and vibrancy within your being. Home is here in the present moment. You have arrived. TA DA! Welcome home. Cheers to your soul rising, dear one.

Kerry Ferber is an Intuitive Guide, creator of Divine Gaia Codes™ and Grounded Grieving® here to bridge you back to your heart and the heart of this planet. She empowers souls to trust in their personal truth, embody their fullest essence, and confidently beam their inner light to live a more empowered and vibrant human experience. Although Kerry currently lives in Europe, she considers herself a traveler and a global citizen of this wondrous planet.

Website: www.kerryferber.com

Instagram: www.instagram.com/kerry.ferber

Youtube: www.youtube.com/@kerryferber

03

Awakening the Miracles Within

By Nicole Sanguinetti
San Jose, California, USA

As a psychic medium, intuitive, and empath, my journey to awakening and accepting my gifts has been filled with several spiritual awakenings.

I will never forget the first time I *saw* Spirit. I was just ten years old when my grandma passed away. As my family gathered at her home to take care of her affairs and arrangements, I spent time doing what she and I loved to do together: swimming. As I played in the shallow end of her pool, I took a breath and blew it out so I could sink to the bottom and see how long I could hold my breath underwater.

I remember having the distinct feeling that someone was watching me. I opened my eyes under the water and noticed the shadow of a silhouette standing over the pool. I popped up out of the water to check, but no one was there. I took another breath and sank back down to the bottom of the shallow end.

The feeling of someone watching me did not subside. In fact, it became stronger, and I started to get anxious. As I opened my eyes again, I noticed something even stranger than the shadowed silhouette I had seen reflecting into the water a few moments before. I glanced over to the edge of the pool and saw two legs dangling into the water!

I immediately popped up again, expecting my mom to be the one with her feet hanging into the pool. But no one was there. By this time, I was starting to get spooked, but I continued to swim. I took one more breath and blew it out hard, forcing myself back to the bottom of the pool.

When I opened my eyes, I saw two legs, two *whole* legs. There they were, standing right next to me. When I followed the legs upwards, I saw a floral-printed skirt bathing suit. The exact bathing suit that my grandma wore all the time. I jumped up out of the water fast, breaking the spell of whatever had just occurred, and ran out of the pool screaming to my mom, "I saw grandma. *She* is in the pool!"

Thus began my initiation with the Spirit World.

As a kid, you'd think I would have been more open and accepting of what would become my "new normal," but that wasn't how things moved along at first. I was born and raised as a Catholic. These things were not accepted or allowed to be spoken about.

When I started to see even more Spirits after making that first contact with my grandma, I was told not to speak about it. Growing up, I was bullied a lot. From my wildly out-of-control curly hair to my ability to talk non-stop (or, as my teachers called it, being "disruptive towards her peers") to my consistent anxiety. The last thing I wanted to add to my plate was another reason to be labeled as "weird."

So, as I began to sense and see more Spirit visitors around my childhood home or while out at large family gatherings, I kept everything to myself. It was such a scary and lonely time. No one I could talk to about what I was sensing. No one to compare experiences with. No one that could understand what these visitations felt like.

I did my very best to hide my gift. I tried to ignore the Spirits that would visit me at night while I was trying to fall asleep. I refused to share the messages they would ask me to share with others. I would literally *hide* under the covers when I heard ghostly footsteps down the hallway of my house. This continued into my teens, and then my gift shifted.

When I started high school, I noticed that it wasn't just the dead that I would sense, it was also the living! Whenever I was around others, I began to notice that my mood, my energy, and my own feelings would shift. If my mom was sad or upset about something, I would take on those feelings as if they were my own. If a friend was stressed out about an upcoming test, I would start to feel scared and worried, too. I would experience cold sweats, a racing heart, and a feeling as if I was going to pass out at any moment.

I would often find myself asking others if I looked okay or if I was pale because I was convinced that something was wrong with me. It drove everyone crazy, including myself. But no matter what I did, I couldn't stop it. Then, the panic and anxiety attacks started. Every. Single. Day.

I started to be afraid of going anywhere but my own bedroom. I didn't want to leave my house to go to school. I had no idea what on earth was going on with me. It was so isolating and frightening. And because I didn't feel like I could tell anyone what I was feeling or what was happening, I started to lean more on my faith. I prayed to God to put me on a path that would help me understand what I was experiencing. I was so tired of being scared every single day, and I wanted to find a way to live freely from my daily energetic anxiety and Spirit visitations. The moment I got out of the way of my own fears and asked the Universe to guide me toward help and understanding, everything began to *shift* in my world.

Not long after, I met my first spiritual mentor. Initially, I started working with her to understand the energetic anxiety and panic attacks I was having. Through our work together, I discovered that I was an Empath.

An Empath is a person who is highly sensitive to the energy and emotions of those around them. This was one of the reasons why I would take on the emotions of others around me! Finally, having a word to describe what was happening to me when I was around the living felt like a *huge* relief. I realized that I wasn't crazy or losing my mind; I was just hypersensitive to the energy around me and needed to learn how to work with it rather than against it.

I started researching about my newfound Empathic abilities. My nose was constantly in a book, learning new energy-clearing techniques and protection methods. The more I leaned into understanding my newfound gift, the lighter and brighter I felt! As I opened up to this gift of mine, I started to gain a new appreciation for it. Instead of being scared of what was going to happen when I was surrounded by others and their energy, I felt empowered. This ability felt like it was protecting me from things that didn't serve me. And when I leaned into it and began to accept it as a part of my identity, my gift for sensing Spirit began to get stronger and clearer!

The visits from Spirit had become more frequent. I would often see loved ones of my friends who had passed, asking me to deliver messages to them. I began having dreams about the people in my life and their loved ones coming through to tell me about major life events that would be happening soon (marriage, babies, new jobs, etc).

When I recognized that my connection with the Spirit world was building, I knew that it was time to seek out my spiritual mentor again. Through working with her, I had come to understand my empathic abilities, and I was determined to figure all of this out. I trusted that the Universe was guiding me on my spiritual path. There had to be a reason, a name for what I was experiencing. I didn't want to be afraid anymore, so I took another leap of faith.

"You are a medium, Nicole, a psychic medium," my mentor told me. The words hung there in the air for several moments before they sank in. *Mediumship.* The word was equally exciting and scary to me in the beginning. What would it mean for me if I chose to open up more to this gift? How would others perceive it—or me? There were so many questions swirling in my mind, but the excitement and curiosity sent me down the path of developing my gift.

I took time to reflect on the moment when I encountered my grandma in Spirit and why it was so important to me. It made me wonder, *'How could I use this gift to help others?'* To connect them with their loved ones who had passed on.

As I began to work on developing my newfound mediumistic abilities, my old fears and anxieties reared their ugly head. I remembered what it was like to be the little girl who was called different, odd, loud. I remembered what it felt like to be scared of being teased and ridiculed. I remembered how *scared* I was to not be accepted by others. And these old fears and stories began to keep me stuck in a holding pattern. There was a version of me who felt deeply called to open and awaken this gift so that I could help others. But there was a bigger part of me, the fearful part, that just wanted to be "normal" like everyone else. I constantly felt stuck in limbo and didn't know where to turn until I decided one day that it was time to tell someone who I knew would support me no matter what. My mom.

My mom was my everything. My best friend. My guide. My biggest cheerleader! I never kept anything from her until I learned that I was a medium. I was so scared that she would be upset with me because of my family's religious beliefs. But I was so lost; I knew I couldn't go on without telling her. I needed someone to know what I had learned about myself, and that person was her.

I'll never forget how *excited* she was when I told her! She could not have been more happy. When I told her how scared I was to be "found out," she immediately told me, in the most loving way possible, that I simply could not live my life in fear. This was a God-given gift, a part of who I was, and it was important to embrace it.

This gift didn't scare her away or make her think badly about me at all. Her love and acceptance of it actually inspired me to do the same. She told me that this gift was meant to be shared and that I needed to use it to help others in their time of need and grieving. With her blessing and guidance, I slowly began offering readings, sessions, and in-person gallery events.

She supported me every step of the way for ten years as I worked on my mediumship development and held space for my clients and for the Spirit world. She was by my side in my work until she passed away in 2022. Her passing led me to an even deeper initiation into my work as a medium. I never knew how deeply painful grief could be or how healing mediumship would be until I lost her.

When she passed, a friend of mine, who is also a medium, gave me a reading and connected me with my mom. I am a medium, yes, but I am a human being first. My grief was so deeply painful and raw in the beginning stages of her loss that I could not connect with her in the way that I could connect others to their loved ones in Spirit. The reading that my friend gifted me with completely changed my perspective on the work of mediumship. It brought so much hope, healing, and peace to my heart. Through my deep grief and pain, I was able to connect with the essence of my mom's Spirit, and it was the most intensely magical thing I had ever experienced.

Right then, it felt as if all of my worries, fears, and anxieties about my truth and my mediumistic abilities were washed away. I decided then and there that the best way to honor my beautiful mom in Spirit would be to fully love, honor, and accept myself. What has followed has been nothing short of miraculous. The way that Spirit has led me to help others on their healing journeys has been fulfilling and magical. With each reading I hold space for, I fall more and more in love with this work. It has become a dream come true!

I was afraid for years to embrace my spiritual gifts and awakening. The world is not always an easy place, and it can be scary to feel or be "different." But the truth is that we are all uniquely beautiful in our own way. Through our own spiritual awakenings and personal experiences we will discover more about who we are at our core, at a soul level, and what it is that our Higher Power and Higher Self want us to know. The gifts that you will discover about yourself are the exact miracles and magic that this world needs! So, if you are scared to embrace your truth, or maybe you feel unsure about what it will look like on the other side of your fears and worries, know this…

You are meant to shine! You are worthy! The world needs your magic now more than ever. Trust yourself, listen to your heart, and follow your intuition. The Universe has a Divine plan for your Soul's journey and when you embrace all of the parts that make up who you are as a whole, that is when your Soul Will Rise!

Nicole Sanguinetti is a psychic medium and spiritual mentor who has dedicated her life to connecting the living with the Spirit world. She is passionate about helping those who are grieving to find peace and hope through the healing work of mediumship. She blends her psychic wisdom and spiritual expertise to guide those who are ready to discover their own magic within!

Website: www.lovelightandmagic.com

Instagram: www.instagram.com/nicole_sanguinetti

'Unlocking the Magic Within' Podcast:
www.lovelightandmagic.com/podcast

Book a Reading: www.lovelightandmagic.com/book-online

04

Embodiment, Trust, and Self-Empowerment

By Holly Poitras
Amesbury, Massachusetts, USA

It was a sunny, warm Fall day in early November 2021. I was leaving for a group trip to Egypt later that evening. I was to embark on this trip with 15 other women. I only knew a few of them, and I was starting to feel anxious about the idea of traveling to Egypt by myself.

I went for a walk to try to calm my nerves. I sat by the water, and then I sat by the trees. I closed my eyes and started to silently cry as I felt the sun kissing my face, trying to remind myself that I'll be okay. I thought back to how I initially heard about this trip and how I had full-body chills and a knowing right away that I would be attending.

Suddenly, I felt the warm embrace of someone wash over me. It felt tingly and extremely loving. I then heard, "I will be with you. Your ancestors and I will be protecting you. There is nothing to fear." It was in this calm, loving, familiar voice that I saw in my mind's eye that it was my deceased grandfather, who passed away a few months earlier that year. I could also sense that there was a group of my ancestors around me. I couldn't see them per se; it was a knowing, a feeling of being swarmed and protected by loving guardians.

My grandfather's side of the family is from Lebanon and Syria, so it wasn't surprising that this crew "showed up". However, it was somewhat startling because this was the first time I had clearly heard and seen my grandfather since his passing. For a second, I felt like I was in Disney's *Mulan* movie, with him talking about my ancestors and me embarking on this journey; I was waiting for a sassy, small red dragon to show up and present himself as my main guide.

Despite this being bizarre for me, it was also extremely loving and calming. I instantly felt the anxiousness resolve, and I had a clear knowing that I would be safe and protected at all times. I sat outside for a few moments longer, reminding myself that the same sun nourishing me in that moment will also be there in Egypt as well. The sun has always felt like an old friend to me. I wasn't going to go there alone, I had a lot of love and support. I just had to trust...

Everything flowed easily and effortlessly on my arrival to Egypt. As I landed, I heard in very clear words, "I am home." I turned around to see if someone was saying that behind me, and it was just me. I then thought, "Great, I'm hearing more voices, this will be fun." I made a mental note to be sure to have a colleague perform a neurological exam on me when I returned to the states.

I was starting to question my sanity at this point. It all felt very clear, though. My heart felt an opening and a warm sensation around it. Despite the scientific part of me that works in medicine wanting more "proof", this did feel unquestionably accurate to me. This was all the proof I needed to trust myself.

Throughout this trip, I had a lot of beautiful and interesting experiences. It was beyond a privilege to be there with the amazing group I was with. As deeply beautiful as it was, it was also challenging for me. I had strange experiences of feeling wired but not tired, so I couldn't sleep much, but I felt well-rested at the same time.

I could also physically feel other people's energy fields pushing into mine, which was bizarre and overwhelming. I had constant headaches and burning sensations throughout my scalp, and I felt like I needed a lot of space from people. I hadn't experienced any of this before, so I truly thought I was going insane.

Fortunately, I had an amazingly intuitive group facilitator who lovingly pulled me aside multiple times and reassured me that I wasn't crazy and to just trust and let this process unfold. At one point, I was walking through a busy marketplace and thinking dark thoughts that were judgmental and cruel. They didn't feel like mine, but they were coming from my mind, so I assumed they were somehow mine. The group facilitator, again, pulled me aside and said, "These thoughts you are thinking are not yours." She started spraying her herbal rosemary spray around me as she spoke. I went from crying to laughing because she was always so supportive with her remedies. She advised me to take a shower and be sure to wash my head with water, and I'd feel much better. She was right.

The following morning, I spoke with her at breakfast, and I told her, "I think I have experienced feeling other people's emotions most of my life. I'm grateful you told me this now. I just wish I knew sooner." I thought back to the challenges of feeling so empathic most of my life. I had always felt alone because I felt most people didn't understand me, especially my family. I had experiences as a child that I didn't feel comfortable sharing with most people because seeing ghosts was not something the Catholic religion was keen on. However, I also reflected on the beauty and privilege it was to be able to feel so deeply.

This trip was one of the most incredible experiences of my life, and it was a catalyst for my awakening experience. I also noticed that the more I opened up to my gifts, the more I would be met with my past wounds.

My awakening process has been like nature, a spiral-like process, and having my facilitator's support in Egypt was the most "help" I have had in this awakening process. I have had to navigate a lot of weird and uncomfortable experiences mostly on my own, in a way to learn to trust myself. I feel that my soul chose to have very little help from others in this incarnation as a way to learn that the best way to trust myself is by learning through my own experiences.

Since Egypt, I have been on a few other group retreats, and although they were profoundly beautiful and healing, they were also challenging, as I would get sick on each trip from subconsciously taking on other people's pain and wounding to try to help heal it for them. Knowing what I know now, it would have been helpful to have known this sooner. However, I trust that this is what I needed to learn.

I also realized that experiencing all of this has made me more empathic to want to help others, especially to empower more women. In the temples in Egypt, I could feel the immensely powerful strength of the women who lived in those ancient times, and it made me wonder how we've come so far from this, with so much female suppression, jealousy, insecurity, and fear of speaking up. It has made me curious about how we can get back to being our supportive, courageous, and fierce selves. Reclaiming our power (in a healthy way) starts with acknowledging our wounds so they no longer can have power over us, feeling our anger and not suppressing it so we don't project it onto others, and using our voices to speak our truth.

Journaling and being more connected with my body has helped me trust myself and be more aware of certain wounds. I also believe that people can have ancestral or past life wounds as well. I think a lot of people in the spiritual community talk about "love and light," but we need to remember that we can't bypass the darkness (our wounds) because healing our wounds is what makes us more authentic and helps us remember our true essence. This is why doing the work to heal my wounds has been helpful in this process; it has helped me remember what I came here to do.

Upon reflecting on my experiences (and witnessing others' experiences), I have narrowed it down to three practices that have helped me the most. I am sharing them because I wish someone had shared them with me years ago. We all have different plans and paths, so if it doesn't resonate, or if you want to try it a different way, then feel free to pick and choose what feels best for you.

1) Start to practice to check in with yourself DAILY.

Before AND after you go somewhere, take a few deep breaths and ask yourself, "How am I feeling?" Notice any sensations in your body. For example, I notice that I feel tightness in my throat or constriction in my abdomen before or after hanging out with certain people who feel draining to me. It's my body's way of trying to help me be aware of this, and it encourages me to be curious and possibly to journal about the experience, as it sometimes connects to past experiences that need to be acknowledged and felt.

I also noticed that after conversations with certain people, I start out feeling great, and then I would leave feeling exhausted, angry, or whatever THEY were feeling. I eventually learned that I was subconsciously taking on others' emotions because of childhood patterns that I developed that were unhealthy, and once I started to heal these patterns, I stopped taking on so much.

I eventually learned that if I left a situation feeling emotions or thoughts that weren't mine, I didn't have to take them on. I could acknowledge them and say, "This is not mine. Please remove this from me now, transmute it to love, and give it to earth as an offering." Our bodies (and souls) know what to do, we just have to be aware of how we feel so we can direct the flow of energy.

2) Sit in silence for at least 5 minutes a day. Try to work up to 20 minutes daily.

This has been the hardest practice for me to integrate. However, it has been the MOST effective one. We live in a society where we are constantly being tempted to be distracted. Whether it be music, podcasts, TV, or phone alerts, the list goes on. Wireless headphones have been wonderful for some things, but they also make it easy to completely check out from reality. Sitting in silence can help us cleanse our energy and move with more presence throughout our day. You're more able to discern which energy is yours or someone else's because you will be more familiar with how you feel at baseline. You will also be able to make decisions more easily because you won't be as overstimulated.

I used to walk around with headphones on throughout most of my day, so I didn't have to talk to people or make eye contact with them. I used headphones as armor to avoid reality and not have to feel so much. I realized that I was staying in my head as a way to ignore my body, and I found this ironic, as one of the beautiful things here about our experience on earth is to be able to feel and experience our senses. Being present allows us to be aware and experience more. To smell the fresh cut grass, to smile at a stranger, to connect with others, to connect with nature, to feel and acknowledge whatever our body is trying to tell us, this is what we are here for. To feel, to connect, to be present.

3) Practice trusting yourself.

Before you run to your friend or colleague with a problem or question asking what you "should do" (something I have done many times), first sit with it yourself. Take a few deep breaths, and ask your body the question. Do you feel any sensations around your heart? Do you feel your body contracting? Expanding? Leaning forward or backward? Only YOU know what is best for YOU. Yes, most of us have that one person in our life who seems to know us better than ourselves, but ultimately, we do know what is best for us. We forget that our body is our most powerful divinatory tool. And just like other modalities, the more we practice it, the stronger the connection becomes.

Now, I am not suggesting that people go to Egypt to accelerate their awakening process. I believe that there are moments and events that onset our own awakening processes whenever they are meant to happen. Looking back, there were other events in my life that caused other awakening experiences, such as actively choosing to work through my wounds and the endings of unhealthy relationships. I do think that these (and many other types of experiences) are also catalysts for awakening.

My intention in sharing my story is to help other people on their paths feel less alone and more empowered. True empowerment doesn't come from wealth or external accolades but instead from healing our wounds through feeling and trusting what our bodies are trying to tell us. I do feel many more people will continue "waking up" at an exponential rate. I see this increase in awakening amongst friends and colleagues. I feel that others may also struggle with questioning themselves and wanting scientific evidence to support the "weirdness" of awakening, so I hope to have my story be of help to that community, too. Lastly, may you also find the courage to trust yourself, empower others, and speak your truth.

Holly Poitras firmly believes we can unfold our truest essence by acknowledging and healing our shadowy aspects or wounds. From working in medicine and having more of a scientific approach, she has experienced and witnessed the remarkable ability to heal. Holly works with people who are open to healing or learning more about spirituality. She does 1:1 healing sessions to help people ease into their own spiritual gifts and incorporate practices to help them learn to trust and empower themselves. For those who want to dive deeper and heal from their past, she uses various modalities such as inner child work, ancestral healing, somatic practices, astrology, and mediumship, and she ends with a personalized energy healing ceremony to help integrate this process.

Website: www.lightningrosehealing.com

Instagram: www.instagram.com/lightningrosehealing

05

Becoming Grace

By Grace Niu
Sydney, Australia

*It is only until you are no longer are who you want to be
that you will discover your soul essence.
It is only until you no longer care about the end result
that you become a master of manifestation.*

I probably don't need to tell you that there is something truly amazing about you hidden inside that you need to bring forth because if you are reading this book, you must already be feeling the weight of this 'hidden treasure' you are carrying.

It is no small task to bear such a 'jewel' without sharing it with the world. You may be agonizing about how to bring such a rare treasure to light. It has kept you sleepless at night. Restless during the day.

You may feel daunted and intimidated, especially with the words 'soul purpose' or 'legacy' being thrown around so lightly these days. Your nervous system tends to freeze up the second you hear the phrase 'quantum leap' spoken. Again.

So may I suggest 'let's forget about it' for a few moments and hear a story. My story.

STOP THE FIGHT TO GAIN THE WORLD

I was in disbelief walking out of my fertility specialist's office. After 5 years of TTC (trying to conceive), where modern medical science failed to offer any explanations, I finally seemed to get an answer—but not the one I was hoping for:

"The level of 'Natural Killer Cells' marker is high in your womb. So instead of implanting, your immune system considers the embryos as foreign bodies, therefore fighting it off..."

Excellent. As a queen of problem-solving, somehow, I conveniently ignored the alarming fact that my body was at war with myself.

I feel, at this time, I should tell you a little about myself. Growing up in 1970s China, I was brought up as an only child with the single aim of achieving excellence. Like a good soldier, I have a mind of steel, and I believed in the famous saying, 'where there is a will, there is a way,' and if something doesn't work, try harder.

At the age of 40, I was traveling on a pretty predictable, high-achievers path. I was extremely efficient, superb at delivering what others wanted, at work, in the family, or in any social situation. Of course, being a perfectionist comes with that. And who wouldn't like a cute baby? Little did I know that I was just about to hit with a giant plot twist the Universe set out for me.

Being a warrior (later on, I learned this is written in my Four Pillars of Destiny Chart according to Chinese Astrology), of course, I wasn't giving up easily just because of some 'killer cells.' But the more I fought, the more my body rejected. Long story short, 24 months later, after numerous failed IVF cycles plus a small fortune, I finally collapsed on the 'battlefield,' admitting defeat.

As I was mourning the death of my motherhood, I couldn't help but wonder:

- Why did it feel like the entire Universe was against me? Or am I fighting the shadow of myself?
- Do I even want a child? It was really too late and shameful to

think about that at this stage, Grace! But is it?

- There seemed to be some mystical, unexplainable, yet benevolent force at work that was powerful beyond measure, conspiring me to 'drop the sword' and come home. At that time, *co-creation* with the Universe had not entered my vocabulary yet.

One night, lying in darkness, awake, I remembered some advice from a wise mentor: "Allow things to fall, fall apart, fall into pieces. It may also fall into place." That's what I did. For the first time in my life, I opened the fist I was holding so tight and let things fall. I stopped trying so hard to make my life fit into a template.

It was a major turning point in my life—the very start of my spiritual awakening journey. Surprisingly, I didn't fall apart. As my body relaxed, I felt mostly relieved. The world around me literally took on colours. I noticed the seasons changing, trees blossoming, and the cycle of the moon. I was moved by the symphony that nature produced so effortlessly. I felt the grandeur of a more textured, more imaginative life as it longed to be known.

I couldn't stop crying for a while, mostly because the state of transcendence and beauty was something that I'd never experienced before. As soon as I stopped the fight, a new Universe opened up for me. As soon as I surrendered to the inevitable, I began to remember who I was.

So now, the question: *How to bring the hidden treasure to light? How do you know?*

Here are two things that I came to believe to be true:

First, whatever ends up leading to your 'hidden treasure' is neither going to be something obvious nor is it going to be like a billboard on full display saying, 'Your life purpose! Fully explained here'. It is going to show up subtly, clue by clue, and it will unfold gradually. Be grateful for this. It is not because the Universe is playing 'hard to get,' it is mostly due to the fact that our capacity to receive at such a divine level can be quite delicate. Think of the light bulb blowing out its fuse if the current is excessively strong.

When these tiny clues start to show up, most people will not notice. Likely, they are being consumed by their own dramas, anxieties, and insecurities in life. But if you are conscious and open enough, your destiny will purposefully yet unmistakably create an aperture for the magic to slip through. It will send you the Universal physical and emotional signals. You will feel it and be fascinated by it. It feels like an obsession or déjà vu.

Like a seed, it may require you to nurture it at the start. Cultivate it. Follow that fascination. Be curious enough to plant it deeply in your creative soil and grow it. Soon enough, you start to 'stumble upon' the right people. Serendipities will play out. The right guidance will show up at the right time. This is when you know you are on the right track. These tiny clues will eventually turn into something, igniting the miracle you never saw coming.

I've never had a childhood dream of becoming a Feng Shui Master or a Destiny Mentor. But I inched toward it. Clue by clue. By the time I looked up from the trail of the 'breadcrumbs' I had followed, I was completely consumed with a passion to transcribe the 'unseen energy' through the language of Feng Shui and Chinese Metaphysics.

Becoming an Energy Alchemist and Destiny Mentor ended up being my purpose after a decade of devotional pursuit, but it only worked because I said 'Yes' to every single tiny clue around me. And I followed it persistently.

Second, your soul mission has to be first and foremost *about* you and *for* you. This means you are not required to help humanity, heal others, or save the world. Such an intention can put a 'devastating strain' upon your soul and most likely kill your mission before it even comes to light. So unburden yourself and travel light.

I originally set out to learn Feng Shui with one single aim: to find out 'what caused my infertility.' Somewhere along the way, I not only got my answers, healed myself, and created Feng Shui Serenity, but I also happened to find my calling. And by merely sharing my story, I inadvertently ended up healing plenty of others. But I didn't have such an intention to begin with.

If you are at the start of your transformative journey, the most vital thing to keep you on track is this: Do whatever makes you feel alive. Engage in childlike wonders. Follow your own impulses and obsessions, and be creative about it. Trust the magnificence of your own becoming and the vaulting scope of your capacity. Unravel whatever makes your heart reverberate.

The rest will take care of itself.

And if, eventually, you intend to share your gift with the world one day, you need to be extremely selfish at this point and forget about others and humanity for a second.

Confused? Let's talk about the concept of paradox.

THE PARADOX OF DESTINY

'What am I here to do, and how can I best live out my destiny?' I get asked this eternal and universal question almost every day.

So here is the central paradox about Destiny: 'Your Destiny is predetermined, and you are the creator of your own Destiny.'

Your capacity to hold the two opposite ends of the spectrum is in direct proportion to how quickly you can leap into the new iteration of yourself and eventually experience the magical overabundance of life.

We live in a world of duality.

Everything is the perfect expression of its opposite.

Everything holds an opposite truth, all of which are true.

I spend almost every living minute of my life learning how to decode your Destiny Chart so we can be divinely guided. At the same time, I also feel at peace that *'Something unknown is doing we don't know what'*, said Sir Arther Stanley Eddington.

I need to know. I don't need to know.

I emphasize the idea that the vital role of your home's Feng Shui can ultimately determine each major aspect of your life, i.e., health, money, family, and relationships. Yet I also trust your home's *'terrible* Feng Shui' could be the very *'catalyst'* that leads you to the biggest discovery in your spiritual awakening.

It matters, it doesn't matter.

Your brilliant Destiny chart could be the exact curse and reason for why you haven't done anything remotely 'interesting' with your life so far. Even with a chart that seems perfect from the theory perspective, you may find yourself waiting for your luck to arrive without taking any aligned action.

The ancient Greeks believed that the steps taken to avoid fate are the same steps that lead to it.

29 years ago, fate stepped in after my US visa was declined twice. The divine hand flipped the switch to Australia. Little did I know I would meet my future husband of 22 years in four years' time.

18 months ago, I took every step to ensure its perfect Feng Shui while we searched for our next home. I was certain there was an inexplicable force at play because the lake house we ended up buying was neither 'Feng Shui perfect' nor did it fit with the timeline. And it was nestled in a location we didn't even know existed 12 months earlier. The only way I can explain it is: 'I was being guided.'

Destiny is that exterior force that, once in a while, you get to experience as if you are being gently propelled and being carried along. It is powerful and mysterious but generous. Something you can't explain, plan, or repeat. It is the belief that life is not merely a series of meaningless accidents or coincidences but rather a tapestry of events that culminate in an exquisite, sublime plan.

If we are to live life in *harmony* with the Universe, we must possess a powerful faith in what the ancients used to call 'fatum'—what we currently refer to as Destiny.

COMMUNE WITH THE UNIVERSE

The Universe never says no.
It either says yes, not now, or I have something better for you.

As you travel deeper into this journey, one crucial thing to learn is *'how to commune with the Universe.'* Because it gives you the sense of faith that no matter what happens, you are not alone.

Finding that unique channel that speaks to you will be your saving grace, the touchstone to discover your hidden treasure.

To me, this channel happens to be the home I live in. My home is my medicine, the portal that leads to my next evolution. It is through each of the homes I live in that I see my lessons. I receive my healing, protection, and guidance. It is through this mystical bond that weaves between me and my home, and my journey on Earth, that I get to access the world beyond.

Without this deep sense of relationship, you will miss out on an incredibly important concept - To Co-Create with the Universe. You will take on 'the world' unnecessarily. You will wear 'martyrdom' as bravery. You will fight the unwinnable war against yourself.

What an absolute relief to know that the Earth you inhabit has the power to ever hold you so compassionately only if you allow it.

How delicious it feels to move out of the energy of trying, struggling, and stress and into the allegiance of your heart.

How comforting it is to realize that the process of this spiritual awakening can also become a gift of healing, prophecy, insight, and growth along the way.

As you surrender to this soul's medicine, your mental anguish is soothed. Your physical body becomes soft and rested. Your attitude to life turns more curious, open, still & receptive. You no longer have to drive the unfoldment of your desire into form. You let go of the 'timeline' and instead trust the 'timing'. You rest in assurance that *daily* action & effort is enough.

It is from this place of increasing stillness that divine healing occurs. Great activity and inspiration will flow. So much will simply emerge, transpire, and emanate out of you.

It is in this frequency that you become a vessel. Your future path emerged. Yet you feel inside as though you are doing nothing at all. Even whilst so much is happening through you. This is the journey.

This divine life you have right now wants to be lived richly, and it wants to be lived through you.

♡ ♡ ♡

Grace is an internationally renowned Feng Shui Master, Destiny mentor, teacher, and speaker who has created the successful business Feng Shui Serenity after following her own intuition away from a 15-year career in media to explore her soul purpose.

She believes when you begin to touch the invisible thread that connects the Seen and the Unseen, the greatest mystery is unfolding around you.

She currently lives a quiet life with her husband in the lake region in NSW, Australia, where changing lights, serene peace, and sunset are her greatest inspirations. Her sole aim in life is to experience life fully through each small, unexpected, easeful mercy, magic, and delight.

Website: www.fengshuiserenity.com.au

Instagram: www.instagram.com/fengshuiserenity

Podcast: www.fengshuiserenity.com.au/podcast

Services: www.fengshuiserenity.com.au/work-with-me

06

143

By Kenda Sheriff
Lake Lotawana, Missouri, USA

January 4th, 2017, at 9:38 p.m. I woke to intense contractions; I was 36 weeks and six days pregnant. It seemed too early for our baby to make his debut, but as a winter storm blew outside, the barometric pressure seemed to be affecting my body. Panicking, I began to time my contractions... every two minutes. It was time to wake Cole.

We began our journey to the hospital, and with white knuckles, Cole carefully navigated the roads. With over six inches of fresh snow, we knew it would take much longer than the usual 30 minutes. As my contractions quickened, I began imagining us delivering our first child on the side of the road.

As we reached Kansas City's infamous Plaza, we were overwhelmed with gratitude, knowing we were now within a few miles of the hospital. Approaching a red light, we slowed to a complete stop. Fogged from my heavy breathing we gazed through the small opening of the windshield, we were in awe of the beautiful scene that lay before us. Still up from Christmas, the Plaza lights twinkled like diamonds, emeralds, sapphires, and rubies perfectly hung along the Spanish-style architecture. With no other souls in sight, we sat silently as if we were centerpieces in a beautiful snow globe ever so gently shaken up.

Just after midnight, we were admitted into labor and delivery. Today, January 5th, 2017, would mark our son's birth day, and little did I know

I would also begin the first day of my new life.

I was able to labor down and safely deliver our son at 6:31 a.m. As he was laid across my chest, I was overcome with love. I took off his tiny hat to get a better look at the life I carried. I exclaimed, "He sure doesn't look quite like I'd imagined." Not good or bad… just different.

I started seeking reassurance from the nurses as he felt incredibly small and wasn't latching on to nurse well. They assured me there was nothing to worry about. Having lost a full night's sleep, I assumed my anxieties were a mixture of exhaustion and hormones. As two more days passed, our baby was still hardly latching and now weighed only 4 lbs. 2 oz.

Thanks to an earth angel behind the scenes, our doctor finally ordered a series of tests. A sonographer came to our room to perform a head ultrasound, and as he casually moved the transducer back & forth across his head, he stopped and walked silently out of the room. We found ourselves saying, "That can't be bad news, right? He probably forgot a supply…" Well, he didn't return, and as we waited to figure out the mystery, we were greeted by a new doctor.

Dr. Hulsing sat next to me, and with tears in her eyes, she reached for my hands and stated, "Your son has Complete Agenesis of the Corpus Callosum. This means he is missing the millions of pathways that connect his brain's right and left hemispheres". I am certain she said more, but all I could focus on was, "Your child is missing a part of his brain." The light in my world went out; it was as if the day turned into night.

Before we could move to the NICU, we needed to give him his name. After the uncertainty his diagnosis brought, we felt added weight in choosing his name. My husband offered up a Hail Mary; we'd share our pick with each other via text message. By some miracle, we sent each other the same name, McCoy Wesley.

After a week of being in the hospital, not leaving his side, I was encouraged by a nurse to take a break and go for a walk. As I set off to visit the chapel, I noticed an outdoor courtyard. With the sudden urge to step outside, I walked through what felt like a portal into the winter night. Surrounded by snow, I stood still, breathing in the icy air and staring straight up at the sky. The snowflakes sparkling like stars joined the tears as they fell down my face. Time stood still. I felt as if I was being held, being held in the way I'd imagine angels would hold you in a loving embrace.

Once ready to return inside, I noticed a small plaque near the door. Wanting to pay homage to the unexpected healing I felt, I bent down to read the inscription. In capital letters, it read "SAINT MCCOY". I was thankful I followed the nudge to venture outside as I had recieved such beautiful confirmation.

As the months passed, I found myself living in a dual reality. I was overwhelmed with worry about what the future held for my little love, yet I was intrigued by my heightened sensitivities. Was it my postpartum hormones raging through my body, or had something cracked open within me? Either way, I felt as if I had a new superpower.

I was noticing people's names, repeating numbers, reoccurring animals, and words like "Kundalini" that were not a part of my previous vocabulary. Leaning into curiosity, I would google their meanings to see if they somehow applied to what I was going through. Amazingly, each message felt aligned! It was as if the universe was leaving me breadcrumbs, and if I chose to follow the path, I'd advance to the next level. While I've always been deeply intuitive, I've never noticed these types of synchronicities before.

We soon learned that McCoy had a rare genetic disorder called 1q43q44 deletion syndrome. I was mixed with emotions ranging from devastation to relief of having answers. To ease my mind, I leaned into the familiar feeling I had when I heard the numbers within his deletion. Instantly recalling that 44 was an angel number, one of divine support and protection. Yet I couldn't pinpoint why 143 felt so familiar. *143, 143, 143.* It was ringing so loudly in my ears! Then, it hit me! As a teenager, I'd communicate through pagers using numbers as codes. *One*-letter word, followed by a *four*-letter word, and ending with a *three*-letter word.

I Love You

It was at that moment I knew that McCoy is here to show us what love is, and I am here to model that love to the world.

Floating in the liminal space between two worlds, I no longer felt like I fit in. The warmth of my baby's body pressed against mine was the only thing keeping me tethered to the ground. Often awake between 3:30-4:00 am. I'd look down at his sweet face, and think of when Dr. Moylan said, "A baby's brain is miraculous; it can do things that science cannot explain how or why."

Early on, I had a feeling that McCoy would likely encounter major challenges like physical disabilities, cognitive delays, and being non-verbal. With those in mind, I often sat in deep contemplation of miracles. *Do you get one miracle in a lifetime, or are they unlimited? Are they only reserved for big instances, or can they be in the mundane too?* It felt open to interpretation, so by removing all the constructs, I chose to view everything as miraculous!

I began to see the world through a new lens. Each day, I led with intention. I'd match his pace and provide the support and tools he required. We'd celebrate each "gemstone" he'd reach as if it were the most beautiful thing we'd ever seen... because it was! In this experience I was gifted a new appreciation for my own body. Realizing I had previously taken so much for granted, and with this new awareness, I gave myself grace for what I hadn't previously known.

The following months hadn't come easy. We found ourselves in dozens of doctor and therapy appointments. It became evident that I needed to speak up and become my child's advocate. I found strength in trusting my instincts when advocating for what was right for McCoy, but as somebody who never "rocked the boat," it was daunting to ask for further explanations or to disagree with medical professionals. It was not long after I integrated advocacy into my being that the universe accepted my challenge, and as if to call my bluff, it began to ask me to step up further and become my own advocate.

I found I was being tested in all areas of my life. At work, clients who I previously allowed to take advantage of my kindness now bullied me into situations that were uncalled for. At home, I was receiving pushback from family members when my decisions didn't align with their opinions. Friends had begun to fall out of my life because I found I could no longer tolerate gossiping and lack of self-awareness.

Having witnessed how fragile life can be, I came to terms that my previous default as a "people pleaser" no longer served me. I needed to trust myself in a way that felt so uncomfortable that I often forgot to breathe. Slowly retreating into myself, I began to take action steps in separating myself from all things that no longer resonated.

Searching for ways to cope, I decided to listen to podcasts on my commute to work. Right away, I found two I was interested in: Kaitlyn Bristowe's *Off the Vine Podcast* and one on astrology called *The Cosmic Calling* with Natalie Walstein. Kaitlyn's podcast gave me the normal girl chatter I desperately missed and the escapism my mind needed, while Natalie's gave me new knowledge and guidance my soul was craving.

It wasn't lost on me that when I was younger and going through a rough patch, I'd read my horoscope for insight. So for my 35th birthday, I took this a step further and treated myself to my first natal chart reading with Natalie. It was enlightening; seeing the colorful pie chart layered with planetary symbols simply filled me with excitement. Finally, a language I could understand! How brilliant it is that the blueprint of your soul was written in the stars the moment you were born.

In the Fall of 2018, I gave birth to our second son, Ledger. My heart grew bigger still. Like a puzzle piece, he completed our family. From the day he was born, there was wonderment in the sparkle of his eyes, a daily reminder for me of all the magic in the world. I declared to the heavens that I wanted to be a guiding light in my children's lives and to raise them to be good humans.

I was experiencing more love than I'd ever felt, and as we were nearing Ledger's first birthday, a crippling fear crept into my body. I became paralyzed with the thought that I could lose it all, and I suddenly felt as if I was going to die.

Needing support I searched for a therapist, and as I skimmed their bios, I quickly realized that no one quite felt right. Next, I searched for a Life Coach, and after coming up short, the universe gave me another breadcrumb by showing me a vision of a woman. Unsure if this was a figment of my imagination, I embraced my curiosity. Could I find the woman with short blonde curly hair, light eyes, and beautiful bone structure?

I refined my search again and added "spiritual". I couldn't believe it; she was real, and her name was Phoenix! She offered coaching through her business, Spirited You. Walking through her door, instantly I knew I was in the right place. At the end of our first session, she mentioned she had an upcoming program, and she expressed that it was right up my alley!

She shared a few details of the year-long commitment, and while I was excited to deepen my intuition, I was nervous investing on a whim. With two kids and a full-time job, I wanted to discuss with my husband the time and cost investment I was committing to. Without hesitation, Cole encouraged me to invest in myself! Two days later, I received a bonus check that was within a few dollars of the amount of the program. It was like I was being rewarded for saying YES to myself and for following yet another breadcrumb!

I was surprised to learn I had signed up for a Shamanic Apprenticeship. Trusting in my vision, I hadn't taken the time to read Phoenix's bio, and it turned out she is a practicing Shaman.

Within this group of divinely orchestrated women, I found myself feeling right at home. I was learning the meaning of holding space for others as well as allowing others to hold space for me. Being taught shamanic healing modalities while simultaneously working 1:1 with Phoenix, I began to work on creating boundaries and healing traumas. Recognizing my sensitivities and empathic nature as a gift was life-changing. As I worked to heal my childhood wounds, the parallels to my present life were undeniable. I was doing the work, and as I faced what I buried in the dark, I could begin to see glimmers of light shining back into my world.

After being grounded in my body again, I finally decided to say aloud to Phoenix the fear that was weighing me down. In a raw whisper, I cried, "I think I'm dying." She looked at me and said with love and conviction, "Yes, you are, you are living a shaman's death."

After reflecting on the past two years, I now understood that a former version of me did die. It was in the experience of knowing that the light won't seem as bright until you've ventured into the dark. With new clarity, I understood it was the path I needed to walk to find myself again and reawaken my soul.

In a lake community outside of Kansas City, MO, Kenda Sheriff shares a home with her husband, Cole, sons McCoy & Ledger, and their dog, Fable. In 2006, she began to use her Interior Design degree in both the Residential and Commercial fields. Outside of her love for design, she felt a calling to go deeper than physical spaces. Along her journey, she found that design begins from within. In 2017, Kenda followed her inner compass and began dipping her toe into the world of inner healing. Studying under world-class mentors, she dedicated herself to practices of Astrology, Mediumship, Angel Messages, Crystals & Energy work, and Shamanic healing. True to her Piscean nature, she shows up each day with the intention of bringing love and magic into the world.

Instagram: www.instagram.com/of_stars_and_sea

07

You are Who You are Looking For

By Pippa Kate
Manly, New South Wales, Australia

It is said that only through pain and suffering do we come to know the divinity within. I have yet to meet anyone who can disagree with this statement, and in my experience, it rings true. Suffering is like an internal wake-up call. When it rings as a break-up, a retrenchment, a death, an illness, or a sudden expected event, we have a couple of options in how we might respond. These options feel like the steps to awakening.

The first option is to blame the world, the second is to blame yourself, and the third is to find something deeper. In these three steps, I found not just myself but my calling and connection to that something deeper, which continues to challenge and awaken me each day. For me, this wasn't something that happened overnight or in a sudden rush, but rather unfolded over a period of 10 years and will no doubt continue to unfold throughout my life in ways I can't yet anticipate.

Let me explain.

Up until I was 28, I worked in advertising. When I was in high school, I had set my sights on 'corporate domination'. I wanted to rise to the top, earn a lot of money and, in the process, prove myself to everyone I met—I had a huge chip on my shoulder. This unrestrained motivation and drive allowed me to do just that. Each year, I would set goals of how

I wanted to be promoted, how much I wanted to earn, or what I wanted to buy (like a house or designer bag, etc).

All of these goals were heavily focused on what the material world could bring me if I just worked hard enough. Each year, through focus and pushing myself, I would reach them. To the point that I found myself at 27 working in the job that I always wanted in a multi-national advertising agency on a global account with enough money to buy an apartment and have my immediate material needs met... and yet I wasn't happy. Far from it.

This is a story we hear more and more frequently. Although I had achieved what I wanted and had no external needs that I couldn't fulfill, I felt incredibly empty and had this deep sense that I didn't belong. So, in typical fashion, I went back to my list of goals and decided the reason I was feeling so empty was because 'love' was missing in my life, so I added 'a relationship' to my ambitions, believing that this would fill that internal 'void'. Little did I realise, it was a 'god-sized hole' that wanted to be filled, not one any external, human love could meet.

As I turned 28, that goal of a relationship was 'fulfilled' at least in part. Little did I know at the time I was in my Saturn Returns (which occurs between 28-30) and so I was cosmically in a time of great upheaval and karmic awakening. As soon as this relationship started, it was over, and for reasons I couldn't fully understand at the time, I fell into a sense of deep discontent and mental instability that I had never before felt in my life. I felt helpless because there was nothing in the material world or in another person that could make me 'feel better'.

Little did I know, this was my first 'wake up' call. Although I couldn't see it at the time, what I was experiencing was a blessing and the universe was making me so uncomfortable that change would be inevitable as well as welcomed. That's something beautiful about the divine, it has all the time in the world for you to learn what you need to, and it will never rush you into realisation.

As such, my first reaction to the 'call' was to blame the outside world.

I looked for fault in the other person I had been in a relationship with and came up with reasons (beyond me) as to why things hadn't worked out on my 'goal sheet' as planned.

As a part of this search, I started coping with my internal discomfort by 'numbing out'. If I couldn't work out what was wrong with the external world, I would just ignore it. So, I started running, working harder, travelling more frequently, and spending money on ridiculous things like designer handbags and shoes in the hope I would get a 'hit' and somehow feel better. I quickly learnt that nothing external could really do it. Everything I strived for to distract me left me still empty, unfulfilled, and no closer to any form of mental stability or peace. I was slowly learning that there was nothing outside of myself that could make me feel 'whole'. Yes I could get a quick hit, but nothing that would bring lasting peace.

This continued for a year or so, and as I moved jobs from working in advertising to being a business consultant, my inner state of discontent continued unabated regardless of what I shifted externally. It didn't matter how big the project was that I worked on, what I was earning, how good of a job I was doing... it didn't touch the apathy I felt within.

Until a time came when I listened again to that inner call—that listlessness and jarring sense of unease—and instead of trying to fix something outside of me, I turned my eye of 'judgment' upon myself. If it wasn't the external world that was creating this suffering, it must have been me, and I was partially right (just not in the way I expected).

In looking for an answer, I believed I must have been doing something wrong. I was the common denotator in the problems I could see in my life, so I needed to change myself. This was a brief period of time laced with self-pity, victimhood, inner criticism, and shame. None of which helped fill the whole within. In fact, that just made it more obvious, for when you blame yourself for not getting what you want, it creates a stronger inner judge and little else.

It wasn't until I was walking past a yoga studio one Friday (after having practiced yoga in my early 20s as cross-training to competitive rowing at university) that I thought maybe that place had the answer I was looking for. I'm not sure why, but there was an inner tug and a pull to show up the next day and try.

Running hadn't worked, blaming myself hadn't shifted anything, and I knew I needed to help myself. So, the inner call was finally answered by something that could show me a path that was greater than myself. Again, I didn't know that at the time that I signed up to that yoga class. I thought it was just something I felt motivated to do.

That's something I've noticed in life (to date) is that it's when we think there is nowhere left to turn that the divine intercedes and, through its grace, shows us a way (without stopping us from learning the lesson we need). Often, that 'way' has been right in front of us all along. It's not the thing that creates a lot of effort or is particularly exciting—in fact, very often, it's simple, plain, and yet we can feel the soft call of what to do coming from within (even if we don't know why).

As I moved through that first yoga class, it came to the end of class (maybe the best part of the class) when you lay in Shavasana, and for some reason, my body wanted to sit up. As I sat, a sense of deep peace descended over me. My body started to rock, and all of my thoughts stopped for the first time that I could remember.

This is what I had been searching for. This is what I thought I could get from a promotion at work, from buying something new, from a relationship, and even from blaming myself. Yet, this peace had never been outside of myself—it had always been with and in me. I had just never known to look there. It had no words, it just simply was—total, joyful, absolute presence.

As soon as I felt that blissful peace, the class was over. I had received a taste, and now I naturally wanted to drink from the fountain. So, yoga became an obsession, a daily practice that was totally focused on finding that inner happiness again and again.

This is something I notice happens a lot: when we have transcendent experiences, we never want them to be a one-off, and so the ego goes about trying to re-create the exact setting to bring that transformational energy again. In my case, that was to the point of always sitting in the same place in class and sitting up during the end of the class in hopes of catching my peace again.

Now, there were classes when that peace called once more and many classes when it didn't even remotely show up. This was an energy totally uninterested in my demands, desires, or compulsive habits. What I learnt was that no two individual awakening experiences are the same—even within one individual. A beautiful lesson for me was to find acceptance with this and, in the process, to start to trust in something bigger than me that I would be given exactly what I needed, when I needed it.

At first, this spiritual connection was only through yoga, as I wrongly believed it was the only place I could find that bliss. When the peace turned out to not have a pattern I could understand, I decided I needed to learn more. So, I enrolled in Teacher Training in the hopes of learning more through the Vedic tradition.

This interest and search for answers then moved from Hinduism to Buddhism and meditation. I hadn't grown up in a religious household and was naturally apathetic to any type of organised spirituality. Slowly but surely, the universe brought me books and teachers—who had blazed a path of peace—into my orbit to learn from. Slowly, the search within became deeper.

I was no longer in a place of constant suffering and mental anguish, but rather, I was slowly learning not just that peace existed within but that it could be cultivated through meditation. So my practice moved from Asana to counting my breaths. In fact, the way I started meditating was really simple. I had no mantra or guidance, beyond sitting and mindfully counting my breathing until I lost count and then starting the process all over again.

This became a practice I did every morning. In times when I felt that inner sadness and emptiness start to appear, instead of running from it or needing to achieve something to not feel it, I would sit, breathe, and quickly I would find a little splinter of inner peace to tide me over. Just like yoga, sometimes meditation would be profound, and other times it was incredibly boring. What I noticed, though, was that, as I continued this discipline for about a year, my mental health improved, my sense of contentment in the world returned, and I started to feel joy again.

That might sound like the end of the story, but it's not...

What I found is that as my sense of happiness returned, my practice started to slip away. In small part because I was finding a tiny bit more inner peace, but mostly because the external world wasn't grating on me so much. In turn, I moved away from yoga and from meditation—even though a deep longing to connect with the divine remained.

It's a strange thing to say, but this is a really important part of any process of awakening. You can find that, as you start on the journey within, the terrain changes. Sometimes, the universe will give you a little break before something big happens again. It's rare that someone has one awakening experience in their life, and that's it. Yes, there are exceptions, but my experience has been that we have many awakening experiences in accordance with our karma and the pace at which our soul is ready.

For me, this break happened right before my next awakening, which wasn't as unfamiliar or painful as the first. I now had some tools in my back pocket and a greater sense of faith in something bigger than 'me'. So when I found myself being called to step away from my career as a business consultant, as the company hit financial pressure, and my health was suffering, I was scared but did so with a greater sense that everything would work out. There was less striving within me for things in the material realm or to change circumstances that were out of my control.

In the process, the universe met me and helped me by putting people on my path who could support this transition out of the corporate world into my own business—astrology (a story for another day)—the greatest of which was a Guru in India. It was through connecting to the divine outside of myself (in the form of a Guru) that I realised that the divine was within me. That was the peace I had experienced in the yoga studio, and it could be cultivated in anyone regardless of their position, spiritual knowledge, or beliefs. Although this journey of life hasn't finished, and the awakening process within will most definitely continue, what I have learnt is that in the suffering is the divine. That when things feel the hardest, when you feel empty or down, that is an opening gifted through the grace of source to help you remember what lives within you. What we're all looking for is within; it's as simple and as hard as that.

Pippa Kate is an astrologist and mythologist. She believes that we are all aspects of the universe being made aware of itself and that astrology is a spiritual practice to aid in this journey. Her work blends goddess astrology, mythology, and embodiment as a means to realise that the cosmos lives within each one of us. She offers 1:1 astrology readings, group cosmic meditations, and runs Full + New Moon 'Ritual + Readings' to help harness the power of each lunar cycle.

Website: www.pippa-kate.com

Instagram: www.instagram.com/iampippakate

Youtube: www.youtube.com/c/PippaKate

Courses: www.courses.pippa-kate.com

08

Moon Child

By Kailanianna Ablog
Honolulu, Hawai'i, USA

I felt Her before I heard Her.

Maybe it was because I had spent years distracting myself with school, or because I had assumed responsibilities that weren't mine to take. Perhaps it was due to a subconscious denial of what was meant for me.

Regardless of the reason, it was finally quiet enough for me to listen, and She had my full attention.

It was a humid day at the end of May, and I had settled into my *goshiwon*, a small room meant for students studying for exams. I arrived in South Korea a few days prior to prepare for my 2019 summer semester at Yonsei University's Sinchon Campus.

The decision to spend a semester in South Korea for school was one of the first times in my life that I chose myself—one of the few times that I chose to put the familial weight down.

I was about to start my junior year in college, pursuing a Bachelor's degree in Anthropology with a certificate in Korean language. My childhood interest in films like *The Mummy* and the Indiana Jones franchise made Anthropology an obvious choice for my field of collegiate study (though I was not planning on taking artifacts while donning a whip and neat hat).

The month before flying to Korea, my boyfriend and I had reached one of our first milestones: we had been with each other for a year. It had been about three years since I started writing for my college newspaper, and I was balancing (with various levels of success) my involvement in two honor societies, a K-POP dance cover group, and my familial obligations as the eldest daughter and oldest sibling.

Being the eldest daughter and oldest sibling is a humbling privilege. I love my brothers and am happy I am their sister in this lifetime. That said, as fellow eldest daughters may attest, it is a position in which many, myself included, were given responsibilities they did not ask for nor were properly prepared for. Like many firstborns, the urge to "do more" instilled itself deep within my bones from a young age.

I was born during the cusp of Capricorn and Aquarius to parents who were college freshmen. While I acknowledge my caretakers did the best with what they could at the time, I was conditioned to put others' needs before my own and taught that I could not safely express my emotions— that my inner voice could not be trusted. When I would cry about not being able to see my parents because of their college classes or work, I was told that I should be grateful that they were "doing this for me." When I expressed anger or sadness, I was often told that I "shouldn't feel that way."

To soothe the sting of consistent invalidation, I chose to pursue other means of support. I would push myself to get good grades and scholastic awards and join extracurriculars that I enjoyed enough to stick with them. While my ambition in this regard helped expand my networks and develop my logical and critical thinking skills, my inner child was left in the dark. The stunting of my emotional development, including unhealed trauma from my biological parents' divorce, led to years of pent-up anger and suicidal ideation (all of which I eventually expressed to my family, healthcare provider, and therapist).

Those I told about my mental health issues would often ask me if I had tried to find God as a means to heal. In most cases, I smiled at that.

Growing up in a multicultural Catholic household (with one family member dabbling in Wicca), ideas of greater powers, free will, and energy were not foreign to me. Although I was baptized as Catholic, attended Catholic private schools, and attended Sunday Mass somewhat consistently, spirituality called to me more than religion.

The concepts of beings beyond our comprehension, the transmutation of energies into intentions and actions—that made more sense to me than religion. I remember questioning why believing in other beings was a sin—because if God created everything we know, why could he not love those "other beings" in the same way he loved us? It also did not sit right with me when I was taught that my loved ones who did not believe in God, even those who were "lukewarm," would go to Hell unless they repented.

Along with that, it felt like a smack in the face to be told that things I was experiencing for myself were illogical—that anything that was not from God was wrong.

The first spiritual, perhaps paranormal, phenomenon that I witnessed occurred when I was about three years old. I was sandwiched between my biological parents, who were fast asleep. I don't remember what time it was, though I knew it was still nighttime as evidenced by the darkened skies I saw out the window. I was wide awake and alarmed that I couldn't find one of my plush bears, which I brought to bed with me.

I turned on my side, toward my Mother, and something—an inner knowing, perhaps—told me to look over her shoulder. My gaze trailed the curve of my Mother's shoulder and settled on something: the plush bear.

Except it wasn't on the bed behind my Mother: it was levitating a few feet away from the bed, rotating in small circles.

I was confused as to why the bear was floating there, but I did not feel like something was wrong. I stared at it, blinking profusely, and somehow fell back asleep. When I awoke, I peered over the side of the bed, where I saw the bear levitating. It was now laying in a heap on the carpet. I climbed out of bed to retrieve the plush and held it to my chest.

While that would be the first and last time I witnessed an object levitating, déjà vu and dream recollection would become common occurrences, with one instance of my classmate and I having the same dream. We were at an outdoor party, and both recalled that we had passed each other, met eyes, and that I was wearing a white lace dress.

While I wanted to dive deeper into why these things were happening, religious messaging in school and invalidation from a few family members continued into my adolescence and influenced my silence and denial of what I know now was meant to tell me that I was meant for and worthy of more.

When I graduated from high school, I became agnostic. While I recognized that religious teachings could be helpful and provide guidance for people, I knew at that point that things meant for you would not hurt you so much.

I found my way back to spirituality in late 2018, when I finally chose to accept and acknowledge it as something that best reflected and supported my worldview. Most of all, spirituality encouraged me to trust my inner voice again.

By the time I touched down in Korea, I started watching "Pick a Card" tarot readings on YouTube and felt drawn to mantras, Reiki, and the use of sound frequencies to cleanse spaces. I also learned about starseeds—souls from other galaxies that chose to reincarnate on Earth to help humanity—and believed that I could be a Sirian starseed.

Like my decision to study in Korea, I chose to realign myself with my core beliefs and follow practices that encouraged growth, not suppression and shame. Due to that choice, the paths I had subconsciously blocked became open again.

And like a Mother searching for their child, She found me within the music.

I was in my *goshiwon*, sitting cross-legged on the bed, playing a YouTube video with frequencies meant to shield against negative energy and bad luck. My eyes were closed as I took deep breaths, my hands cupped in my lap as the music flooded my ears.

About halfway through the video, the sensations began.

The skin along my scalp began to feel prickly as a gentle heat spread along my back. It felt as though someone was standing behind me, though I knew logically that was not possible. My back was facing a wall, and I would have felt the bed shift if someone had been in the room with me.

My eyes shot open, and I cast my gaze over my right shoulder. I was met with an empty space.

The concept of "beings unseen" within spirituality was not unknown to me at the time, as I related it to my understanding of ghosts, angels, and demons. I learned that people work with deities and energies, an idea that fascinated me. I also knew that it was possible to dispel negativity, and in that moment, I felt compelled to do so by saying it out loud.

"If you mean any harm, you are no longer allowed in this space," I said, ignoring how my heart started to beat faster in alarm.

I tried my best to sit still as the music continued. The heat never receded from my back—even when the video ended. I did not feel unsafe, but I knew that I definitely was not alone in that room. I never felt such an energy like that before and I accepted that if it was there, it had something for me.

"I know you're there." I spoke again as the warmth began to focus on the center of my back, as though someone had placed their hand there, "Who are you?"

A voice, one I never heard before, came through my right ear.

"Mama."

The breath that came out of my mouth was shaky. The warmth moved from my back to my right shoulder, and my eyes flickered to my laptop. With the warmth radiating behind me, I opened Google and started looking up goddesses who had the phrase "mama" in their name. After a few minutes, I came across the goddess called Mama Quilla.

"Mama. Mama Quilla." I repeated as a sudden wave of emotion crashed through my core, "Is that you?"

"Yes."

I took in another breath and started crying. It felt like I was finally home.

According to what I found, Mama Quilla is the Incan goddess of the Moon and marriage, protector of women, and regulator of menstrual cycles. She is also an embodiment of the Feminine. Like any history buff, I loved learning about the Mayan and Incan people in Social Studies class, but the topic of mythology and pantheons never came up. What gave me pause at this revelation was the fact that Mama Quilla is a Moon Goddess and is associated with silver. I have loved the Moon since I was a kid, and silver is both my favorite color and metal of choice for jewelry.

From that day on, Mama Quilla has been with me as a guide and a Mother figure for my inner child. She manifests as a warmth that gathers over my right shoulder, and it is through her that I learned that I am clairaudient.

With her guidance, I started tarot reading and now offer them to family, friends, and folks who kindly inquire. Mama Quilla has only made herself visible once: during a tarot reading I was doing over Discord during the height of the COVID-19 pandemic.

The client I was reading for said they saw an orb (Mama Quilla) form over my right shoulder and fly into the deck of tarot cards I was holding.

Working with Mama Quilla and reading tarot cards have healed my fear and wounds around invalidation and being seen as incorrect, as well as reestablished trust within myself and my inner voice. As a child, experiencing invalidation and hearing the things I wanted or believed in were wrong dealt heavy blows to my sense of self-worth.

It is through my spiritual work that, while I am still healing, I am in a much better place.

Over the years, I've started working with multiple deities, all of which are feminine. Mama Quilla is the Mother figure for my inner child, Mahakali is who I work with for my inner teenager's healing, and

Lilith is who I work with in my adult life. I've been told that my tarot readings are accurate, and while I do not claim to predict the future, what I've seen in the cards has come true. I've taken up Reiki and am a Level II White Light Reiki Practitioner.

The validity of spirituality tends to be contested, especially by those who rely on hard sciences. From a logical standpoint, my clairaudience and inner knowing may be forms of self-preservation. I choose to believe it is something more.

My (agnostic) biological father asked me once: "What do you think when people say that you are working with demons?"

I told him, "How could I be working with demons if they are encouraging me to heal and help others?"

Spiritual awakenings can come in many forms. Some may experience it early or later on in their lives. For me, I was always awake. I just chose to ignore it until I finally decided to stop. On this path, I've learned that the things meant for you will never miss you or hurt you. Your heart knows what it wants and needs. Sometimes, all you need to do is choose to listen.

♡ ♡ ♡

Kailanianna (Kai) Ablog is an Oʻahu-born journalist-turned-archaeologist of Pacific Islander and Southeast Asian descent. Having been raised in a multicultural household, ideas of religion and spirituality were introduced to her at a young age. This provided tools for Kai to gain new perspectives as to how beliefs inform the ways humans do the things they do. Part of Kai's mission is to study and capture the nuances of the human experience through her work, with hopes of reminding people of their autonomy and empowering folks to think critically and use kind discernment while moving through life. When Kai is not writing, pulling tarot cards, or practicing Reiki, she may be found enjoying a matcha latte or bubble tea, listening and dancing to K-POP, or reading. You may also spot Kai galavanting in Kaimukī, the neighborhood where she was raised. Instagram: www.instagram.com/empressstarseed

09

Dark Night of the Soul and the Blue Star Being

By Emma Wertheim
Sydney, Australia

I believe awakenings happen continuously throughout our lives, right up to the moment of our death and beyond. Each one is an important lesson in faith, trust, and letting go. A perpetual dance that returns us back to our hearts.

In my experience, awakenings are often small, with gems of insight garnered with time. It's the cataclysmic ones that become defining landmarks in our life story—that shift the very foundation of our inner and outer reality, leaving us wilted and hollow, clinging on for dear life.

What I also know, after almost half a century on the planet, is that awakenings are nearly always born out of struggle.

"When you pass through the waters, I will be with you; and when you pass through the rivers, they will not sweep over you. When you walk through the fire, you will not be burned; the flames will not set you ablaze." - Isaiah 43:2 (NIV)

Awakenings can sometimes be referred to as the dark night of the soul, shadow work, existential or spiritual crisis, or "entering the void." We all face these times in our lives when our mettle is tested and the sword of our resilience is forged. It's where a glimmer of faith or hope burns somewhere deep within.

The term "dark night of the soul" comes from 16th-century Spanish mystic Saint John of the Cross, who describes it as a profound spiritual crisis where the soul feels abandoned by God. This intense suffering is seen as a necessary step toward spiritual union with the divine.

First, before I share my own story of entering the void and experiencing one of those poignant awakening milestones, I'd like to paint a picture of where I was in my life and everything that led up to that moment.

The Grunge Years

It was the 1990s, and grunge vibes were in the air.

I've always been a spiritual seeker and creative soul at heart. I doodled on bed quilts, walls, and myself. I would literally draw on everything. I also loved photography, acting, and dance. My ex-professional ballerina/ artsy mother naturally encouraged all this.

Yes, I was that annoying 16-year-old, asking all the big questions like: "Does God exist?" and "What happens after you die?" But even elders I spoke to at the time left me with more questions than answers. Surely someone knew something?

Guided by an intuitive sense that "there must be more", I explored my own and other religions and various spiritual traditions. I would turn up to free meditation classes after school with other attendees three times my age. I had a Bat Mitzvah, and attended Christian church services. I also went to Hare Krishna gatherings, and was a frequent visitor to metaphysical bookstores, devouring books on various topics like Buddhism, mindfulness, and Paganism.

My inner seeking and sense of discord with the world were expressed in an outward manner. For me, it was the only thing I could do that made sense at the time. I went through grunge, goth, medieval (my favourite), and hippy phases. I lost myself in the feelings music stirred in me.

At home, my bedroom became an oasis, my retreat from the realities of teenage angst. I had the most amazing purple and blue lava lamp, a '60s fibre optic rotating light (I wish I still had it!), an original red cane peacock chair, and Janis Joplin-style scarves covering most surfaces. It was all about the ambience and soft lighting. Most nights, I'd burn candles and incense, cast love spells, or write letters to a shaman living on Dharug and Gundungurra Country/The Blue Mountains. '70s music was on repeat all through the night.

My imaginary world sprang to life in the quiet hours of the night. I dabbled in many things. In reality, I was looking for something deeper, something that would fill my being with calm and hope—not imaginary—but real and visceral. I was keenly aware that something was missing.

Little did I know I was about to go through two of the most difficult years of my life.

Dark Night of the Soul

Let's descend...

I'm not getting out my mini violin here. Everything is relative, of course, and I'm sure there will be people reading this who have experienced things beyond anything I have encountered. I simply wish to paint a picture of my own dark night of the soul between the ages of 17 and 18.

It wasn't just one event, but a barrage of things—like an out-of-control bushfire.

Here's the highlight reel:
- My parents went through a separation and divorce.
- The family home was sold.
- I was in my final year of high school.

- We had money concerns.
- Mum got hit by a car.
- Dad had surgery and complications from it.
- My grandfather had two major surgeries, and my grandmother had one big operation (I was very close to them).
- I had undiagnosed endometriosis and suffered debilitating periods each month.
- I had an ovarian cyst the size of an orange, which ruptured—I needed emergency surgery and spent a month out of school recovering.
- I went through my first major relationship break-up.

So, it had been quite a year. Then, everything crescendoed at my 18th birthday party.

Around midnight, I was driven by a friend to the local hospital. I became unwell during the celebration and felt like I was about to die. Perhaps it was the first of many panic attacks or something else—I'll never know for sure.

I was lying in my hospital bed with the festivities still happening back home, feeling alone and scared.

I remember silently calling out to God and the great beings of light with every part of me, begging them to spare my life. If they did, I promised to dedicate myself to an esoteric path. That night, I made an earnest pledge to my soul.

Suddenly, it was as if my mind's eye opened, and I saw a scene, like a movie playing out before me. There were beings sitting around a table—like a grand boardroom table (think Downton Abbey but more grandiose)—discussing and pondering if it was my time to leave Earth or if I should get another shot at things.

Then, I sensed they had reached an agreement. I'd get to stay on and continue with my life. But with that decision came a message. They shared an intuitive sort of language, not words, so to speak. And what they had to say was not what I expected. You need to understand that at this point, I thought I'd already gone through the toughest of times.

Their message was, "Everything you have gone through leading up to now is nothing compared to what you will go through in the years to come if you choose to walk a spiritual path in life."

They told me that choosing a spiritual path is not for the faint-hearted. It's incredibly hard, but the rewards are equally great. It would take discipline and dedication to walk a path of inner transformation; Real WORK—harder than any chosen career path or life challenge.

Strangely, at that moment, I also felt a sense of relief. The weight of everything I'd been through in recent years lifted off me. I saw that all I'd been caught up in was preparation for the real work to come. I also saw that I needed to get off my butt and onto a spiritual path ASAP!

A couple of years earlier, through a very dear girlfriend of mine, I had found an esoteric school. This place felt like 'coming home' with its teaching based on meditation and cultivating inner stillness. I could feel the living truth of it in the people who were part of this community, with its roots in what is known as "The Fourth Way" pioneered by George Gurdjieff.

There is a saying that crops up in many mystical traditions: "When the student is ready, the teacher will appear." I knew I had found what I was looking for, but the truth is, after being welcomed and meeting its teacher—I wasn't ready at that time. Despite my enthusiasm, I was a bit of a hot mess and had more life lessons ahead of me before I could make a real commitment. I was also quite young.

But knowing this school existed was like a little lamp of hope, burning softly in the background of everything else I had going on. It quietly buoyed me through those turbulent teenage years.

Now I was ready. My birthday night spent in hospital was an initiation of sorts. Without this, I sometimes wonder if I would have spun off the side of the planet in my "double-Gemini-ness". The "Work", as it is often called, literally saved my life and forever changed my trajectory.

And the other blessing of that night was Mum turning up to the hospital. She sat at the bedside with me, held my hand until daybreak, and then took me home.

The Blue Star Being

A few months after joining the esoteric school, I was still living at home with my mum. I was going through a phase of not wanting to sleep on a bed. I slept on the floor—zen-style.

Lying on my back one night, I found myself suddenly awake, or it felt like that anyway, as I was definitely asleep. My bedroom was on the top floor of our two-storey, semi-detached home. I was gazing up and watched as the bedroom ceiling completely dissolved, revealing the most magnificent night sky—an inky expanse of millions of twinkling stars. I had never seen anything like it. It was like the sky was breathing, and I was breathing with it.

Then I noticed one star, in particular, twinkling brighter than all the rest, like a diamond. My attention locked onto this star, and to my complete amazement, I realised it was moving—travelling toward me. I had no idea what was going to happen next.

As the star came closer, I realised it wasn't a star but a radiant entity of blue light, the most beautiful being I'd ever laid eyes on. She was dressed in simple garb of feminine expression. Her clothes were billowing around her as she floated closer, moving with purpose and intention. She had dark, almost black hair and a milky pale complexion similar to my own. As her face came into view, I noticed it was filled with an expression of pure love. I kept wondering, "Is this my soul?" But then I thought she was too magnificent for that.

Closer and closer, she came. What was going to happen?

Now, just metres away, without slowing, she entered my body, and in that same moment, I sat bolt upright, wide awake, breathing hard and fast.

77

I sat completely still in bed, coming back to the room and looking up at the ceiling firmly in place again. I couldn't quite believe what had just happened. But I could feel the energy of it still coursing through me. It felt like I might have been slightly glowing in the dark! I was also drenched in sweat and very hot. I went straight back to sleep and had dreams of resting in ancient groves surrounded by exotic birds stroking me softly with their wings.

I haven't ever been able to fully articulate what I felt that night because I've never known anything so exquisite: that sensation of being completely held in the energy of a holy presence.

My dedication to soul work was sealed in deepest reverie. I was "all in", fully committed to walking a sacred path with a hand-over-heart pledge to face any future challenge with open arms, inviting in the big soul lessons, letting go of fear in the process. I felt naked, reborn.

The Light of a New Dawn

My teacher at the esoteric school would often talk about how we are physical beings on earth having a soul experience, bringing spirit into matter. That's the real transformation. Many spiritual teachings talk about this.

For me, as a member of a school that cultivates the sacred within, the most beneficial daily ritual has been meditation with breathwork—it's made me a calmer and better person. Also, in more recent years, I've incorporated the sacred energy of Hasta mudras, ancient yogic hand postures, into my meditation practice. Through this work of stillness, energy, breath, and awareness, I've found a space within that has nourished my soul and given me great peace over the decades. It has seen me through many challenges and all the gifts of this life.

My lived belief is that there is much to be gained from introducing small rituals and disciplines into daily life, like meditation, mudras, or breathwork, whatever practice sings to your soul. These tools help you move into a heart-centred space and integrate the mind with more balance so your decisions become more grounded and aligned, allowing a truly magical life to take shape.

Awakening seems to me like a continual journey of unfolding, a way for us to grow—to delve deeper and reach higher, as great mysteries reveal themselves in the polarity of light and dark and all the shades in between.

♡ ♡ ♡

Emma Wertheim is a Guringai/Sydney-based meditation, yoga, and sacred dance teacher with a special interest in yoga mudras. Since 1995, she has been part of an esoteric school with origins in The Fourth Way movement, dedicated to cultivating stillness as a foundation for transformation in veryday life.

She is the author and artist behind Yoga Mudra Oracle, which was created in collaboration with husband, artist, and writer Steve Denham. This project communicates the ancient wisdom and multi-dimensional benefits of yoga mudra hand postures.

As a graphic designer, intuitive digital artist, and photographer, her creative work is inspired by spirituality. Her work is featured on book covers, websites, greeting cards, and oracle decks, expressing a sense of peace and hope while reminding us of the ebb and flow of mystery woven through daily life.

Website: www.emmawertheim.com

Instagram: www.instagram.com/emmawertheim_

Facebook: www.facebook.com/emmawertheim.mudras

Youtube: www.youtube.com/@emmawertheim

10

Healing from Within: My Story of Transformation Through Medical Astrology and Holistic Remedies

By Angela Hendry
Zurich, Switzerland

My spiritual awakening came when I least expected it, and it felt like the rug had been pulled out from under my life. At the time, I was experiencing what I thought was burnout. Having spent years in the high-pressure world of corporate HR, I knew all too well the feelings of stress, exhaustion, and frustration that come with the territory. My life had become a series of relentless cycles—working long hours, sacrificing self-care, and living in a state of dis-ease. It was in this state of depletion that my awakening began.

What sparked my spiritual journey wasn't a conscious choice. It wasn't me sitting down one day and deciding I wanted to live a more spiritual life. No, it came like a tidal wave—uninvited but ultimately life-changing. Physically, I was burnt out; emotionally, I was drained. I had chronic health issues, from asthma to frequent UTI infections, and a general sense of being unwell. I was overweight, anxious, and feeling utterly disconnected from my own body. But instead of addressing my body's cries for help with more rest or self-care, I kept pushing. Like so many people, I was caught in the mentality that hustle and productivity equaled success. It was only when my body gave up that I finally listened.

At first, I had no idea what was happening. It felt like a complete breakdown—mentally, physically, and spiritually. I didn't have the language for what was going on, but it was as if my soul had finally reached a breaking point and was demanding attention. I remember lying in bed, feeling as if my body and spirit had nothing left to give. I had spent years trying every health fad, every self-help book, and every diet, all in the hopes that something outside of myself could fix me. And yet, here I was, more lost than ever. I felt like I was grasping at straws, looking for answers where there were none.

I didn't realize it at the time, but my soul was speaking to me. It was urging me to stop, to listen, and to heal. What I had once seen as burnout was actually the doorway to a spiritual awakening. My soul had been trying to communicate with me for years, but I had ignored the signs. The chronic health issues, the deep sense of dissatisfaction with life, the feelings of being out of alignment—they were all symptoms of a deeper spiritual disconnection.

Through this awakening, I began to recognize how essential it was to pay attention to my body's wisdom and energy. I studied and received certifications in various holistic modalities, starting with aromatherapy and herbs. Over time, I expanded my knowledge and training to include movement, yoga, meditation, breathwork, minerals, sound, and energy practices. As my journey unfolded, it became clear that I needed to explore Medical Astrology, which provided deeper insights into the patterns and needs of my body.

Each modality played a significant role in helping me reconnect with parts of myself I had forgotten existed. As I deepened my understanding, I realized that everything I had learned over more than a decade, was already reflected in my Medical Astrology Chart. I only wish I had known where to look earlier, as the answers were there all along, hidden in plain sight. This realization marked a turning point in my journey.

Now, I help others explore their Health Astrology Charts to find the answers to their health and wellness questions. From my own Medical Astrology Chart, I learned several key things about maintaining my well-being: I need to keep my body warm, regularly detox by sweating, and pay extra attention to my mental health, especially during the colder, darker months of winter. Hard and sweaty workouts are essential for keeping my mental health in balance. In addition, I take Mimulus flower essences to manage anxiety and prevent worry spirals, and I eat warm foods and Calcium Phosphate-rich foods like lentils, beans, wheat, parsley, raisins, strawberries, and blueberries to support my Astrological Health Blueprint. I ground and support my root chakra by working with rutilated quartz for stability, drinking plenty of ginger tea, and using vetiver essential oil for warmth, grounding, and overall well-being. This understanding has transformed the way I approach my health, and I now use these insights to guide others toward their own healing and transformation.

As I began to embrace my awakening, the biggest challenge was trusting the process. Awakening often feels like you're being torn apart and put back together, but in the moment, it's hard to see how things will ever fall into place. I had to let go of control, let go of the notion that I could fix everything with the next "big thing," and surrender to the healing tools that actually resonated with me—yoga, meditation, sound healing, and aromatherapy. These holistic practices were what saved me. They reconnected me to my breath, my body, and my spirit and ultimately led me back to myself.

One of the most profound things I learned was that healing is not linear. It's a journey that ebbs and flows, and it's deeply personal. Through my spiritual awakening, I realized that we often look for healing outside of ourselves, but the real work is internal. No tool or practice will work unless it aligns with your soul's blueprint. My journey wasn't about becoming a "better" version of myself; it was about returning to who I was all along—someone who could listen to her body, honor her soul, and cultivate real well-being.

I also learned that what works for others may not necessarily work for you. Take ice baths, for example. When everyone I knew was doing them, I jumped on the bandwagon, believing it would help me feel better. But for me, it had the opposite effect—I got sick each time I tried it. Only later did I realize that my Saturnian energy thrives on warmth. My body needs heat to function optimally, which is why activities like hot yoga, eating spicy foods, and sweating work wonders for me. Medical Astrology offered me a framework for understanding my unique constitution, and it helped me stop comparing my journey to anyone else's.

Today, in my forties, I am healthier than I've ever been. I'm free of the chronic ailments that plagued me in my twenties and early thirties, and I've found a profound sense of peace and alignment. My life and work have completely transformed. I no longer view health as something to chase or fix. Instead, I see it as an ongoing practice of self-care, listening to my body, and staying in tune with my spirit. The joy and fulfillment I experience now stem from this deep connection with myself—a connection I was missing for so many years.

For those navigating a spiritual awakening, my biggest advice is to be gentle with yourself. Awakenings can feel overwhelming, especially when your old life starts to crumble, and it's easy to fall into fear or doubt. The most important thing is to trust your process. Each person's awakening is different, and that's okay. Don't rush it, and don't feel like you need to "fix" everything immediately. Instead, take time to cultivate practices that nourish your mind, body, and spirit. And most importantly, listen to your inner wisdom. You already have the answers within you; it's just a matter of trusting them.

Self-care is not a luxury during a spiritual awakening; it is a necessity. You are in the process of becoming who you are meant to be, and that requires energy. It is easy to get caught up in the intensity of the spiritual experience and neglect the physical and emotional aspects of your life. I always remind my clients that taking care of your body is taking care of your spirit. The two are not separate. Your body is the vessel through which your soul operates in this world, and it must be cared for accordingly. This is where tools like Medical Astrology become invaluable. They provide insight into what your unique body and soul need to thrive.

If you're struggling with how to integrate your spiritual awakening with your physical and emotional health, know that there are tools available to help guide you. Medical Astrology, for example, can offer incredible insights into your health blueprint and provide the shortcuts I wish I had known earlier in my journey. There is no need to struggle or suffer for years, as I did. The secrets to your health and well-being are already written in the stars, and with the right guidance, you can unlock the radiant health you deserve.

The beauty of awakening is that it never really ends. It is an ongoing process of discovery and growth, and each layer you peel back reveals more of who you truly are. Trust that every step of the journey, no matter how challenging, is bringing you closer to your authentic self. And remember, you don't have to do it alone. There are guides and tools available to help you along the way. Your spiritual and physical health are deeply intertwined, and when you nurture both, you create the foundation for a life of fulfillment and joy.

Angela Hendry is a Professional Coach currently studying Music Therapy at the University of Arts in Zurich. She is an international Yoga Teacher (E-RYT 500), Medical and Health Astrologer, Aromatherapist, and Sound and Energy Healer, with a diverse background in Psychology, Business, and Human Resources. As the founder of Modern Moon Mystic, Angela helps clients achieve radiant health through holistic practices, including Medical Astrology, Yoga, Breathwork, Meditation, Sound and Crystal Healing, Aromatherapy, and Herbal Medicine. Having personally overcome a range of health challenges, Angela is passionate about guiding others on their wellness journeys through customized programs.

Website: www.astrovitality.com

Instagram: www.instagram.com/astrovitality_official

More Links: www.linktr.ee/astrovitality

11

Entering the Blue Lily Portal

By Michelle Cowell
Brisbane, Queensland, Australia

I've been fascinated with Egypt, ancient cultures, and places like Machu Picchu, Mexican temples, Stonehenge, stone circles, and the sacred lands of Japan and Hawaii for as long as I can remember. I yearned to travel, and in my younger years, I absorbed so much information about these places, researching and dreaming. I am an Aries Sun with a Leo Moon with Aquarius Rising, an adventurer who loves watching Indiana Jones, and someone who is curious with an appetite for self-discovery.

As part of my 'muggle job', I travelled to Japan twice a year, where I was introduced to Reiki, which is a Japanese ancient healing practice, and I immersed myself in its fascinating culture of chaos and zen. Here I discovered shinrin-yoku (forest bathing), tea ceremony, and other mindful practices. At this time, my spirituality consisted of working with botanicals and nature, crystals, creating personal rituals, and celebrating the moon cycles and the wheel of the year.

My spiritual awakening was significantly activated when receiving my Usui Reiki First Degree Attunement (Shoden). During my attunement, the music speakers in the room started crackling, and I saw in my mind's eye a large number of spirit guides and star family gathered around me. It was as if a veil had been lifted, yet reality had been shattered. I could feel and sense my higher self (soul) and spirit showing me the way. I was being energetically aligned with a higher vibrational path and consciousness.

A week after my attunement, I began noticing that non-aligned, stagnant energetics started falling away. It was intense and painful. Like the Tower card in the tarot, old forever-long friends started exiting my life, which was a deeply emotional time. I started feeling triggered by the people I met or worked with, which I realised was a mirror into myself that required exploration and healing. I no longer wanted to watch or read the news or resonated with 'fear-based' messaging. I started craving more nutritious meals, and alcohol no longer appealed to me.

As I moved through the Usui Reiki Second Degree and Reiki Third Degree attunements, life was literally changing before my eyes! My higher self was calling me to dive deep into shadow work, which is never comfortable. To descend into the underworld, reflect on my life, and experience a dark night of the soul (which felt very much like a nervous breakdown). As I was searching for meaning, I felt completely isolated and was unsure of my purpose. *Why was I here? What direction in life do I take?*

I was learning that time and space were one and the same; there is no past or future—everything lies in the present moment. I saw that everything that happened to me was actually FOR me and was all part of a soul contract I had agreed to before entering this Earth School experience.

As I rose from the depths of the underworld to see the light, I felt compelled to undertake my first spiritual pilgrimage. However, I didn't know what this looked like or where I was meant to travel to. When scrolling through websites one afternoon, I saw a spiritual pilgrimage taking place in Hawaii, and deep within my soul, I knew I needed to sign up!

Four months later, I was on the Big Island, experiencing life-changing transformative moments. I undertook my first past life regression and discovered that I lived in both Lemuria and Atlantis. I heard myself speak while under a trance and express past life moments in detail. I learnt that I was a Starseed and felt strong connections with particular star systems and beings, which explained a lot in relation to how I felt growing up—that I was a black sheep and didn't really 'fit' into society. There was so much questioning going on in my mind during this trip. *Was I making this all up? Was I going crazy? Was the UFO-shaped craft in the background of a photo of myself real?*

The next phase for me was around the theme of 'Trust and Surrender' a.k.a. following the breadcrumbs that the universe was literally dropping in front of me, left, right and centre. My higher self was pushing me to set up my own spiritual business, which was way outside of my comfort zone! Nevertheless, I listened to, showed up, and followed the calling, and 'Soul Starr Studio' was born, offering Reiki and Crystal Healing Soul Sessions. I started working with clients and being of service to humanity.

Enter Egypt—Hathor's sistrum was vibrationally calling me from beyond the veil. By now, I knew better than to ignore any spiritual callings, so I booked my flights and tour and started packing! A few weeks before I departed Brisbane for Cairo, I started receiving a 'download,' a calling to birth sacred ritual oils into the world infused with Egyptian energetics. I followed this advice and purchased litres and litres of almond oil (again, questioning my 'crazy'!). Here I was in this ancient, sacred land, immersing myself in history, hieroglyphics, and potent energies. It was yet another learning about the importance of trust and surrendering to the understanding that if it is meant to be, then it will.

Before entering any temples or sites, you are required to go through a security check, including x-ray machines with an array of items that are not permitted to be taken into such sites. I was reading on the sign that one of these items included oil of any kind. Here I was, waiting in line at security, carrying bottles of almond oil concealed within my backpack, literally experiencing heart palpitations around them being confiscated. But alas, trust and surrender—I was through security, my bags inspected via x-ray machines, and I entered into all sites without a word about what I was carrying in my backpack.

During my second day in Cairo, I found myself being seated at an enormous shared table by the hotel waiter for breakfast. Why did he not seat me at the available tables for two instead of a table for twenty? Five minutes later, my question was answered. A group of Japanese people were seated beside and around me. Suddenly, I experienced a compulsive feeling to introduce myself, in Japanese, to the lady seated beside me. *But why?* I looked over at the group and noticed a Japanese man drawing Reiki symbols over his breakfast. I took a deep breath and then, in my broken Japanese, introduced myself to the lady seated beside me, and asked if she could speak English. And what do you know, she could! She was part of a sacred 'Ryujin Reiki' group. I had never heard of this form of Reiki before, but obviously, this meeting was not one of chance. We exchanged contact information and parted ways.

Also during this Egyptian pilgrimage, the deity Horus was revealed to me, and a spiritual jigsaw puzzle began. I could see layers and layers of shrouds in my mind's eye that were part of an even greater self-awakening. I realised I was on a highly personal mission to discover who and what I really was.

As I immersed myself in the Karnak and Luxor temples and sacredly entered the Valley of the Kings, visiting tombs of ancient Egyptian Pharaohs, I noticed an Egyptian eagle would be circling the site or would sit on the temple structures watching me. *What did this mean? What was the mystery here?*

During this two-week pilgrimage, there were many more breadcrumbs dropped, which was wonderful, but each breadcrumb led to even more questions. The name 'Followers of Horus' had been given to me. *Who were they?* Another piece of this enigmatic puzzle. Once back in Brisbane, I journeyed through a period of energetic integration and just 'knew' I needed to revisit Egypt and sail deeper into my personal transformative journey, with daily synchronicities becoming stronger and more prevalent in my life.

Two months later, I found myself on the Gold Coast, Australia, overlooking the ocean while undertaking a Ryujin Reiki workshop and being attuned directly from Master Kawashima, the founder of Dragon God Reiki. Our meeting in Cairo was not by chance; this was universal alignment. This was followed by further attunements in Tokyo, Japan, two months later when Master Kawashima 'happened' to be running a workshop on the one day I had off whilst I was there on a business trip. There was no going back now.

Egypt had not yet finished with me! I returned to Cairo, filled with excitement, this time as part of an all-women's spiritual pilgrimage. Laying in the King's Chamber of the Great Pyramid in deep meditation, smelling blue lilies while hearing the beautiful hum of crystal bowls, I left my body and experienced two separate meditations taking place at the same time. I astral travelled out the top of the Pyramid, through the Orion star system, and out into the universe, receiving hidden information whilst I was simultaneously in-body undertaking a different journey of scent and chakra alignment.

At the Temple of Dendera Complex, I experienced a flashback to when I was there in a past life. However, it looked very different from today. The Goddess Hathor guided me, along with three other ladies, as we subtly left the larger group and climbed up a ladder, squeezing through a tiny entrance hole to be given direct entry into a small sacred chamber dedicated to Hathor. As her image on the wall looked down upon us, I heard a humming in the ether, and my entire body started vibrating. I could actually see the skin and hairs on my arm moving with the deep hum of this temple. We were experiencing something powerful, magical, ancient, and sacred. The word 'Devotion' was provided to me, and the veil lifted further.

The following morning at 4:00 am, we boarded a bus that took us to the Aswan Low Dam, where we climbed into a colourful motorboat and sailed to Philae Temple, located on a small island in the dam.

The only way to reach this ancient, sacred temple complex is by boat. As the sun rose, painting the sky in soft shades of orange and pink, I stepped onto the wooden ramp. My feet touched the ground, my heart filled with immense love, and my mind filled with a deep knowing that something magical was about to happen. Philae Temple is dedicated to the Goddess Isis, as well as Osiris and Horus. Past life memories danced before my eyes. I recalled journeying here many moons ago in BCE as part of a group that was travelling up and down the Nile River on a pilgrimage from temple to temple all laid out to reflect the Milky Way in the skies above; however, I wasn't Egyptian.

On 8 April, 2024, during the solar eclipse inside the temple's inner sanctum, the Knot of Isis, an incantation is recited and I am spontaneously initiated into 'The Priestess Path' with this group of women, by Isis herself, who is being channelled through our Spiritual Guide—all unplanned and totally unexpected. In my mind's eye, I saw the blue lily open to reveal her golden centre, pulling me into her magical portal. What a powerful astrologically aligned gift!

To be completely vulnerable and answer my own question of 'Who and what am I?' I have come to discover that I am a fractal of source energy and I am here reliving the pattern of a past life. I am one of the Followers of Horus with Starseed connections who escaped Atlantis through a portal / stargate into Egypt via the Sphinx. Through my travels, I am collecting information and codes I have left for myself to find and am awakening to the truth of the past, which is very different to the one we have been taught. I have learnt to be okay with being the black sheep. I've experienced many awakenings (so much more than I can include in one chapter). I continue to peel back my layers of life conditioning and feel that I can now be of service to others. To help with the next wave of global awakening that will take place on this beautiful planet, to be an empowering spiritual guide for others, as I would have loved someone to be there for me. It can feel quite daunting going through it alone. Once your inner knowing has been roused, there is no turning back!

Mother Gaia is ascending, as is our consciousness.

We are living through a time that has been predicted through the ages. We are exceptionally fortunate to be here to witness this global ascension and collective shift in humanity.

As I close this chapter, I deeply thank my higher self and my spiritual and galactic family for their loving support and guidance. My awakening journey continues with a pilgrimage to Bali in 2025 where I will enter the portal of 'Devotion' and discover the meaning of this sacred word given to me in Egypt.

My key takeaways:

1. The Awakening process never ends. We're forever remembering and feeling into the mystery of being a soul having a human experience.
2. Trust yourself—do not second guess what you know deep within or are shown by your spiritual guides / higher self.
3. Surrender to the universe—you are safely held.
4. Connect and work with trusted spiritual mentors and healers who have been through their own awakenings. They identify with how you feel and can lovingly guide you through the process.
5. Seek out a like-minded supportive community, whether this be in person or online.
6. Challenge yourself and transform—live an aligned, authentic life.
7. And the big one—you are NOT going crazy!

Michelle from Soul Starr Studio is an Usui Reiki Master, Crystal Healing Practitioner, and Spiritual Guide who creates high-vibrational ritual oils and botanical products based on transformative spiritual pilgrimages.

Michelle works with embodied energetics and chakra balancing and is highly passionate about targeting the root of imbalance for a well-rounded healing experience. She feels it is a great honour and privilege to be part of her clients' healing journey. She believes that healing is a layered approach that brings us back to homeostasis. Her sessions hold a high vibration of love, compassion, integrity, and authenticity. Michelle looks forward to working together with you to reawaken and align your divine spark.

Website: www.soulstarrstudio.com.au

Instagram: www.instagram.com/soulstarrstudio

Services: www.soulstarrstudio.com.au/general-2-2

12

The Way it Was and The Way it is Now

By Lisa McConnell
Greenbank, Queensland, Australia

Back in the beginning, I had always had hopes and dreams that my awakening would happen the way others' have—a big moment, followed by a sudden complete opening—where one moment I couldn't see energy or spirit, and the next I could. Then, the world would suddenly be filled with the sights, sounds, and everything else from the otherwise unseen realms. This was my dream because I always believed I was better at dealing with something after it had happened than planning for it and preparing for it to happen bit by bit.

This was not how it happened for me.

Growing up, I felt alone, the black sheep, the odd one out. I still feel that way now, but I don't care as much. I realised not too long ago, when I was in one of those moments of despair about why my awakening hadn't happened like I wanted, that the reason I wanted it that way was because I thought nothing interesting had or would ever happen for me, and that if I had an easy connection to spirit, then I wouldn't be lonely anymore.

What actually happened was a series of smaller events, which collectively have opened me up and allowed me to adjust and not freak out when something new happens. I didn't realise how much the fear of seeing or hearing was actually holding me back. I had plenty of those moments when I was a child of waking up in the night and thinking the clothes in my wardrobe had a face, or that a shadow from the street light was a spirit watching me. They may have been, may not have been, but either way, I was freaked out in those moments—and that fear stayed with me.

Cut to my early 20s. When I started learning healing techniques (kinesiology, reiki, theta healing, and sound healing), I discovered my intuition was pretty on point—I could pick things up in those that I was working with that they hadn't mentioned or that weren't listed in the charts I used. I never thought much of it because I thought it was something that just came with the territory. When I realised that others couldn't do it, that it wasn't natural to them, I shied away from doing it so they didn't feel less than. Outside of classes, I still had to follow the "rules" of the technique I was using, but I eventually learned that following the rules was holding me back, and I allowed my intuition to lead the way.

Life continued on for years like that.. nothing much changed. I was growing pretty annoyed at the universe (and myself) for not delivering on this magic event I was after, this one event that would change everything, and when something did come, it absolutely wasn't what I expected!

The Covid lockdowns in Sydney meant that I had to stop seeing in-person clients and move to fully online. This was something I was toying with anyway, but I always loved the connection from an in-person session.

At the same time, I got the idea that I needed to offer my sessions intuitively, meaning I just tuned into the client and gave them whatever was coming through rather than relying on the structure of the technique I used. This pushed me so much, brought up so many fears and worries, but also opened me up more than I could imagine! After each session, I was absolutely buzzing with energy, and I could FEEL what clients were feeling.

I was getting messages from spirit and loved ones, but they all came through as feelings or knowings. I would feel a string of thought in my mind, and speak it, rather than listening to words and repeating them back.

This was what I consider to be the first of two moments that I call awakenings. During this time, too, I had great success in my business, and was honestly feeling like nothing could stop me.

But then it did stop—whether it was my own doing or not, I don't know, but it stopped. And if I'm honest, it still hasn't come back yet after three years and LOTS of healing work.

The next awakening moment that came was only seven months ago when I was diagnosed with pneumonia and hospitalised for a week for intravenous medication because I was unresponsive to the usual medication. As it turned out, I had some unknown bacteria causing the pneumonia, rather than one of the usual 15, so it really was a strange occurrence.

I should backtrack here and mention that I also only believed that the only way I could have a proper spiritual awakening was if I was "in hospital" (or similar) because I didn't have time to have a breakdown! I had read stories of people being bedridden for weeks whilst the awakening happened. I couldn't do that! I had a job, and a family, and a mortgage… I needed to function.

Back to the hospital. I was admitted, put on oxygen, given the IV for my medication, and basically advised to just take it easy and let this thing pass. On the second night after I was admitted, I had my moment…

I don't remember the specifics, and I do know that prolonged constant oxygen can stop REM sleep and cause hallucinations, but I had what I believe to be my biggest awakening yet.

I remember it being about 3am, I was almost asleep, and suddenly, I felt like there was something after me. I opened my eyes, clawed at my face to get my oxygen off, got out of bed as soon as I could, and stood in the corner of the room, arms around myself, rocking side to side, repeating over and over, "I am safe, I am safe, I am safe." I don't know how long I did that, but I do know it took a while for me to settle enough to get back into bed.

When I did sleep, my dreams were so vivid and scary to the point where I didn't want to go to sleep at all because I knew I would dream something I didn't want to see. During the next day, I did guided meditations, and I could SEE the energy. I remember vivid pictures of energy swirling all around, and I could sit back in awe at the energy moving as I did the meditation. In another meditation, I had a full experience as if I was in the Troll family from the *Frozen* movies—that vision started because I tried connecting to the trees and bushes I could see through the window.

I was seeing in a way I had never seen before, and I was absolutely loving that experience! Sadly, that has somewhat reduced now, but I am still more visual than I was before.

During my fourth day in hospital, I heard a voice very clearly call: "Lisa Robyn Bialkowski"

My response was, "Huh? That's not my name?"

Voice: "That is the name you were born with."

Me: "Ok, yeah, fair enough."

Voice: "This is your initiation..."

I can't even begin to explain how stunned I was, and as much as I tried, I couldn't tune in anymore and got no further answers that day.

After that, however, other interesting things happened. I found I could talk to my body and tell it to pay attention and listen. I was having a big coughing fit, and I just yelled in my mind, "Body, STOP," and the coughing stopped. Every time I was coughing after that, I would tell my body, "Cough if you are bringing up gunk, but otherwise, no." My coughing reduced significantly. Also, when I was struggling to get comfortable, I would close my eyes, and I'd see levels (like in a spirit level tool), showing me exactly how to arrange the bed so that my body was the most comfortable.

After my hospital stay, I discovered in meditation one day that my pneumonia was planned by me as an opportunity to have my initiation/ awakening! However, as my pneumonia was worse than I'd apparently planned, it was decided that I would allow my body to rest (by watching TV) rather than experience the full awakening. I was sad at discovering this, thinking I'd wasted my one and only opportunity. However, I now see that if I had walked out of hospital still seeing as vividly as I could, hearing the voices as I was, I wouldn't have been able to go back to normal work/family life afterward. I would have needed much more time alone to integrate. So again, I had my confirmation that a big awakening story wasn't for me.

The awakening experience did have some unexpected benefits—it allowed me to see that a relationship I thought was important wasn't important to the other person, and I was able to walk away much easier than I thought. This also involved me leaving a long term job, which I had been trying to do for a while anyway, but always felt guilt over. The guilt was gone, I saw the relationship for what it was, and I was able to move on with ease.

It also showed me that issues I'd been dealing with for years were also related to that relationship. So, in my leaving, I also released a whole bunch of belief systems related to those issues that I thought were mine but... weren't.

The other thing I feel like I learned was the absolute depth of our souls—obviously, I don't know the full extent, but seeing and experiencing as I did really showed me that there is so much more to us, more to the world we can see, and especially the world we can't see. I feel like it opened me to feel and get to the depths I was craving rather than living and experiencing superficially. So many situations where I would get really stressed over, I don't stress anywhere near as much.

However, there are certain topics, like my healing work and the impact I want to leave on the world, which now weigh more heavily. I feel like this is because I got to briefly see the depth of what is available, and because the work I do with clients accesses that depth, too, I want to be in that more!

My day job, which I always thought was going to be the main whilst I have my business on the side, now seems like such a waste of time and energy. It should be left to those in the field who are passionate about it. I felt so deeply it's about being where the passion is, following your heart and having faith and trust that it will all work out. Granted, the faith and trust part is harder for me, and breaking the habit of a 20+ year career is also hard, but I'll get there.

I also see now just how much I want to control everything—and I never thought I was a controlling person! But I wanted my awakening to happen a certain way, I wanted so many things to be a certain way, and they never were. I held so tightly to controlling how things should be that I completely stopped the flow of the universe moving through me. This, unfortunately, isn't something I've managed to overcome, but I'm working on it daily as I can now see when it's happening.

On the plus side, I am so much more open to spirit, I have been connecting to the Akashic Records, channeling Arcturian beings, and even Light Language is coming in! My work with sound healing has also developed so much more. I have also learned that my emotions play a big role in my ability to connect, and I have had to increase my grounding and clearing on myself to help.

I would love to have another awakening experience, and hopefully I will. Next time, I would tell myself that I'm OK, I'm safe, and just to RELAX! Relax and allow the energy and universe and your soul to do its thing, because I'm sure it's all planned out and it's all meant to be. And the longer you fight, the harder you make it for yourself. Also, don't distract yourself from what is needed... Don't doom scroll instead of meditating... Don't watch TV when you should do a quick emotional release. I know it's hard in the moment, but flowing with the energy and allowing it to move through you completely is so much easier than trying to fight it and especially trying to prevent it from happening.

Also, don't diminish the experiences you have. In the moment I thought I'd ruined my awakening by focusing on my physical health, but actually, it was good that I did that. I have friends who tell me just how much I've changed since that experience, how much I've developed and deepened, that it makes me realise that it's hard to see in ourselves what others see—so don't discount anything because you never know the effect it could have overall.

Lisa is an energy worker with over 19 years of experience working with healing modalities, including kinesiology, reiki, theta healing, sound healing, and even remedial massage therapy. Lisa has a passion for using these techniques to help clients clear their pain—both physical and emotional, to help them live a life that leaves behind the idea of "I just have to live with this...." Whether that is trauma, abuse, or physical pain, through to aligning with goals and clearing the path to a better tomorrow, Lisa wants to help everyone release all the things that hold us back from living the life we want.

Website: www.energiahealth.com.au

Instagram: www.instagram.com/energiahealth

InsightTimer: www.insighttimer.com/energiahealth

13

Waking Up to Radiance

By Rebecca Zaccard
Butler, Pennsylvania, USA

Sometimes, things have to dissolve, have to completely deconstruct, to make room for what's possible, for what your soul is calling you towards. I urge you to trust that inner knowing, that part of yourself, deep inside, that is leading you on a path toward awakening. It doesn't have to make sense to people on the outside (oftentimes it won't). It doesn't even have to make sense to you, your brain, or your ego (oftentimes it won't). As long as it brings harm to no one, and it's your intuition leading you, then take the step, follow the call, say yes.

In the summer of 2018, I attended a breathwork workshop with a friend. In a room full of people lying on yoga mats with eyes closed, breathing in and out at a rhythm, I saw, in my mind's eye, a blue goddess with many arms.

I did not know her name, I did not know her image, but I saw her. She wasn't fearsome, but she had power. I went home that night and google searched and found Kali, the Hindu goddess of radical transformation— the goddess of death and rebirth, the awakener, the wild woman, the ego destroyer—and then I went about my life. If I had been paying closer attention, I would've known my life was probably about to change.

In early 2020, from the outside, my life looked beautiful and full. In many ways, it was, but despite the career and life I had built in Los Angeles, I constantly felt like I was on the edge of burnout and overwhelm. I was exhausted from juggling so many different plates and was borderline obsessed with being perfect. I felt so much pressure, so much stress, and so much worry.

My husband, Steve, and I loved our lives in LA, but we were searching for something more career-wise. I was desperate to quit my day job so that I could focus all my energy on sports hosting, and Steve wasn't fulfilled in his work either. He grew up on a farm in Western Pennsylvania, and he knew that he wanted to revitalize it in some way. After much cajoling on his part, we decided to temporarily move to rural Pennsylvania to turn that family farm into a hemp farm. Our plan was to go in April of 2020 and be back in LA in under a year. That isn't exactly what happened.

In mid-March, we were at a crossroads. We weren't ready to go yet, but the world was starting to shut down. We made the decision on a Wednesday, and by Saturday night, we were packed up in the car with our two cats and whatever else we could fit. LA locked down the next day.

I didn't want to leave LA, not really. I didn't want to leave the friends I'd made, the life I'd created, but the deconstruction of my old life (thank you, Kali) awakened something in me that had been asleep. So many things my ego had been attached to were now gone—who was I now? Who was I without all those things?

Steve was working around the clock to get our farm and brand going, and I was working from home, often alone, in our apartment. It was hard and it was lonely, but in the quiet, in the solitude, my daily practices started to blossom. As the outside world shut down, my inner world opened up.

I started practicing yoga in my living room, learning about crystals and experimenting with oracle decks. I journaled a lot, I cried a lot, and I started studying astrology. I had always been intrigued by astrology, but I didn't know my birth time, so I never went as deep as I craved. My days were so FULL in LA; I was so busy and bordering on burnout, but now, I had nothing but time, so I ordered my birth certificate and dove all the way in.

I started to see myself. I started to wake up to my magic and my intuitive gifts. I felt my Shakti rising, I felt my power come back to me, I felt the stirrings of my soul, all as I learned who the hell I truly was. I also felt fear. The awakening part isn't always pretty because you awaken to the dark as well as the light. There were aspects of my personality, though, that I had always felt were flaws, and suddenly, I saw them for the gifts they were. I started to learn that when I flow WITH the energy of who I am at a soul level instead of against it, there's so much more ease and grace available. I began to embody my truest self and flow with the movement of the Cosmos.

I did, eventually, quit my day job to focus on building our businesses; however, I was still operating from the old paradigm about work, productivity, and worth. I was putting pressure on myself to work in a certain way at certain times, and I thought if I wasn't busy or stressed, then I wasn't really successful. You'd think moving across the country, a global pandemic, and a total career shift would be enough leveling of my old life, but I brought the old beliefs with me.

The more I attuned to the wisdom of the universe, though, the more I had to release those outdated ideas. I had to learn that sometimes the energy isn't going to flow, and I could try and push to adhere to my plans like I used to, or I could tune in, re-align, and allow. I invited a more Divine Feminine approach to my work, trusting myself and the universe along the way.

But now it was time to get out of my living room.

As the pandemic started to get under control, I was able to build community in this new place. Cultivating your practices in solitude is powerful, but it can be even more so in community. In addition to that, as the world opened back up, so did my hosting career. I had more gigs, more interviews, and more travel than ever before, all on top of helping to run our businesses. I'd be lying if I said I wasn't afraid that the burnout, perfectionism, and ego attachments that had plagued me previously would resurface. Could I invite in ease and flow rather than worry and stress? Could I embody my full self and be an entrepreneur, a host, and a magical being who aligns her life with the movement of the planets?

Yes, I could.

But it took and takes practice. I practice a lot of gratitude, a lot of grounding, and a lot of shining light on the shadowy parts, the people-pleasing tendencies, paying attention to the times I dim my light. I do my best to maintain my rituals while letting them morph and adjust as necessary. When I have challenges, I am intentional about honoring my feelings, moving through them, and then hopefully seeing them for what they are—opportunities to learn a deeper layer of the lesson. I am still navigating how I can embody my most authentic self in order to best serve the greater good while simultaneously doing this deep excavation work to release worry, perfectionism, and this belief that I need to fit into a single category. It's ongoing and never-ending. Because the deeper we go, the deeper there IS to go. There's a new layer to uncover, to learn, to integrate. It's a spiral, a back and forth, an up and down. It's wild and sometimes brutal.

It's also so, so worth it.

As I continue my practices and continue to get to know who I truly am, my intuition is easier to hear and feel. This guidance sometimes shows up in dreams, during meditation, prayer, or in a conversation. Most often, though, my intuition speaks to me through feeling. I get the chills, and/or I cry. You know I'm really online when I do both.

One morning, I was free writing about the mounting pressure I was feeling and wrote, "I am a conduit for my divine gifts." I got the chills, and tears sprung to my eyes. An intuitive jackpot. This truth helped me to further let go of my ego and to remember that we are all here to share the gifts we are given—it's one of the best ways we can serve the collective—and to not do so is to do a disservice to the world. I was able to get out of my own way and let my gifts shine. I was able to find flow out in the wild.

But still, I wasn't done.

I had moments when my guides were so loud in my sleep that I had to politely ask them to quiet down. Once, I woke up in the middle of the night and downloaded an entire product line. I didn't even turn on the lights as I scribbled down notes in the journal next to my bed. Those notes became the Cosmic Collection, an astrological bath and body line designed to align the energy of each sign, one of our offerings that I am proudest of, and another important step on my journey to sharing all parts of myself.

I had awoken to my gifts, but as usual, there was deeper still to go. I felt a soul-deep call to incorporate astrology further into my career. It had been so impactful for me in discovering and embodying my full self and in inviting more flow and ease into my life, that I needed to share that gift with others. But this was the scary part. It's all well and good to be spiritual and woo when I'm alone or with like-minded people, and it's a whole other thing to share that part of me in a bigger, more public way. I had to face the fear that if I shared my magic, my multi-dimensional nature, I might get ostracized, lose jobs, or just generally freak people out. It was time to come out of the broom closet.

I did so, little by little.

I always choose a word of year, or rather, the word chooses me. In 2024, that word was Radiance. In March of that year, as I was winding down after football season, I found out that I did not get a full-time hosting position that had been on the table (which was my dream before leaving LA). Surprisingly, I didn't feel disappointment. It felt like a gift because I now had the space to follow where I was being led, even if it didn't make sense to people on the outside. Immediately, I signed up to get my Astro Pro Certification from Soulshine Astrology. I was so lit up to help light other people up. I started my classes, built a website, and launched Radiance Astrology (it turns out that "Radiance" was much more than my word of the year). I started teaching workshops, blogging, and interpreting birth charts. It was Aries season, and I was unstoppable.

And then, in April, my dad died.

Everything did, in fact, stop. I can't begin to explain the depth of the loss of suddenly losing him. The grief is immeasurable, and I am one of the lucky ones. Lucky because I had a dad as funny, loving, and supportive as mine. Lucky because I know he underwent such a beautiful transformation in this life. Lucky because he left me with so much insight and love. Lucky because I know he is not truly lost, I know he is still with me, and it is still the deepest pain I have ever felt.

When he was in the hospital, he coded, which means his heart stopped while my mom, Steve, and I held each other and cried in the waiting room. I begged for him to come back. I begged for more time. He did come back, but not for long, just long enough for him to impart a little more wisdom. A few days before he passed, he shared that when he coded, when he momentarily died on that table, that he became God.

He left us with that reminder of who we really are. Souls in bodies. We are all divine, and we are all connected. I was always searching for God outside of myself. I was searching for myself outside of myself. God is within each of us. We ARE God.

He also taught me about radiance. As I grieved, I thought, *how can I be radiant now? How can I shine when I feel this much pain? How can I follow through on all these commitments that I agreed to before I lost my dad?* I learned, and am still in process of learning, that there is nothing more radiant than someone showing up in their full expression, even when, and perhaps especially when, it's messy, complicated, or painful.

My radiance is not contingent on being happy. It is not contingent on being accepted, categorizable, or perfect. My radiance is me, mess and all. My divinity is me, mess and all.

So here I am, in my full radiance, which means sharing my grief, expressing my magic, not hiding the mess or the witchy or the woo, saying yes to writing this chapter, feeling worthy of sharing my insight and my gifts—while still in process of discovering them—in hopes of inspiring others to do the same, in hopes that we can raise the vibration of this planet full of darkness and beauty through our energy, our voices, our actions, and through showing all the way up in the way only we can.

♡ ♡ ♡

Rebecca Zaccard completed her Astro Pro Certification in August of 2024 and is the founder of Radiance Astrology—offering readings, magical products, and more. She is Co-Owner & COO of family-owned hemp farm and brand, PENN'S CHOICE, edibles brand Cosmic Candies, as well as a dynamic speaker and live event host for the Packers, the NFL, and more. Rebecca lives in Western Pennsylvania with her husband, dog, and two cats. When she's not on the mic or running businesses, she's probably curled up with a book, on a walk near water, or belly laughing with the people she loves the most.

Website: www.radianceastrology.com

Instagram: www.instagram.com/rebeccazaccard

Astrology Readings: www.radianceastrology.com/radiance-readings

More Links: https://qrco.de/RadianceAstrology

14

No Mud, No Lotus: The Journey of Dark and Light and Everything in Between

By Kirsten Sorensen
Brisbane, Queensland, Australia

I believe that we can have many versions of our journey and life path playing out at one time. All of these versions are unique to us and based on our individual and sacred soul blueprints, which were decided upon before our birth into this world. These paths appear in front of us through various phases of our lives—key, pivotal moments that create twists and turns, taking us into our future and next ways of being. I believe that these paths have many directions, with our souls determining which way to go at any given moment. It's a beautiful conjunction of serendipity and fate, mixed with our soul's higher knowing, which ultimately leads the way. One journey that I believe we all have in common is finding our way back to our true selves, our soul identity, and our purest essence.

This coming back to self can occur in many ways—there are infinite possibilities. Many paths and forks in the road may appear along our journey, with each creating the next opportunity like a never-ending series of doors opening and closing. On a human level, this can occur with what can be incredibly painful and intense experiences—life-changing moments that will ultimately shift the trajectory of everything going forward. This is how my personal story of awakening and coming back to self begins...

Just over ten years ago now, there was a moment in time that changed everything. A moment that I can look back on and pinpoint an exact shift in my timeline, where a true split between everything before and everything afterward occurred, altering my life forever.

I was twenty-one, living in London, England. My calling to be there came from a higher place. I remember seeing a sign in the window of a travel agency, and at that moment, I decided I would move away from my home and family in Brisbane, Australia, and spend two years living and working abroad. Everything happened so quickly—it was meant to be, and it was all falling into place perfectly. Everything felt like a dream. I was overseas and in love with the world around me. It felt like such a magical time, and I remember seeing the beauty in everything. I was on cloud nine.

One day, not long into my spirited adventure, a devastating event transpired, and my world would never be the same again. I call it my initiation. A life-altering event, changing the world as I knew it. Many parts of me died in this moment... and in the months and years afterward. The lens of innocence that I saw the world through was shattered as I experienced a traumatic series of events at the hands of another. I became a statistic... one I sadly share with one in three women worldwide. I went into a deep state of shock, and looking back now, I can see that I highly likely experienced a fragmentation of self and a long period of disassociation. It would take me approximately five years to start to emerge again and to begin to heal from my experience.

All of my emotions, the pain and shock that I had experienced during this time, were pushed down, deep beneath the surface of my being. I completely hid and turned away from what I needed to feel. I lied to those around me but most of all to myself. I was *truly* disconnected. One could call it the Dark Night of the Soul... I was in the depths and darkness of the muddy waters, unable to see a clear way out. However, as the wise quote by Thich Nhat Hanh goes, "No mud, no lotus."

For the first five years after my experience, I was in a serious relationship and living life as per society's expectations. I was deeply reliant on my inner masculine, going through the motions as per society's conditioning. Throughout all of this, I could feel that something was missing. There was a deep feeling of being lost... being confused... I felt alone and very uncertain about who I was, what I was doing, and why anything and everything existed at all.

What I realised after some time was that I was craving a deeper connection—a connection to myself and everything in the universe that surrounded me. I was desperately wishing to truly understand myself, my place on earth and why I was here.

My relationship was the place where I had put all of my energy. I poured everything that I had into the other rather than taking care of myself and reclaiming my power that was hidden away. There were many inner truths and signs from my higher self that I had ignored. It took me five years to come to the realisation and decision that I needed to part ways with my partner. I needed to be alone to do the work, to tend to my own needs, and to try to heal. My higher self had taken over. They knew enough was enough, and I couldn't run from myself any longer. I knew from a higher place that I needed to find myself, not knowing what this meant... but I knew I was deeply lost. I was craving depth, connection, and most of all, to be authentically me. This was something I had never truly known—it felt like a deep mystery that I needed to uncover.

My relationship with myself began from this moment. My soul was leading the way and spoke to me through deep inner knowings, synchronicities, and symbolic dreams. Potent truths that would land in my mind and in my heart. Truths that I had to listen to and investigate deeper through self-reflection and introspection. Surrendering into the abyss was required. I needed to let go of all expectations, of my mind's limiting beliefs and conditioning from society. A surrender into not knowing and not needing to know.... a trust in my higher self and in something greater than I could see and logically understand.

There are clues from spirit and the world beyond what we can see that appear in our paths, almost in complete mystery. They are inklings and feelings from deep within that we can choose to follow, with a knowing that they are ultimately occurring for our greatest good. My connection to the liminal space and the world that exists beyond the veil of this human illusion are what have guided me to where I am today. The path of dropping in and surrendering to the mysteries of life, connecting to what is unknown, what is magic, and what is true, is something we can all do whether we realise it or not. We all have our own unique gifts, and these will open up to us in our own exact, perfect, and divine timing throughout our lives.

I began my journey of self-inquiry through astrology, learning all about my unique birth chart and understanding parts of myself for what felt like the very first time. I was able to see my divine connection with the universe and with the stars that I had gazed at so deeply in complete awe since childhood. The sense of personal power that I gained through learning about myself in this way was indescribable—*I felt so incredibly seen.*

Soon after, I started working with a kinesiologist through my very first energetic healing session. This was the first time I had felt my own energy and innate power. I could feel my energy pulsating throughout my entire being. I was guided to balance my divine masculine and feminine through the simple task of holding my hands apart, aiming to bring them together in a prayer position. I remember the feeling of my hands not wanting to connect—my masculine and feminine were completely out of balance. There was intense power in this moment—not only through actually feeling this physically as a sensation throughout my body (something I could tangibly feel for the first time) but also in the learning that I had gained about what I was feeling emotionally and metaphysically. I had opened the door of my healing journey, one that I could not keep closed any longer.

There was a period of a few years where I worked with many incredible healers and mentors through lots of one-on-one work. This was absolutely needed whilst I was in my initial phase of self discovery as it enabled me to have many amazing shifts whilst being held and supported. I was able to dive with complete devotion into the personal medicine I so desperately needed.

Along my journey, I have worked with deeply intuitive, strong, and wise women. They have guided me with such gentle love and care, and I treasure them greatly. Each woman that I have been so privileged to be guided by has been so embodied in their own personal wisdom and medicine, leading with authenticity and deep reverence for the work that they do. They have taught me so much through just being themselves and stepping into their own divinely aligned calling in this life.

Some of these women have become dear sisters and friends. This sisterhood has opened me up in so many ways. There is such beauty in divinely aligned friendship—through deep soul conversations, knowing the connection is beyond this world and time. The community that I've developed with these like-minded women has taught me so much, with the greatest learning being just how crucial forming genuine connections with others is!

Something else that I have learnt and have great certainty in knowing is that we are all one and all divinely connected. Those that we meet are our biggest teachers; we can see ourselves in others just as they can see themselves in us. Most of all, *we are not alone*—especially in our journeys to awaken!

Over the last few years, I have connected with my spirit team and the world beyond what we can physically see. Many of my guides are powerful animal spirits, such as Emerald, my Lemurian dragon guide, and Pluto, my black jaguar power animal. I met Pluto for the first time through a sacred shamanic drum journey. She greeted me as I dived deep into a waterfall, her emerald green eyes piercing through as she came in and out of my sight with great elusiveness. She has visited me over and over, guiding me in my dreams and in many other sacred journeys. She is within me, protecting and holding me in my power always. She is connected to the planet Pluto, holding both dark and light with her transformational Scorpion energy. I am guided by her in all that I do. Her wild and untamed wisdom breathes within me.

At the beginning of my journey, I wanted to rush through *everything*, including what I thought were spiritual milestones. I was stuck in my masculine and in a deep pattern of needing to be in control. This was not going to work in the realm of the unknown! There are universal laws and a natural order of things that we must follow and surrender to.

I was stuck in wanting to control everything, including my own awakening journey. I had ideas of the way it would play out and the happy ending that I thought would magically appear after I completed each step in a perfect, specific order.

One of the biggest lessons that I have needed to learn throughout has been patience. The art of letting go and relinquishing to universal timing, aligning myself to the flow of the universe, and just being present have the hardest but most freeing lessons. What I know now is that our awakening is all about the journey and that there is no true end. We will always be met with struggles that change depending on where we are and what lesson we are next being required to learn. The fact is that nature works and relies on cycles and natural ebbs and flows—this is the circle of life. There are no highs without lows, and the brightest of rainbows will always come after the biggest of storms!

Throughout our lives, we will have many moments in the void—this is where our souls await the next step of their reclamation and their journey to clearing all that blocks their path to truly shining as one's brightest self. Our soul waits in the mud as long as it needs to, rising up through the waters just like a lotus does—emerging and opening with our life-giving force, the sun. Just as we watch the sun rise from the east and move through the sky each day, soon to be met by the moon each night, we also move through darkness and light. You are not alone, as you are guided by your highest self each and every day.

Through my awakening journey, I have learnt firsthand that the depths of our despair will bring us the greatest capacity for our enlightenment. My suffering and darkness are what have allowed me to feel and understand like nothing else. It has brought me depth in my character and resilience and trust in myself and my capabilities. I am grateful for all that has transpired in my life—the 'good' and the 'bad' have made me exactly who I am today. The twists and turns in my path have brought me awareness like nothing else could. From a higher perspective, I am comforted to know that my soul has chosen this path... as has yours.

Kirsten Sorensen is in love with the stars and is ruled by the planet Venus, being born with a Leo sun, Taurus moon, and Libra rising. She is a qualified Emotions and Metaphysical Kinesiologist and Advanced Usui Reiki Practitioner living in Meanjin (Brisbane), Australia. As a 5/1 Self-Projected Projector in Human Design, she observes the universe with complete awe and is intrigued by the magic of all that exists around us. She is a spiritual branding photographer and visual storyteller who is led by her heart and soul. She craves depth and authenticity in everything she does and is a student through life itself, seeing every moment as an opportunity for growth and deeper understanding. She is here to help others move through the more difficult parts of their awakening journeys, guiding them to deeply understand themselves through her intuition, presence, and insight, leading them to heal themselves with infinite love and gratitude.

Website: www.kirstensorensen.com.au

Instagram: www.instagram.com/kirstensorensen.energyhealing

More Links: www.kirstensorensen.com.au/offerings

15

The Shift: From Barely Surviving to Embracing Soulful Wellbeing

By Marie-Christine Laroche
Quebec City, Quebec, Canada

I was born and raised in Quebec City, Canada. From a young age, I was taught that the only way to success and abundance was through good grades in school and a public sector job with a pension plan. The road had been mapped for me: I was to go to university to obtain a degree in a healthcare discipline. The belief encoded in my brain was that this was the only way to financial security.

By the age of 13, I had already lost track of who I was. I always looked outside of myself for validation and had completely given my power away to others. I tried to decipher what was deemed valuable by society and strived to align myself more and more with that. I wanted to please my family and to play it safe, so I walked along the road most taken, even though it didn't feel right. A straight-A student, I had read society's rulebook, and had mastered how to live by it.

At 39, on paper, my life was a dream. I was married, had kids, a lovely house, an apparently healthy body, and a job in healthcare. In spite of my amazing track record, I was on the brink of burnout...

I felt alone, even though I was constantly surrounded by people. I was exhausted and overwhelmed by responsibilities, and I felt trapped in a spiral over which I thought I had no control. I was no longer living; I was barely surviving. The woman I was, no matter how accomplished, was oceans away from the joyful, curious girl I had once been.

It was from that place of exhaustion that I began my spiritual awakening in 2019. Following the guidance learned in a self-help book, I started to wake up an hour before everyone in my world. This small change allowed me to sit in stillness by myself every day. In the morning silence, finally uninterrupted by multiple demands, I began to craft a daily routine that would soon lead me back to some inner peace: stillness, exercise, new learnings, and journaling. I took a meditation class and integrated a twice-a-day 20-minute practice. I moved my training sessions to the early morning and started to jog outside while listening to self-development audiobooks and podcasts. I also bought a journal and made sure to pen down a few words about how I felt every day. These words, on top of providing an energetic release, would also become a tracking tool and a witness to my constant improvement.

Progressively, I began to reconnect with all that I was: my passions, my talents, my desires, my sources of joy and energy. It was in these peaceful moments, when I pressed pause on my fast-paced life, that I realized I had strayed so far away from my authentic self and made so many choices from a place of fear.

The path and wishes of others had become my own. The apparent constraints and limits of the world around me had become closed doors to which I did not hold the key. But now, things were starting to shift inside of me. I could feel my soul pushing, wanting to emerge, to express itself, and to lead the way. It showed through small things at first, like daring to wear colored nail polish instead of my classic French manicure or only wanting to have deep conversations while steering clear of small talk. Something was changing for the better, and I was starting to see it.

In 2021, I came across a podcast that was talking about Human Design (HD). Intrigued, I generated my chart online and booked a reading. I had always been curious about astrology and had visited the same medium for many years. I was well aware that there was more to life than this 3D physical world, and yet, I had never accessed more than most people.

The HD reading was my first step into a whole new world! I learned how I was energetically designed to function optimally. Suddenly, I understood why I had been struggling with finding my voice and why I had been such a good soldier, taking on everyone else's pressure. I also discovered why it was so easy for me to understand the root cause of problems and fix them, while it seemed really hard for other people.

And the star on top of the tree? I realized that my life purpose was to learn to love myself as the colorful visionary being that I was and to guide others, to give them permission to live as their true, beautiful, and unique, authentic selves. My heart, I discovered, had this unique ability to love humanity in all of its extremes and to raise other people's frequency through the power of my loving and caring words.

It was one of those aha moments when the light suddenly turned on, and I felt so much love and acceptance pour into my whole body, knowing that I had always been meant to be different! I, the proper little rebel, had a reason to be, and my fitting into society's mold was not serving humanity. It was certainly impacting my health and wellbeing negatively.

I needed to learn more; I needed to dive deep! I had never been so passionate about anything in my life! I was back on a path, I was evolving again, and I was feeling alive! That's when I committed to learning how to analyse HD charts in depth to better understand my loved ones and help other people find meaning and purpose in their own lives.

This knowledge alone completely revolutionized my parenting skills and my relationship with my husband. I no longer wanted them to be a certain way, as I now understood who they were designed to be. Instead, I acknowledged the unique beings they were and focused on walking them home to who they were meant to be with love and compassion.

As I studied HD, I was drawn to learning more about Western astrology. I felt like there was a missing piece in the puzzle of my life, and this ancient practice really allowed me to go even deeper into my purpose, my abilities, and my understanding of the influence of celestial transits on my daily life.

The phrase "as above, so below" suddenly took on all of its meaning: I could absolutely see how those planets had impacted my past and, therefore, get a hint on how they would impact my future. This got me to think that my life had possibly been planned and that my date of birth had possibly been chosen in order for certain events to unfold in this lifetime for my soul's evolution.

This new awareness led me to read and learn more from doctors and hypnotherapists who specialized in past life regressions and who had written extensively about the soul's multiple lifetimes. I went ahead and experienced two past life regressions to satisfy my curiosity and learn more about my own soul's history. I explored Buddha's teachings and discovered the concept of karma. I gained an understanding of how karmic relationships and soul contracts were at play in my life, not to bring on hardships but to allow my soul to learn the lessons it had come here to learn.

As I lived more and more in alignment with my human design and followed the path laid before me by the Universe, I noticed how much I had changed. I was happier, brighter, healthier, and filled with joy and new dreams. I was at the forefront of the pandemic, and still, I was filled with light! My body was drained, but my heart and soul were shining bright.

I had stopped social drinking, no longer watched conventional media, and rarely turned on TV. I found peace within myself, and the outside world did not influence me anymore. I was undergoing a radical transformation, and even though I had no notion of where it was going to take me, I trusted that it was all happening *for* me.

By 2023, I had received five different metaphysical readings and all of them pointed to my ability to connect with other dimensions. While this surprised me, it felt exciting because I had always admired people who had those skills, wishing I could have them myself. I had heard that readings activated something in you, that they awakened dormant parts of you. That year, I experienced this truth for myself.

Other lightworkers had taught me about the existence of Guides and Beings of light and the ways in which they connected with them. Because I now knew and believed it was possible, I decided to give it a try. I had been meditating twice a day for nearly four years when I first connected with my main Guide. To my surprise, it was subtle, easy and felt just like pure love. Over time, other Guides and Beings of light began to come through during my meditations, always offering enlightening guidance and different perspectives on the events of the day and those to come. I even got into the habit of asking to be shown images of the highlights of my day during my morning meditation, and inevitably, these scenes or faces always ended up showing a time later in the day! Now, if I could see some of what would happen, could that mean that some of my life was pre-planned?

This newfound ability marked the beginning of a very different life for me and the end of existence as I had known it before. I no longer needed outside validation, and I felt a profound sense of self-love. When in doubt, I simply connected with my Guides and asked for their loving guidance, which would quickly reassure me. Not only that, I began to recognize and trust the signs and opportunities presented to me by the universe and my life became so magical! I stopped pushing and trying to control and instead learned to allow the story to unfold... most of the time!!!

Seeing how beautiful it was to live in such close contact with other dimensions, I decided to go further and explore my psychic abilities. I joined a group and practiced every week with people from all over the world. One day, as I was listening to another member's personal difficulties, I felt a strong desire to help coming straight from my heart, and I spontaneously started channeling her Guide. It took both of us by surprise, but I allowed it to come through as I could see the words made sense to her and were exactly what she needed to hear in that moment. This was the beginning of my channeling practice, a precious way to guide myself and others through the many hoops of life.

I, the fast-paced worker, had learned to harness my feminine energy and to allow communications to move through me as a vessel, without trying to interfere or judge, in full acceptance of whatever came through. I had learned to trust what I heard and to transfer the information, knowing that the words would make sense to those they were addressed to, whether I understood them or not.

Today, I can affirm that the wellbeing daily routine I put in place back in 2019 (and upgraded over the years) was the solid foundation that allowed me to build my multidimensional abilities. One thing I have learned is that to be able to sustain the demands of these connections on a regular basis, I needed to ensure that my human body would be rested, well-hydrated, and exposed to low levels of stress.

As an embodied soul, I accept and recognize that I am here to live a human experience. As such, I do not strive to live only from the soul, constantly plugged into other dimensions. I enjoy the beauty of all my physical senses and the unique pleasures of human love. My soul and my human body continue to learn to live as one, harmonizing their respective energies and trusting and nurturing each other. I have also become quick to notice any disconnection between them, as this phenomenon brings tremendous discomfort and misalignment for me.

My spiritual awakening occurred over the span of five years. The path was shown to me progressively, one stepping stone at a time. I was guided to build solid foundations and daily wellbeing routines that would support the skills that were to come. I was divinely supported through it all and it was trust that made all the difference.

Nowadays, when I sit with friends with the intention of guiding them, I see past the words spoken and straight into the soul's needs and genuine intentions. I hear the guidance offered by guides, beings of light, and even crossed-over loved ones sometimes. I am eternally grateful for the gifts that have been bestowed upon me, and I use them wisely, with the utmost respect, to help improve people's wellbeing.

At 39, I had given up on my livelihood and joy and believed everything would go down from there. Now, at 44, I feel like my life is just beginning! I keep learning, growing, teaching, guiding, and helping others, just like I did in my youth, but with newfound abilities and the wisdom of a woman who has already experienced half a lifetime.

I am living proof that when you reconnect with your soul, you can transform your life and glow from the inside out!

Marie-Christine Laroche has spent the past 20 years in service to others. She is passionate about preventative health and soulful wellbeing. She strongly believes that we can all contribute to making this world a better place by taking charge of our own wellbeing in order to live meaningful and purposeful lives enhanced by harmonious and respectful relationships with others and with ourselves.

Facebook: www.facebook.com/mcl.71883

16

Surrendering to the Sacred Chaos of Saturn

By Jennifer Birge
Lake City, South Carolina, USA

My spiritual awakening didn't come with soft light or gentle whispers—it began as a violent unraveling. Each layer of who I thought I was was torn away, one after another, exposing every belief, every fear, and every hidden part of myself I had yet to confront until only the raw truth remained.

I had spent three years in Wisconsin, living in a stunning spot on Lake Michigan, with 10 acres of country land where I envisioned building my homestead. It felt like my dreams were finally aligning. My business was thriving, I was earning more than ever, and I was deeply passionate about my creative work.

But as time passed, I began to notice how stifled I felt, unable to express myself outside of my online career. I was in a relationship that, while outwardly stable, left me feeling suffocated. Every time I tried to share my thoughts, my partner either dismissed me or reacted with anger. It mirrored my childhood, and eventually, my body broke down.

As I delved into astrology, I yearned for deep, authentic female friendships—connections that truly resonated with who I was becoming. In the process, I began attracting more spiritual web design clients, each one igniting a new facet of my awakening. Some of these clients even evolved into the meaningful friendships I was craving. Synchronicity led one of these clients to become a mentor on my journey. After receiving a few Reiki sessions from her, the stagnant energy within me began to shift, but it came at a cost. I became very ill. For months, I was so weak I could barely breathe or speak—my throat and heart chakras were deeply blocked, reflecting my struggle to express myself.

One day, as I lay on the floor choking on a massive ball of phlegm, I started blacking out, accepting that this might be the end. At that moment, I felt a breath come from nowhere, releasing the blockage that had suffocated me—both physically and emotionally. After that, I vowed never to let anyone silence my voice again.

What happened in those seconds of death's kiss can only be described as a walk-in soul exchange. It wasn't clear to me then, but it became evident later. What I knew immediately after was that it was a wake-up call urging me to reassess everything. I realized I needed a fresh start in a new place. I made a list of what I wanted in my new location, and Asheville's pull became undeniable as synchronicities kept appearing. So, I packed my car, left everything behind, and embarked on an 18-hour drive with my dog. The moment I saw the Blue Ridge Mountains, an overwhelming sense of home washed over me, and I knew this was where I was meant to be.

Asheville, North Carolina was the first place where I felt truly free. It allowed me to explore the spiritual practices I'd always been drawn to but were forbidden in my strict Pentecostal upbringing. For the first time, I could express myself fully—dressing as I wished, speaking freely, and stepping into a world that felt like it had been quietly waiting for me.

I didn't realize how profoundly Asheville would transform me—and how challenging that transformation would be. When I arrived, it felt like the doors to a magical world opened. I stepped into my spiritual gifts that seemed to just magically appear out of nowhere.

At first, everything felt beautiful and liberating. I was making new friends, having soul-nourishing conversations, and feeling spiritually fulfilled. I felt deeply connected to this place. But as much as this spiritual exploration brought joy, everything else in my life seemed to unravel. The contrast was striking—freedom and connection on one side while my world fell apart on the other.

It wasn't until years later that I was able to see why. I had unknowingly planted myself on my "negative Saturn line" in astrocartography. Saturn, the cosmic taskmaster, became an unrelenting teacher, embodying lessons I had spent my life avoiding, especially surrounding my father. But the lessons were mine to learn, and they called me here—to a place that would become both my toughest teacher and the safe container I needed to dive deep into my awakening. Slowly, I surrendered to Saturn's demands, facing the discomfort instead of fleeing. Over time, I embraced this place, recognizing its role in my journey and the transformation it brought.

The irony was hard to ignore: why would I fall in love with a place that felt like it was punishing me? I had visions of putting down roots, settling into these ancient mountains, and letting this be my sanctuary. But life had other plans, and watching others around me flourish, building homesteads and lives that seemed to blossom effortlessly, felt like salt in an open wound. Why did they get to thrive here while I unraveled?

Asheville felt like home, but not in the gentle way you'd imagine. It was a "familiar hell," a haunting echo of my childhood, with its unforgiving edges and inner battles I thought I'd left behind. Yet the pull was undeniable, almost like an invitation to confront the deepest parts of myself—one ego death after another. And yet, I've never known a place more beautiful, more inviting, or more connected to my soul in ways I can't fully express in words.

I was plunged into a dark night of the soul, and nothing went untouched. My location had changed, but otherwise, everything seemed the same—yet my life felt like it was disintegrating, and my nervous system, already frayed from the near-death experience, finally snapped.

The mountains and waterfalls became my escape, my constant. Each step into nature felt like a reset, a whisper of hope: "Things will get better if I just fix this." I clung to every "aha" moment, certain that uncovering the root of each challenge would bring the solution. I'd retreat to my spiritual toolbox, determined to mend every wound, believing I could fix it all. Each new layer of awareness brought a rush as if I were inching closer to my essence. It was addicting.

The struggles pushed me deeper into spiritual practice, seeking healing wherever I could find it. I immersed myself in reiki, astrology, sound healing, human design, gene keys, books, spiritual courses, and ancestral connections, heavily relying on my spirit team's guidance. Spirituality and nature became my anchor, eclipsing the creative work that once grounded me. Hours were spent in meditation, energy work, and wandering the forest.

I desperately tried to control everything, manipulating energy to align with my desires. I threw myself into daily astral travel and lucid dreaming, longing to escape my body. After my near-death experience, being in a body felt unsafe, and I yearned to return to Sirius, wishing to bypass the human experience altogether. My spiritual ego swelled, mirroring my mother's self-righteous religious views—a harsh truth I had to face. The lessons were humbling and relentless, like living in a constant state of breakdown, trapped in the Tower card on repeat. The irony hit when it showed up so often that I finally tossed the deck in the air, yelling, "Fuck this, I give up."

Surprisingly, this journey led to self-acceptance. Through these practices, I began to embrace parts of myself I once disliked, realizing my intensity and sensitivity had a purpose. For the first time, I felt genuine love for who I was. This acceptance also softened my view of others. What was once a challenge became an exploration. I learned to see people with more compassion through the lens of childhood wounds, communication, attachment styles, and astrology.

Two years into my spiritual journey, I believed I'd found my twin flame—a love that consumed me for four intense months. When he left unexpectedly, just as we were about to move in together, I was shattered, sinking deeper into the dark night of the soul.

Over these six years, my life became a series of intense karmic connections. Each relationship and friendship burned brightly, teaching me painful lessons that took months or years to process. It started to feel like this was my path—fleeting, powerful connections that forced me to grow through their inevitable pain and the soul work they demanded.

Four years in, I ended up back at my parents' house after my business collapsed, needing to reset financially. Those four months were some of the hardest of my life. It felt like stepping into a time machine, back to my childhood—everything the same, from the house to my parents' routines. The biggest revelation was uncovering the truth I'd blocked out: my alcoholic, verbally abusive father had been the source of most of my childhood trauma. I'd always blamed my mother, but being there, reliving it all as a more evolved version of myself with new tools to cope, I couldn't unsee what was now so clear. By the end of those months, I found the strength to stand up to my father. That confrontation marked the end of our relationship, and the next morning, I left for good.

Saturn took my father's place, teaching me what he couldn't. I returned to a nearby town, hoping for a fresh start, and bought an RV to renovate and live in, with a five-year plan to buy land and create my homestead. But deep down, I could feel myself on the wrong path, making decisions that didn't align with my truth, resisting the reality that it was time to leave. For two years, I found myself in a karmic situation that forced me to confront and release deep-seated guilt and shame, pushing me toward the right track for the next phase of my life. Ironically, this connection was with someone who shared my father's birthday, presenting the same lessons my father couldn't teach—just in a different form. So much of my life seems to revolve around the dynamic with my dad and our soul contract for this lifetime. Every challenge and breakthrough seems to be tied to that thread.

During this phase of my life, it was easy to be consumed by my Scorpio stellium and neglect my Sagittarius stellium—my two superpowers that, when combined, balance each other out so beautifully! "Let it be easy" has become my mantra, a gentle reminder to release the resistance and surrender to the flow of life.

The dark night of the soul was tough, but facing Saturn's intensity showed me I don't have to live in seriousness alone—I can embrace joy, too. Though my mind still struggles with it, little by little, my nervous system is learning to feel safe in joy.

I transitioned from being a workaholic to working only as much as needed, learning to appreciate the little things I once overlooked. My work now reflects my true passions, and I no longer take on clients just for financial reasons. I've set stronger boundaries, improved my communication, and let go of people-pleasing. Saturn has taught me that life doesn't always go as planned and that I won't always meet others' expectations—and that's okay.

In my eagerness to heal, I dove in headfirst. I pushed myself far beyond my limits, bulldozing through layers of trauma in a rush to be "fixed," spurred on by social media's seductive promises of swift, magical transformation. It seemed like everyone else was emerging fully healed after short, intense journeys, and I fell into the illusion that I could do the same. But true healing doesn't work that way—marketing does.

Healing demands patience—it's not a checklist of wounds to fix but a lifelong journey with peaks, valleys, rest, and integration. The process unfolds as we're ready, and forcing it only drains our physical, emotional, and spiritual reserves. When I began to trust the universe, I discovered the magic in surrender. Every misstep and setback became an opportunity to grow, embrace humility, and let my ego soften a little more.

As someone who craved control, letting go was terrifying. I had to release the identity shaped by childhood trauma, where being hyper-vigilant was my baseline. I believed controlling everything would protect me from pain, but it only created resistance against life's natural flow.

I've come to realize how much I've underestimated the value of rest and self-care, even though they are essential. While I know I am a spiritual being, I am also in a dense, physical body that needs time to let energy flow and settle. Whenever I've pushed too hard, too fast, my body simply couldn't keep up. I often found myself yearning to leave my body behind, craving a return to spirit without even realizing it. But I've learned that I'm here in this body for a reason, and it's my temple during this lifetime. Without it, I can't fulfill everything I came here to do or fully enjoy the beauty of life. It deserves my care, attention, and love.

Every experience has brought its own lessons and insights, revealing that my journey is uniquely mine, shaped by the paths I've taken and the growth I'm here to embrace.

After the most challenging six years of my life, navigating this dark night of the soul with Saturn, I've come to believe we shared some kind of cosmic soul contract. I was called to this place for the karmic lessons I needed to experience, lessons only Saturn could teach. Everything unfolded exactly as it was meant to, and now, that chapter feels complete. It's time to move forward into the next phase of my life, equipped with the wisdom those lessons instilled, allowing me to navigate life's challenges with more grace and strength than ever before.

Now, when I see Saturn in the night sky, I smile. I remember all we've been through and finally understand what Saturn wanted for me all along. Hindsight really is 20/20.

I'm Jennifer Ann, a passionate and fiery creative and the heart behind Coral Antler. I specialize in crafting soulful designs for spiritual entrepreneurs and authors. My offerings span a range of creative mediums, including book cover design, oracle card design, and custom digital and print illustrations.

In addition to bespoke services, I curate a collection of premade brands, book covers, logos, website templates, illustrations, and stock images. You can explore these one-of-a-kind creations and digital goods in my online shop at shop.coralantler.com.

Website: www.coralantler.com/quick-links

Instagram: www.instagram.com/coralantler

17

A Crack is Where the Light Comes In

By Erika Anderson
Lyons, Colorado, USA

I have always been an extremely spiritual person. I grew up in a Catholic family, went to a Catholic school and to church usually two mornings a week. I loved incense and chanting and the feeling of ancient mystery when I looked at the stained-glass images of angels and saints. I loved the awareness I had of the Holy Spirit. To me, it felt like a type of magic I could step into and touch. As a child, that aspect of spirit in my life felt so filled with awe. This wove a thread through my life, where I continued to experience the energy of angels around me. I spoke with them and received messages back often. I never doubted the presence of the Divine in my life.

I talked to God regularly. You could call it prayer, but it felt like a conversation to me. I remember once asking for a best friend. I explained to God how lonely I was and that I needed someone to talk to who really understood me. I felt God answer like a whisper in my heart, saying that I just needed to hold love for my best friend and imagine her. I did that every morning and at night before falling asleep. We'd call it manifesting now, but I imagined what she looked like, even down to her hair color. When the summer was over and I went back to school, I met her on the very first day of class. I knew it was her because she looked just as I imagined. My life forever changed with that friendship, and it was just because I listened to my heart.

I have always been sensitive. Really sensitive. I loved so fiercely, felt emotions so strongly, and shattered easily. Now I know the term for it: HSP or highly sensitive person. I feel things so deeply. When I say this, people glaze over as if to say, "Sure, we're all sensitive." But this is different. I tried explaining it to my husband recently when we walked by a young homeless man with the saddest eyes. My husband slipped him 5 dollars at my asking. I told him, "This is the difference between us: I see him, and I want to go sit next to him, tell him how beautiful his heart is, and cry for whatever pain led him to homelessness. And you can walk by, give him some money and say good luck, and then move on with your day. But 48 hours later, I still think about finding him on the street."

I wasn't just emotionally sensitive; I was spiritually sensitive, too. Since I was a young girl, I was able to see ghosts or spirits, along with communicating with my angelic helpers. I didn't talk about it to anyone, but it just felt normal to be like that. I was aware that there was more to the world than what we can see with our outward eyes, and even though I didn't know what to call it then, the boundary between the physical and spiritual world was thin for me.

As I got older, I started experiencing a lot of anxiety. I didn't know that I was an empath. I just thought something was wrong with me. I felt the energy or emotions of people so strongly, and I just absorbed it all like a sponge. Good or bad, mean or nice, whatever was around me became part of me.

I became adept at masking my feelings and felt I needed to pretend that I was always happy and comfortable. But inside of myself, I was suffocating under a weight I couldn't see or grasp or even understand. Over time, it developed into a constant undercurrent of anxiety, always lingering and exerting control over me. I despised it, and hiding it was becoming increasingly difficult.

So, like many people who live with anxiety, I set out on a path of distraction—a journey of trying to overcome the anxiety itself. I became a high-functioning anxious person, finding areas I could control to channel my anxiety, making it nearly invisible to those around me. I felt ashamed of how I was, and I buried that shame as deeply as I could.

Looking back, I can see how anxiety gradually replaced the quiet, spiritual trust that once lived within me. My deep connection to the Divine was overshadowed not only by the anxiety itself but also by my relentless efforts to control it. Worry and fear clouded my intuition, making it difficult even to recognize, let alone listen to, my inner guidance. For years, I was focused on managing emotions and escaping anxiety instead.

I started down the path of self-improvement, driven by a need to prove I was a worthy person. I believed that if I could work hard and achieve, my accomplishments would affirm my worthiness, and success would somehow make me feel whole. Being diagnosed with dyslexia in my late teens had only added to my anxiety. So, as an adult, I believed that the more successful I became, the less vulnerable or anxious I would feel.

Becoming a mother brought a profound shift in my life. The experience of giving birth to a child I had nurtured within me felt primal, and as I held him, a new kind of love radiated from my heart, awakening my soul to an entirely new way of being. I loved motherhood deeply, yet the miracle of this new life and responsibility shook me to my core. My heart danced between the heights of love and the constant fear that my world could shatter because of it.

Even though I was a successful acupuncturist, a respected healer, wife, and mother—someone deeply attuned to caring for others' needs—I was still struggling internally. Anxiety was my constant companion. As a new mom, I now had a fresh outlet for this anxiety: parenting.

One night, when my son was about three years old, I woke in the middle of the night. I had developed a routine of checking on him around midnight to make sure he was safe. That night, I went downstairs to peek into his room, but he wasn't in his bed. Panic surged through me as I searched his room, looking into every corner. I called up to my husband, saying, "He's gone! I can't find Jackson!" My husband, sensing my fear, started panicking too. We searched every level of the house, checking behind each piece of furniture.

Desperate, I returned to his room, calling on my angels to help me find him. I pulled back his messy blanket, and there he was, nestled deep within the folds of his comforter, sound asleep. He had been in his bed the whole time.

By the time I had my second child, I was skilled at masking anxiety. I had earned two bachelor's degrees and a master's degree and worked both as a nurse and an acupuncturist. Between my work and being a devoted mother, I was exhausted.

On New Year's Day 2019, my sweet, 18-month-old son got sick. He was struggling to breathe. He was vomiting and then guzzling water repeatedly. I told my husband that something felt seriously wrong, even though the hospital nurse line suggested it was probably a virus and just to rest. We hurriedly got both kids into the car and drove to the hospital anyway.

The doctor assessed him and confirmed it was a virus, instructing us to go home and keep him hydrated. But I had this voice in my ear telling me not to listen. I said, "I won't leave until you take some labs to make sure you're right." The doctor scoffed at me until I insisted repeatedly that I would not leave. She relented and drew blood, checking a few of his markers. After a short wait, the doctor returned and told us his labs were dangerously far from normal. She said, "You are right. Something is very wrong, and we need to transfer him to a bigger hospital now." She explained, "He is in a life-threatening condition, and he has type one diabetes." We raced to the new hospital in the ambulance and stayed there for days in the pediatric intensive care unit while he stabilized, and we learned about how we would be living our new life.

I went down a dark tunnel of despair. For months, I grieved the near death of my child. If I had listened to the doctors and not fought back, he wouldn't have survived. I cried for his future and worried incessantly about how I could keep him safe for the rest of his life. I was so mad at myself for ignoring the creeping feelings around his health that I had for months before the hospital. I had been ignoring my intuition for so long and pushing myself so hard that I hadn't trusted those feelings to be real. I became worried that he would die in the night or that I would make mistakes with his care. I was engulfed in shadow, and I loathed myself.

I woke up from bed one morning and started down the stairs for the morning routine of coffee and drawing up insulin. As I walked down the stairs, I realized that I didn't recognize myself anymore. I could see myself from outside of my body like I was looking at myself from across the room as a stranger moving in the kitchen. I felt her dark emotions and the heaviness of her energy. I could even see the looping thoughts in her head that were telling her she was a victim. In that quick moment of truth and awareness, I also saw that I had a choice to be different, and I realized that if I didn't start finding myself, I was going to lose myself forever.

It was that same day that I decided I was going to try to meditate. I had always resisted meditation. I thought, "I can't focus. It's boring and too hard." But on this day, for some reason, I went upstairs and grabbed my laptop. I sat on the floor of my bedroom and found a YouTube video with a chakra meditation. It was a simple, guided meditation led by a man with a soothing voice who also talked about manifestation. It was kind of cheesy, but I watched his videos every day for two weeks. I learned how to sit and visualize or just empty my mind for five minutes, then ten, and so on. One morning, I thought, "I can do this myself," and I put away the computer and led myself through a meditation. And this is where everything in my life began to change.

Inspiration: A mystical force, the breath, bringing in air

As I sat quietly breathing, I could feel my body shift. A powerful surge of energy rose from the base of my spine, coursing through my belly, into my heart, and finally shooting through my crown like a bolt of lightning. Sparks ignited within me, hundreds of them like tiny fireworks bursting. I had no control over it, and yet I felt ecstatic. It was as though someone was tossing little balls of gunpowder inside me, each one erupting into miniature explosions that reverberated through my body. I had no idea what was happening, but it felt amazing—as if each of those explosions broke apart old energy, an aged story that I no longer needed to carry. What had been so tightly wound and stuck in my body was released. I realized later it was something called Kundalini rising, but at the time, I just thought it was a miracle.

What happened in that moment was the beginning of the journey to my true self. I began to crave quiet moments, just breathing or visualizing or being. I realized that in taking that small amount of time to sit with my own presence, I was shifting my understanding of how the presence around me felt, too. I learned which energy and emotions were mine and those that didn't belong to me. I learned how to be responsible for my own energy and not take on others as my own.

Meditation became a gateway to experiencing life in an entirely new way. It opened a portal to my soul and into the oneness of life. The magic that happened when I began meditating evolved quickly. I realized that the soul is boundless and deep, and when I found the quiet space of my heart, I was able to find myself again.

It didn't erase my child's disease or make all my worldly problems vanish. But it helped me rediscover self-love and find beauty in surrender. It shifted how I show up in the world and deepened my ability to sense the presence of others. I realized the immense power I hold in life simply through my thoughts and feelings. I began conversing with God and my angels again, and my intuition expanded to whole new levels of insight and ability.

My spiritual awakening felt intense, even traumatic, but sometimes it takes a sledgehammer to crack through the dense layers for the light to enter. My life now is profoundly different. I feel peaceful, grounded, and grateful for everything that led me here. I no longer strive to prove my worth because my heart knows the truth. Anxiety shows itself to me on occasion still, yet now it holds no lasting power over me. I see it as an emotion or a teacher, not who I am.

The Divine works with me in mysterious ways. I can now hear guidance from the angels, both for myself and others. What began as seeing spirits as a child has blossomed into a gift of mediumship. It feels as though the spirit world was waiting for me to find myself so I could work alongside them. With the ability to feel energy so deeply —and now the awareness to differentiate it—I can connect people to their loved ones who have crossed over. My sensitivity had a purpose all along, and I finally discovered it. I know that my spiritual awakening led me to my soul's true path.

Erika Anderson is a loving wife and mama. She is also an evidential psychic medium and teacher who channels messages from spirit, provides soul and mediumship readings, and empowers other gentle souls to discover their spiritual power.

Website: www.spiritualmediumerika.com

Instagram: www.instagram.com/mediumerikaanderson

Spirit Portal Podcast: www.spiritualmediumerika.com/podcast

Offerings: www.spiritualmediumerika.com/offerings

18

The Sacred Cage and the Key to Freedom

By Ashley Mondor
Saint Paul, Minnesota, USA

"Oh! You must be in the office today… are you in a jail cell?! Those blue cinderblock walls look like you're in a prison." My coworker casually asked in our virtual meeting. If she only knew how trapped and utterly powerless I felt, how I despised this tiny, windowless office. I ended our call with the best smile I could muster before a wave of sadness crashed into me. I buried my face into my arms as hot tears streamed down my cheeks. I tried to muffle the sound of my cries so my coworkers couldn't hear me, but the weight of those walls made me feel like a caged animal.

"Why me, God? What did I do to deserve being put back in this system?" I bitterly thought to myself as my heart shattered into a million jagged pieces. For context, I had spent the last two years being free. I was full-time in my coaching business, supporting clients in healing themselves from heartbreak, divorce, low self-worth, feeling lost, anxious, fearful, etc., but spirit has a funny way of working.

When the end of 2022 rolled around, the momentum in my business came to a sudden standstill. No matter what I said or sold, nothing was working. "GOD! What the hell am I doing wrong?!" I'd plead as I watched the money in my bank account dwindle. The stress compounded as I tried to figure out how to claw my way out of this all-consuming hole that felt like quicksand. I do this work because I genuinely love it. I bring a deep sense of integrity, care, and profound reverence for every heart I have the honor of holding space for—so why send me back to corporate?

A few months later, one of my best friends and former bosses excitedly shared that she had an opening on her team and that she'd love for me to apply, knowing my skillset firsthand. Everything about the opportunity sounded incredible… if you're looking to work for a company that isn't your own, I guess. The salary was a dream, the company did great work in their industry, and I'd get to be on a team of talented women while meeting new people across the world.

You're probably thinking, "What's the problem here, Ash? That sounds wonderful compared to what so many are struggling with… and you're just gifted an opportunity like that?!" But when you've spent the last two years of your life creating your own schedule—shaped specifically around your energy and passion, experiencing what it's like to love every single Monday, and only working in ways that make you feel alive—going back to doing work that isn't deeply meaningful felt like a punishment.

What do you do when you feel like you're trapped between a rock and a hard place? Well, I dove headfirst into depression. Do I remain committed with unwavering belief in my business, praying it'll all work out? Or do I begrudgingly go back to an outdated system that expects you to constantly perform, even when your body, brain, and energy aren't built to be a productive machine for 40-plus hours a week?

The most challenging part was how relentless, persuasive, and dark my thoughts were. How could I sustain my business with so little time left after eight hours in front of a computer? What would my capacity be for creating content, supporting my community, and producing my podcast? What if I push my adrenals to the brink of burnout again?

At one point, when I was frozen in indecision, I remember snuggling next to my fiancé, Nikolai, as I told him, with tears in my eyes and a lump in my throat, "I don't think I can go back. I don't know if I can handle being in a system where the work I do doesn't really matter. What did I do wrong? Why can't I work with people in the ways I love? Why even stay on the planet?" I know that sounds dramatic, but the tunnel vision I had only made everything foggier and more convincing.

With a heavy heart, I decided to apply for the job. I hit submit on my resume and vividly remember my friend texting me with so much excitement at the thought of working together again. I then promptly let my ego take the wheel on a thrilling adventure toward self-loathing, fear, and hopelessness.

To try and lift my spirits, Nikolai took me on a hike to help me process. I remember him holding my hand as I cried when he gently said, "Ashley, your life is beautiful; you just can't see it right now." I looked down at the moonstone engagement ring he had custom-made for me when he surprised me in the National Botanic Gardens of Ireland to propose only a month earlier. The light reflected back to me in these ethereal blues and purples. In that beautiful moment, it was as if the fog had cleared from my mind.

To have a job brought to me in the most divine and effortless way, to be making more money than I ever have, to live in a healthy body, and to walk through life in a relationship that seems as if it were written for fairytales—well, I knew Nikolai was right. So, I decided that I might as well get out of my own way and open my heart up to possibility because spirit MUST know something that I can't see yet.

In April of 2023, at 1:11 p.m., while I was in my car after grabbing coffee, I held the phone up to my ear and watched the rain splash across my windshield as the recruiter offered me the role. I accepted with a gleeful tone and heavy heart. She shared that she'd email me my onboarding paperwork along with my employee ID number, which starts with 111—a sign from my spirit guides that represents soul alignment and new beginnings.

I've been in my job for over a year and a half now, and I can tell you that being placed back into corporate has been one of the hardest and most challenging spiritual initiations I've walked through. For context, I've navigated assault, infidelity, heartbreak, loss, and abuse. But this job is the one that's forced me to face myself and every ego attachment I had to who I believed I was.

I desperately tried to keep my business afloat, but people can intuitively feel that energy. They can sense when you're exhausted and hopeless, even if you try to put a pretty filter over it. I spent a whole year being forced to figure out who I am outside of being a coach and healer— my proudest accomplishments and the foundation of my identity that I had been building for the past seven years.

What does life look and feel like when you're not focused on constantly trying to generate sales or forcing the muse of your creativity to perform for something as fickle as an algorithm? How does my nervous system respond when I finally allow myself to rest after work? What do I actually want to say now that my livelihood isn't linked to the offers I create or the content I share?

What if, for the first time in my life, I had the capacity to focus on my core wounds, limiting beliefs, and subconscious programming around my inherent value while being fully supported financially by this job? What if I allowed this role to take the pressure off me so I could pay down the thousands of dollars in debt I was carrying from investing in my skills and business? What if I could finally see my soul and experience life FOR me? What could I create from this space?

So, I assimilated back into the corporate system... and I was fucking miserable. There's something about working more hours in a day than you spend living your life that is soul-crushing. I did everything I could think of to try and leave: I signed up for marketing programs, launched new offers, and tried to cobble together ideas for working part-time jobs to make ends meet, which, of course, never panned out.

To cope with feeling like a failure and the lack of traction in my business, I guzzled wine damn near daily to help numb the searing pain. However, after one particularly heavy meltdown, I remembered that I had tools to move the energy in my body. I started EFT tapping whenever I felt like burning everything to the ground. On my drive home from the office, I'd park my car, raise the crook of my elbow up to my mouth, and rage-scream my frustrations as tears spilled from my eyes.

My brain would lovingly remind me of what I once had: those long, slow mornings, how every Monday was a blessing, and the way clients would look at me at the end of our sessions with a renewed sense of power and light in their eyes. One day, I needed to go for a walk to process the heaviness I felt in my chest. I remember pleading with God, "PLEASE get me out of here. I'm so tired. I don't want to do this shit anymore!" Then, a crystal-clear voice in my mind cut through the noise, saying, "Do you not trust me?" At that moment, I shifted back into my power. I realized that I was the creator of this cage, and my soul gave me this opportunity so I could remember that I also held the keys to my freedom.

We're given obstacles as a form of evolutionary tension. We're placed in situations to expand beyond our perceived limitations, programming, and societal conditioning. Because of this job, I learned that the obstacles ARE my path. They were given to me on purpose—gifts and opportunities lovingly disguised as confronting challenges that reveal more of who I am at the core of my being.

When you're presented with seemingly insurmountable tests and trials that you'd do anything to escape from but can't, that's when evolution calls your spirit forward. No matter how black and white anything seems, no matter how heavy the pain and despair may feel, what will bring you clarity, freedom, and power isn't grasped in the clutches of your ego but found within the light of your presence.

We think of spiritual awakenings as being filled with rainbows and joy, but for me, it's more like being forged by fire—walking through the flames and compounding pressure to be shaped into something as exquisite and resilient as diamonds. I realized that the more I tried to run away or break free, the tighter my mental shackles became.

Have you ever played with a finger trap toy? The ones where you place both index fingers into a small, braided paper tube? When you try to pull yourself out of the trap, the toy shrinks and tightens around your fingers, making it impossible to escape. The trap gets tighter the harder you try to pull away from yourself. Resistance is the trap. In this job, I learned that acceptance is what unlocks the medicine. I had been with the company for a year when I could finally see with new eyes that this experience has been one of the biggest blessings of my life.

I learned that, to free yourself, you must accept where you are right now. Acceptance isn't the choice your ego craves; it's the one your heart yearns for. Acceptance doesn't mean you're giving up or giving in; it means you're willing to relax into facing yourself or the situation without judgment, shame, guilt, or fear. Self-acceptance is what brings you back to a neutral place of love and clarity–a powerful place from which to move forward.

If I hadn't been lovingly placed in my own mental prison, I would have continued believing all the lies and distortions my ego threaded through my consciousness, which kept me from understanding and embodying the power of my presence. I learned that I'm NOT what I achieve or offer to the world; I'm not my title, business, or the labels I wear as a healer, oracle, or guide. I'm not my ego attachments to pain or suffering, nor the trapped bird I believed I was out of fear. I'm not what I create; I AM the creator experiencing myself through the vast array and richness of what life has to offer. I now know that I AM the cage and the key.

Do I still have challenging days? Well, yeah, that's the gift of being human. But I'm quicker at catching negative thought loops, along with the anxiety or frustration that try to pull me away from the magic of the moment. I sit with what I'm feeling now instead of trying to repress it. I allow myself to feel into those heavy emotions because my body and unconscious mind are sending me messages trying to catch my attention, letting me know I have a shadow-based thought or belief that's asking to be illuminated by my consciousness.

My life has been profoundly impacted. I've let go of alcohol, paid off $25,000+ of debt, and became certified in Coaching the Unconscious Mind and Integrative Hypnosis from Melissa Tiers, a woman I've admired for years. The opportunities materializing because of the shift in my energy have been beyond my wildest dreams! One of those most treasured opportunities includes sharing my story in this book you're reading.

If I could leave you with a gift: You create your own heaven or hell based on the amount of love you have for yourself. Your brain will weave you webs of lies because it loves and wants to protect you, but you will always be invited to expand beyond your stories and limitations. While your brain doesn't truly know what you're capable of, your soul wholeheartedly does. May you find joy in your Earthly journey, valuing each step more than the pursuit of a destination that might not align with your soul's true mission.

Ashley Mondor is a seeker and guide embarking on a new journey of self-discovery. As her work continues to evolve, she loves sharing her inspirations, revelations, and channeled wisdom with those who wish to join her on their own quest for self-expansion.

Website: www.ashleymondor.com

Podcast: https://freeyourheart.buzzsprout.com

Facebook: www.facebook.com/ashley.mondor

Instagram: www.instagram.com/ashley.mondor

19

Answering Your Soul Calling Even If You're Scared or Uncertain

By Kim Coots
Howell, Michigan, USA

My spiritual awakening has been challenging, but what I've received along the way is the clarity, courage, and resources to fulfill my soul's calling. I hope this chapter inspires you to find the blessings on your journey of spiritual awakening, turn wounds into wisdom, and unlock the courage to live your divine potential with love and joy.

I'm honored to share part of my story with you.

I grew up with a mom who was chronically ill and an absent, alcoholic father. Yet, as a child, I felt a magical connection with life and nature. I was content with being an only child and using my imagination to occupy my time.

Life changed when I was twelve. My mom got involved with a man who had a heroin addiction, and we moved across the country to an impoverished area in Detroit. Suddenly, the magical life I once knew was gone, and I felt unsafe.

Then, when I was fourteen, my mother left me with a distant relative who was mean and abusive. My survival instincts told me to stay as quiet and unseen as possible to stay safe. I was devastated that my mother had left me, and I had no contact with her for many months. She never told me where she went or why she left. She said it was too painful.

These experiences formed beliefs that I was unworthy, unsafe, and insecure. As a teenager, I began attracting older men into my life who abused and mistreated me, but I felt like I deserved it. I coped with the emotional pain I felt by cutting my hands and arms with a razor blade, drinking alcohol, and smoking cigarettes.

I also discovered that employment was a way to find the security I desperately needed. At age fifteen, I had three part-time jobs, and I lived out of a suitcase, partying and crashing on a friend's or boyfriend's couch. No one disciplined me, and I did whatever I wanted.

I was living two lives. One was the hard-working, dependable employee who strived to please the boss because that meant approval and money. The second was a tough, rebellious party girl who allowed me to escape the pain and pressure in my life through alcohol.

When I was seventeen, I graduated high school early and received a college grant, so I enrolled. It didn't take long to realize college was not for me, and I dropped out. Life had little meaning and felt so painful that I began planning to end my life. Thankfully, I discovered I was pregnant with my beautiful daughter, Keira. We both almost died during my pregnancy, but our souls were destined to be together in this life. She gave me the meaningful purpose I longed for.

At the age of twenty-three, I was recognized as an Inc. 500 award-winning business leader when the company I worked for became the 26th fastest-growing company in America. Shortly after, I landed a lucrative job as an executive for a 6-billion-dollar company and earned a six-figure salary without a college education. As a young, single mom, I continued to work hard and party hard to balance the stress and pressure I placed on myself to keep me and Keira safe and secure.

I was aware that my past trauma was affecting my life, and I began studying metaphysical healing.

I also secretly became a massage therapist after I had an out-of-body experience while receiving a massage. I was astounded to discover that I could sense and feel stuck energy in my client's bodies during their massage, and I also received information about why it was there to help them release their energy blocks.

I was so fulfilled in my spiritual work. However, I kept my spiritual side secret because I was afraid my business colleagues would think I was weird or crazy.

Keira encouraged me to follow my dream of growing my spiritual business and quit my corporate job, but I was too afraid to leave the perceived sense of security it gave me. I also felt guilty about desiring something else when I had this fantastic job that most would consider a dream job.

A corporate client discovered my spiritual business website and asked me about it. I was terrified my boss would find out, and it would sabotage my business career, so I closed my business. I also joined a religious church because it seemed like an acceptable form of spirituality, and metaphysics did not.

Then, I became physically sick. I wasn't honoring myself or what I felt called to do. Yet, I continually worried that I wasn't enough and wouldn't have enough if I gave up the security of my corporate job. Plus, my family depended on me.

My physical illness drew me back to the spiritual healing arts that I love, and I regained my health enough to function. However, I still didn't allow myself to re-open my spiritual business and longed for it.

In 2019, I felt strongly guided to quit my corporate job and start my own business. Instead of ignoring that guidance like I usually would, I followed that urge. Without knowing what my business would be, I notified my boss that I was quitting. People and resources suddenly appeared when I decided to follow my intuition!

A business colleague called to ask if I offered business consulting, and I said yes. I'd spent the last 20 years leading several multi-million dollar companies. My new business became a six-figure-a-year business consulting company, and it took off without doing any marketing.

I had my own successful business and the freedom of an entrepreneur. Despite suppressing the urge to express my spiritual gifts, I felt like my life was finally coming together safely and securely in a way that I was more in control of. I was still using alcohol, anti-anxiety meds, and comfort food to quiet the voice inside that told me there was something more for me to do.

To quell my spiritual urges, I enrolled in Astrology School. My instructor read my astrological birth chart and told me I'm a medium who can communicate with people who've died. I adamantly denied that I was a medium! What is known as "After Death Communication" freaked me out, and I was so uncomfortable with the topic that I avoided anything to do with it. My instructor gave me the name of a woman who taught evidential mediumship in case I changed my mind, and I filed it away, never planning to use it.

A few months later, my world fell apart when my worst possible fear became a reality. Just after Keira's twenty-sixth birthday, I received a phone call with the news that Keira had taken a drug she didn't know contained fentanyl, and she died of a drug overdose. My baby girl was gone! I didn't think I would survive this devastating loss.

However, something miraculous happened. The day after Keira died, I started receiving undeniable signs from her from the Other Side. In my heart, I knew this was Keira telling me she was okay, but my mind wondered if I was making these signs up because I was so desperate.

Then, tragedy struck again. A week after Keira's death, my 64-year-old mom developed a bacterial infection she contracted after a routine back surgery. Her health declined so much she needed life support to survive. I honored her medical directives and advised the doctors she didn't want life support. My mom died a week later. I was in shock, and I couldn't believe two people I love most died unexpectedly in the same month!

I located the mediumship teacher's contact info that I'd filed away and contacted her. Her evidential mediumship training program was about to start, and although I was scared and skeptical, I signed up. I wanted more proof that the signs I received from Keira were real, and I hoped I'd find them in this program.

I continued working full-time in my business consulting company even though I was experiencing immense grief, and I felt my body warning me that I needed to stop and take time for myself, but I didn't listen. I had enough savings to take time off, but I was worried I'd lose clients if I did. I was also worried about what my business clients would think if they knew I was studying mediumship, so I tried to keep it hidden. I kept putting pressure on myself, like I had for much of my life.

Part of my mediumship training was to provide mediumship readings for other people, and although I was very reluctant, I'm so glad I did. During practice readings, I discovered that Keira was helping me connect with people on the Other Side to share information and messages that their living loved ones could validate. The experiences of these mediumship readings gave me the proof I was looking for that after-death communication was real and that my connection with Keira was, too.

After years of study and practice, I cautiously decided to become a professional evidential medium. I opened my own spiritual business again, helping people who'd experienced the death of a loved one find hope and healing by working with Keira to facilitate a connection for them. I was mindful about keeping my mediumship a secret so my business clients didn't find out, and I struggled with living two lives again.

I felt torn because the healing power of mediumship was so profound, but I also feared losing my reputation and sense of security if my business clients and colleagues found out about it.

I hid my spiritual business again, and compounded with my immense grief, I became very sick. Afraid of disappointing my clients, I forced myself to continue working until I couldn't anymore.

I was diagnosed with organ failure, five different infections, and mold toxicity, and I was on the verge of developing an autoimmune disease and Addison's disease. I was also diagnosed with complex grief, PTSD, and Limbic System Impairment. My brain was stuck in fight-or-flight mode. My illnesses forced me to stop using wine, medication, and comfort foods to cope with my grief and fear because my body couldn't process it.

Doctors recommended I undergo two very invasive surgeries and start lifelong steroids. My intuition told me it wasn't the answer, so I refused all of their surgery and medication recommendations and became my own advocate.

I was searching for ways to heal my body when I was diagnosed with breast implant illness, which is caused by toxins in the breast implants I'd gotten 15 years earlier because I'd felt insecure about my small breasts.

I underwent a 5-hour breast reconstruction surgery. My recovery was painful, and I had to take time off to heal. I reduced my work schedule by 80% to focus on my health.

During this sober healing time, I reflected on my life and accepted that my soul was calling me to serve as the Connector for Spirit I came here to be. I'd denied that calling for a long time and decided it was time to honor it, no matter what. I began doing mediumship readings again and teaching mediumship to others who were called to serve as a Connector for Spirit. I trusted my gut to know what treatments to use and found myself healing. I no longer had five infections, the autoimmune markers were negative, and I began restoring my low cortisol levels through somatic trauma recovery.

Learning to love and honor myself has been a powerful healing balm for my mind, body, and spirit. Listening to the guidance of Spirit while compassionately working through the fears and uncertainty of my wounded self has opened up a new way of being that I love. I also realized that Spirit is my true Source, not my job. Throughout the difficulties of my life, I always had what I needed. I'm delighted and fulfilled to honor my soul calling without the pressure I used to put on myself.

I invite you to reflect on the following questions with non-judgment and compassion. Your answers may be helpful for you in navigating your spiritual awakening journey and answering your soul calling:

- Are you hiding your true self? If so, in what ways can you begin embracing and embodying your gifts to create a life that you love?

- What is your source of security and safety? Can you trust in Spirit, whatever you define Spirit to be, as your Source?

- Do you have a sense of connection with your soul? If so, what is it guiding you to do or be? If not, you can ask your soul for guidance about how to connect and listen to the insights you receive.

- Do you honor your intuition, the voice of your soul?

- What miracles or blessings have occurred on your journey so far?

- Are you willing to ask your soul to help you turn your wounds into wisdom?

- Is there any pressure to be or do what you think you need to for perceived safety and security? If so, can you begin releasing that pressure with compassion?

- Do you feel connected to the divine vessel that is your body and have a loving relationship with your body?

Your spiritual awakening is part of your soul's plan to help you unlock your divine potential and do what you came to earth to do. I celebrate you for your courage and willingness to honor your soul calling, even if you're scared or uncertain. I know from experience that Spirit supports you every step of the way, and you are not alone.

♡ ♡ ♡

Kim Coots is an Inc. 500 award-winning business executive turned Evidential Medium and Spiritual Development Teacher. She is also the founder of The School For Spiritual Development and an Astrologer and Shamanic Healing Practitioner.

The unexpected deaths of her only child and mother changed the trajectory of Kim's life and career. Kim went from feeling skeptical and uncomfortable about After Death Communication to being an advocate and teacher of mediumship after the undeniable signs Kim received from her loved ones on the Other Side set her on a journey she never expected to take.

Now, she helps people connect with Spirit so they can experience divine guidance, healing, and purpose.

Website: www.kimcoots.com

Instagram: www.instagram.com/coachkimcoots

20

A Moonlit Path

By Renee Precopio
Westborough, Massachusetts, USA

The journey to my spiritual awakening entailed over two decades of confusion, denial, ignorance, and obliviousness. Nonetheless, I consider myself fortunate and trust the divine timing. There are so many in the intuitive space who come to terms with our gifts later in life, as others are forced to quite literally confront them at a young age.

Before my awakening began, I'd already held the belief that everything happens for a reason. Even with the limited hindsight I've got now, I know it holds true for my life. In time, I'd experiment with reciting mantras ad nauseam for months on end. Yet, one mantra that has always resonated most is: "The universe has my back, and what's meant for me won't miss me." I'll explain more of the "why" later. But first, let's turn the clock back and admire all of the waving, glittering flags from the universe that I chose to ignore!

Back in K-12, there was more than one occasion walking home where I felt I was being watched or followed. I'd look around and see that I was completely alone. Similarly, pretty much any time I was up late at night and by myself, I'd experience that familiar sensation of skin tingling on the back of my neck. I chalked all of this up to being afraid of the dark or being haunted by images of a few seconds of a horror movie trailer I accidentally saw on TV. Those are all more logical explanations than sensing a spirit, right? And because the universe has a sense of humor and our guides want our attention, they cranked up the dial to activate most of the psychic "clairs" (i.e., Clairvoyance, Claircognizance, Clairaudience, and Clairsentience) decades before I knew what they were.

In late high school and throughout college, the lightbulb in my brain started to flicker and tell me something was going on. I'd have highly specific premonitions (i.e., knowledge of future events) with anywhere from 30 minutes down to 30 seconds of lead time. For example, knowing I'd be called on in class for a specific homework question. Watching someone drop their phone in the exact spot I'd spontaneously been overcome with that very concern one minute prior. Texting a friend I inexplicably knew needed a hug, who replied back she'd been crying alone in her room, buildings away. Bolting upright in the middle of the night, terrified about an active shooter and learning later that the San Bernadino shooting was transpiring across the country at that very moment. Those experiences, and plenty more, occurred in various locations and manifested in distinct ways. The intuitive hits were sporadic and leveraged all of my senses, which made it challenging to connect the dots and all too easy to joke about and dismiss.

I consider myself to be a data person. In 2016, I received my Bachelor of Science in Psychology and held a series of corporate roles in data collection, analysis, and reporting. When these "coincidences" increased in frequency and impact, naturally, I created a log! Okay, fine, I created multiple logs. At the end of 2020, I "randomly" had the idea to track my dreams in 2021 for a new daily journaling practice. Soon, I wondered if I had a "heightened intuition" and listened to a podcast about identifying and understanding your gifts. A couple of months later, I asked my family to get me a psychic reading for my birthday. In secret, I hoped this medium would confirm I was intuitive. In a few short weeks, he entirely validated this deep knowing and added, "You're meant to help other people, talk to other people. You're really good at seeing them." The dedicated student I am, I immediately followed the recommendations to buy crystals for anxiety and grounding, read books on intuition, experiment with divination tools, set dream intentions before bed, and enroll in a psychic development course.

When I started at Nu It School, an online educational portal and community for budding intuitives, my goal was to learn more about myself and the potential of my gifts to help others. That summer, I leveraged their prerecorded activations, attended monthly live classes, meditated, and developed a "Yes/No" system for connecting with my Nana, which I still use today with all spirits. When the 6-month Nuurvana Be Light Program was announced, I trusted my gut and signed up. With live ceremonies, lots of esoteric reading that infused Chinese medicine with psychology (perfect!) and brand-new metaphysical jargon, plus yoga and meditations, this virtual program provided exactly the educational support I craved!

Eventually, it took a turn I didn't expect. We'd be doing psychic readings. Now, you might think, "Okay, Renee, it's an intuitive development program, and you didn't think you were going to actually apply it?!" Well, no. I thought we'd keep trying different exercises to strengthen our clairvoyant visualization and continue with personal healing work. It was incredibly nerve-wracking when we started live practice sessions to observe, be read by, or try reading others! We got paired with Partners in Light—would you be surprised I knew exactly who mine would be before we'd ever interacted? We met regularly to practice and discuss our nervousness and self-doubt that, at times, compounded as the weekend intensive quickly approached. During these workshops, the group engaged in new exercises, read strangers and classmates, and received feedback from peers and the instructors. No pressure, right?

At this point, I was concluding that the evidence of innate intuition in all people was undeniable. I witnessed person after person share completely accurate information and yet doubt every word coming out of their mouth. The pure shock as messages resonated was truly validating for us all. To this day, I still experience that awe and laughter-inducing sense of surprise.

There's a misconception that psychics know everything. We can't! We're people, too! With the human experience comes anxiety, stress, confusion, bias, and fear. We inadvertently block insights. The main, and somehow easier, obstacle to overcome is the concern that a truly objective person in front of you won't connect with your gifts. I've learned that the more I trust myself to wield my gifts for the greater good of someone else, the faster information comes through and the more potent and direct its articulation. If only it were as straightforward when reading ourselves!

Now, where does this information even come from? Is it inner knowing? Are we all actually mediums connecting to a spirit team, whether or not we perceive beings? Are we tapping into an energetic collective containing knowledge of the past, present, and future? Who knows! And does it matter? Despite all the AI chatter right now, I believe intuition can never be replaced by this emerging technology. Yes, supercomputers could run predictive algorithms based on probability, but that's not the same, is it? AI can't connect to someone's energy, process the arc of their lifespan and past lives, or gather wisdom from loved ones who've passed on. To engage with your intuition is to be more powerful than a quantum computer—how awesome is that?

My spiritual journey since graduating and becoming accredited in the Nuurvana Clairvoyant Healing Method has naturally involved some major up-levels. The friendships formed during that program are going strong to this day. One of those friends became my podcast co-host! I've read hundreds of people, incrementally incorporating different language and divination tools as I progressed. My intuitive muscles (yes, muscles, because you need practice to build them!) have grown and expanded into other "psychic clairs". I launched my business, networked, and partnered with local companies for public and private psychic events. I created social media accounts, started running live stream classes on Insight Timer, became a certified astrologer, launched natal astrology services, and designed a digital planner! That's an incredibly long list, and it's the cliff notes version! But it hasn't always been rainbows and butterflies.

Ascension is never a straight line. There are obstacles and shedding that occur both inside and outside of your control. We may feel we're backsliding, lost without a north star, confused by messages and signs, or utterly devastated by material and emotional losses. And don't forget the stigma and pervasive stereotypes around intuitive work! Social pressure, self-doubt, and struggles of everyday life all blend together in a tapestry of low vibrational opposition.

Is this even real? Am I on the right track? What's the best way to tell someone I do readings? When is the "right time"? What happens if "xyz" friend, partner, coworker, neighbor, or family member rejects or shames me? Should I keep this all to myself so I don't end up ostracized? Are there other people out there who feel the same way I do?

Well, the answer to that last question is unequivocally yes. Finding connection and community is crucial to building a support system. However, doing this work inevitably results in some relationships fading or bursting into flames. It's part of the process. As long as you return to your values and high vibe intention, with your feet on the ground, you'll move and live with integrity. In doing so, you'll start releasing the toxic grip of those "witch wound" questions and allow those who don't see your compassionate heart and spirit to happily slip out of your circle. Anyone unwilling to grow with you wasn't meant to stick around anyway.

To underscore that point further, a quick sidebar: I was in a long-term relationship, during which I significantly decreased the time I spent meditating, connecting with my guides, nurturing my yoga practice, etc. However, I received my Nuurvana certification, casually offered readings, and even did one while my partner and I briefly lived together. Not once did he ask about my intuition or spiritual wellness practices. Not a single time. During the week I ended things, I heard it straight from the horse's mouth: "I ask questions if I'm interested." I'll refrain from launching into a secondary sidebar about how utterly apathetic that mentality is and leave you with a mantra: "I deserve to be loved, not tolerated."

Back to the expected energetic shedding that goes hand in hand with ascension. Six months after that breakup, I was laid off from my company of over seven years, and a few weeks later, my granddad passed. These are perfect examples of shedding: the ending of a relationship not serving my highest good, severance from an identity as a corporate employee and loyalty to an organization over my own well-being, and loss of a loved one who believed in me.

In the aftermath of shedding, you can harness that energy and transform it into an up-level—if you understand the assignment given by the Universe! My assignments were abundantly clear: take up space, use my voice and share my truth, be visibly authentic (no more hiding!), and wholeheartedly believe in myself. Remember that long list of accomplishments I shared? I achieved all of that in around 12 months! That's expansion, baby!

Growth can be scary, though. Maybe it's happening too fast, and you're suddenly worried about whether you're truly ready for major change. Maybe it's happening too slowly, and you fear your dreams will never pan out and you'll struggle indefinitely. Maybe it's happening in stops and starts, and you're frustrated that the ride up to the mountaintop is bumpy and stressful instead of awe-inducing.

There's a lot of pressure around personal and spiritual growth that often goes unacknowledged. For example, keeping up appearances, never having a rest day, or carrying expectations of this outcome by that point in time. Or what will people say about you? *You've made the wrong choice and should return to a more "traditional" and "stable" lifestyle.* It's easy to be in your head and get lost in the maze of what-ifs.

The name of the game is Surrender. As a Type A person who adores a good plan and to-do list, truly surrendering is a challenging road. I still struggle against one-off stressors, wants, and circumstances. And yet, hasn't everything worked out as it was supposed to? As a kid, I preferred English and Science classes, and during my senior year of high school, I discovered Psychology, which perfectly fused the two fields. In undergrad, I decided to become a therapist but got spooked by a visiting lecturer. I feared I'd get overly invested in my patients and be gravely disappointed if they didn't make the life changes necessary for measurable mental health improvement.

I pivoted on a dime to focus on research instead. After graduating, I worked in data roles at the company where I spent over seven years. Now that we're back to the top of my story, you see where this is going, right? After everything, I wound up back in one-on-one life counseling that specifically requires me to energetically and emotionally connect with the person in front of me.

Was I supposed to become a licensed therapist all along? I don't think so. My childhood interests pointed me in the right direction: towards people and seeking an understanding of what's bigger than us. In elementary school, we had a unit on tracking the moon's phases before bed. It was an assignment I particularly enjoyed. Decades later, I still look for the moon in the night sky. As a student of astrology with a moon-ruled chart, I grasp more clearly my innate childhood fascination. Regardless of the winding path, I've sought to follow my north star—or, in my case, my moon!

We can't expect the journey to the mountaintop of spiritual ascension to always be smooth, the view ever-dazzling, nor that our gondola never stops for repair. Extended metaphor, I know, but if you have a mantra, vision, or dream that speaks to you on a soul level, you'll find your way. For me, it's, "The universe has my back, and what's meant for me won't miss me." What's yours?

Renee Precopio (she/her) is the Massachusetts-based owner of Read by Renee, co-host of the Synergy to Synastry podcast, and a teacher on Insight Timer. A Nuurvana-certified intuitive and Nightlight Astrology-certified astrologer, she provides virtual psychic and natal astrology readings, meditations, educational classes and resources, and creates yearly planners. It's always her priority to be inclusive of all levels of metaphysical knowledge, and she compassionately guides beginners into and through this world. Renee is constantly dreaming up, sometimes literally, new ideas and ways to help others and contribute to the global ascension.

Website: www.readbyreneetoday.com

Instagram: www.instagram.com/_readbyrenee

Podcast: www.readbyreneetoday.com/podcast

Insight Timer: www.insighttimer.com/ReadbyRenee

21

10:50PM

By Claire Solomon
Melbourne, Victoria, Australia

I was a very serious kid. A deep thinker. I had a lot of wonder about the world but also wondered why no one else had the same questions that I did. I had vivid dreams, saw patterns in people and events, and had random knowledge drop in. I had a deep need to understand the things that no one else seemed into, like stars and planets and auras.

It's 1998, and I'm 14 years old. My bedroom is full of Suns & Moons decor. You know the vibe. It was Saturday morning in my county town in Australia, and Dad asked me if I wanted to go down the street. (Yes, we called it "the street" because there was basically just one).

We walked past a newsagent, and I saw a kit called "Discover Astrology." Each week, you'd get another chunk of info to build into a huge set of folders. There were exciting things each week like tarot cards, runes, crystals, all the things. This was my first Shiny Dot, which I'll explain further shortly.

I've heard people say that astrology is the gateway drug to spirituality, and that kit from 1998 sure was mine. I was absolutely hooked. All this metaphysical information was satisfying an itch in my brain that I hadn't been able to scratch before. It allowed me to shift from the overly serious, deep-thinking kid to one who was ready to dial up the weird.

For the first time, I felt like I had answers to things about myself and the Universe. I even started to feel like I had some kind of spirit team helping me, but I didn't really know how to connect with them. Still, that didn't stop me from feeling plugged into the magic.

Then, as the years went by, life happened. I went to University, and my parents sold the family home I grew up in (my little Suns & Moons cave was gone). After University, I moved to Sydney (which had far more places to go than "down the street," that's for sure). The world was starting to feel bigger and heavier than I had ever experienced before. And not in an exciting way.

I could feel the energy of people and situations deeply and see patterns and paths ahead for them. I had intuitive nudges about what was going on around me and felt like I knew what was going to happen before it happened. But I was in the "real world" now. I was in a big city, with a new job in an Advertising Agency, with humans who seemed very comfortable with life as it was.

I still had big cosmic questions. But no one else seemed the same as me. They felt comfortable in the world. I did not. This turned into a general discomfort rising in me around everything; the way the corporate world was structured, the food industry, big pharma, societal expectations. I had lots of questions but answers that never satisfied me. And no one to talk to who seemed to have the same level of discomfort as me.

In those early questioning days, it felt like I was the first kid awake at a sleepover and was eagerly and anxiously waiting for those around me to open their eyes, to see what I could see, to wake up, to awaken. I was also forced to lead a double life. I still had to pretend I cared about these mainstream paradigms—working 9-5, organized belief systems, patriarchal structures, fitting in, not asking questions—while my soul was pulling me down this other path.

Straddling both realities was hard. That was actually quite painful. Feeling alone while simultaneously surrounded by sleeping people. So, the fun weirdness that I had dialled up when I was 14 had to be turned all the way off. It felt safer to blend in and play the game.

Unsurprisingly, partying and classic dissociation followed. I felt like if I was going to have to play this character in this backward society, I had to pretend I didn't have these strange, untapped wizard skills brewing in me.

Because, you know, we had marketing campaigns about cheese slices to create. Trying to figure out why I was here had to go on the back burner. And within a year that spiritually awakening flame in me was now a tiny ember. That was until 24th March 2017.

But let me back you up a bit. The act of being a "normal person" was a lot, obviously. After a few years in advertising, I decided I was going to travel the world alone (read: run away). As is the divine function of the Universe, about 10 months before this plan of travel, I met my now-husband. We travelled together, visiting 32 countries, and ended up living in London for a few years.

On paper, those years were amazing experiences, but I was still consciously disconnected from life. It felt like the easier option. Bigger city, bigger, fancier advertising job. New countries with more intense energies.

While my now-husband knew me and my abilities (he was there for some strange happenings), he also knew it was a path I had to traverse on my own timing.

That was until I became pregnant with our daughter. By this time, we were back living in Australia. Another big city, another advertising job. Playing the game. But this is where I found my next Shiny Dot. My search for people who were asking the same questions as me led me into the health coaching community, and I ended up qualifying and opening up my first coaching business in 2014.

This is what I like to call The Shiny Dot Effect—when something grabs your attention and won't let go. It might not make any logical sense, but all the signs keep pointing you to take a step toward it anyway. It keeps glimmering there and catching your eye.

I was still working in marketing but had this growing business on the side that was drawing soul-aligned people into my world. Simply seeking like-minded people who also felt the world was mad launched me into my own business.

And here's the thing about Shiny Dots—they only join up and make sense when you're looking back. In the moment, it might feel random or even a little chaotic, but later on, you realize those dots were connecting all along.

So, I remember when I got that positive pregnancy test. I grabbed the kitchen bench to steady myself and broke down in tears. And it wasn't just because this baby thing was actually happening. I felt in that moment that there was some kind of alchemical spark or a society-approved reason to get out of the corporate world once and for all and come back to me, my freedom, my sovereignty. The pregnancy was hard and long (13 days overdue in the peak of the Australian summer). But the labour was harder and longer (62 hours labour. Not a typo).

They say giving birth can be a spiritual experience. For me, it was a moment where everything seemed to come back online for me. It's like someone plugged my abilities back in, and they were in turbo mode. At one point, I actually felt like I was outside my body watching myself. Was it pure exhaustion? Or the divinely timed line-in-the-sand moment where "playing the game" was no longer an option.

In the months that followed, I was propelled into the first-baby vortex. But alongside this, the Universe had started its conversation with me. Loudly. There were unexplainable synchronicities: radios coming on by themselves with a random song that I was just humming, lights flickering when I walked past, repeating numbers everywhere, feeling the energy of people and situations in my own energy field.

So, a spiritual awakening (or re-awakening) had absolutely started. The difference this time was that I no longer had to play a character in the "real world." I could take the time to see where this was heading in the comfort of my own home. And to see how this unfolding was going to manifest within my business. Well, I could have done all of this if I didn't have a very small baby that needed every single part of me.

This brings us to 24th March 2017. My darling Dad had been unwell with dementia for around 5 years. We were due to fly to visit the next day, but Mum called and said Dad was not doing well. I got a very strong feeling that I needed to get on a plane. Immediately. Was it practical? No, we already had a flight booked for the next morning. Did everyone think I was overreacting? You betcha.

With our 11-month-old daughter on my hip, I got straight on a plane, and my husband was to follow the next day as planned. It was like I was in a trance. Something was guiding that journey, and it sure wasn't logic.

We went to visit Dad in the nursing home. He was very unwell and sleeping deeply. He hadn't known who I was for many years or that he even had a granddaughter, but in that moment, I do feel he knew we were in that room.

That night, I got ready for bed. I still felt trance-like. It was weird, but I trusted whatever was going on. I fell asleep and was woken up by the most intense rush of energy through my body that violently shook me awake. I sat straight up and looked at the clock: 10.50pm. I was dizzy, my heart pounding out of my chest, trying not to vomit, my teeth chattering, ears ringing, my body shaking all over.

I sat there for a few moments, trying to figure out what the heck was going on.

Then the phone rang.

Dad had died.

At 10.50pm.

The months that followed were deep, dark grief.

Still navigating this new-mum thing, trying to figure out who I am in a world that I don't seem to fit neatly into, and now this.

You could say I unwittingly signed up for the Spiritual Awakening Acceleration Pack, and the Universe was absolutely not going to let me cancel my subscription.

Casually experimenting with my spiritual gifts was no longer an option. I needed a new dimension of reality—fast. One that explained the afterlife, the unique soul path of individuals, and how they intertwine. I needed to understand soul origins, soul families, and what we do in between lives. I wanted to know everything about the stars and astrological transits. Ultimately, I needed to bring the spiritual world closer to me.

And I needed my business to be the container for my intuitive gifts. I just didn't know what that meant.

My innate curiosity turned into a deep and frenzied digging for answers:

- Who am I, really? What am I being called to do?
- Why do the things that seem to matter so much to others feel absolutely meaningless to me?
- Am I going legitimately crazy, or is there more to what I'm feeling and experiencing?

This wasn't just about reshaping my life and business to be in alignment with my soul gifts (although that did naturally happen). This was about deciding to see what would happen if I fully followed the Shiny Dots as they appeared - without needing to understand the bigger picture at all.

I mean, my life as I knew it had just crashed to the ground. What did I have to lose?

The next Shiny Dot that appeared for me: The Akashic Records. And this one was blindingly bright. So I followed it. I signed up for extensive study and learned to read the Akashic Records. It came ridiculously easy to me. Like I'd done it before (spoiler alert: it turns out I have been an Akashic Records Reader in many of my past lives. Shiny Dot Effect right there). I started offering Soul Purpose Akashic Records Readings, which brought deep clarity to my clients and were so easy and fun for me to do.

The next Shiny Dot called me to get back into Astrology and the intersection between it and Human Design and Gene Keys.

After hundreds of these readings, here's a key question I formulated for my clients that brought all of this cosmic stuff right down to Earth level: What is your soul telling you is the most aligned thing you can do *this week*? What Shiny Dot has been trying to get your attention?

I had no clue that following that one Shiny Dot to learn to read the Akashic Records would lead me to the soul-aligned business I have today. I now help my clients discover why they are here and then do something about it. Because as it turns out, I'm not the only one that thinks the whole 9-5 thing is B.S. I was never alone. I just hadn't found the other people awake at the sleepover yet.

And here's something I want to leave you with: Spiritual awakening ain't a one-and-done. It's a layered unfolding for the rest of your life. And you don't need to lose a loved one or give birth to a baby for 3-5 business days to initiate you into a state of awakening.

Sometimes, it's a build-up of general discomfort within the world over many years. Sometimes, it's seemingly spontaneous—which could actually be astrological alignments crossing your birth chart—pre-planned by you, before you were born, to wake yourself up.

The difference between my first spiritual awakening and all that continues to unfold on-the-daily, is the rock-solid knowledge that with each new layer, I know I'm taking another aligned step towards what my soul planned to do with this life.

Just make sure you're following that next Shiny Dot without always knowing why. One day, you'll look back and see how the Universe was lining them up to glimmer in your eye all along.

Claire Solomon is a Certified Akashic Records Practitioner and Intuitive Business Strategist who blends mystical wisdom with practical insights. She supports those seeking more meaning, connection and soul in their everyday lives. Through grounded, actionable teachings and intuitive guidance, she helps others explore spirituality in a way that makes sense and brings more alignment, clarity and purpose to both their life and work.

Website: www.clairesolomon.com
More Links: www.clairesolomon.com/links

22

From Upside Down to Right Way Up

By Jan Denham
Sydney, Australia

When I reflect on my journey of awakening, how it all began, and where I am now, I get an image of an impressionist painting, lots of subtle moments merging into one another, some clearly defined experiences and others more abstract, yet somehow an overall picture and flow.

Moments of illumination have come and gone, sometimes with long periods in between. Yet I have found that these, what I will call "living" moments, never truly leave you. These moments are different, they fall deep into you and are always there to draw on, like water from a deep well, should the need arise.

It has been and still is a fascinating journey, stages of understanding I have gone through in search of something more and all the many challenges that perhaps I wouldn't have wished for myself, but nonetheless have had their silver lining and led me back to a deeper place of connection.

When I was around four years old, I recall being shown that all was not what it seemed. My family and I were living in Sydney's inner West, and it was the first time I had my own bedroom after sharing with my two brothers.

I remember my eyes being open in the dark in the early hours of the morning. Suddenly, I saw a vision of the world as I knew it to be, except everything was happening upside down.

I recall witnessing this dream-like yet somehow real scene with a child's eyes. I was open and receptive yet didn't feel alone; it was like some friendly but mysterious intelligence was showing me this upside-down state of affairs as if it was an important truth I needed to remember.

I was quietly fascinated as I pondered on the thought: "Was most of life not happening the right way up"?

It was a revelation and, unbeknown to my young self at that time, the beginning of a series of inner awakenings.

Over the years, this experience has come back to me, causing me to pause, reflect, and relive its message. Only recently, I had a timely reminder of the gift of insight it was. And as is often the case, the reminder came left of field. I've found the universe has a way of communicating when needed in sometimes surprising ways!

I'd been involved in a car accident where I lost consciousness at the wheel. In the seconds I blacked out, my car veered across two lanes of traffic and mounted the footpath to find its final resting place in the shopfront of what used to be an iconic patisserie in the suburb I live in.

As I came to, in the flurry of ambulance, police, and bystanders, I was relieved to realise my car had chosen this shopfront as it was vacant, unlike the two businesses running on either side of it. I hadn't harmed anyone or amazingly hit another car, and I was still in one piece, albeit with a black eye and bruised ribs.

I felt a strong feeling of being protected, where I was helped on another level of intelligence, so any harm done was manageable.

It was, in fact, a wake-up call. In the lead-up to this event, I realised I had been ignoring signals that I was overdoing it. In my "drivenness" to tick all the boxes in my life, I had begun to live out of alignment with my connection to something greater and so had begun, as my childhood vision had imparted to me, to live upside down.

This was further imprinted in my being as when I went to pick up my new car, I noticed the number plate reflected the house number and first letter of the street and suburb where I lived when I had my vision.

I was quietly astounded and once again felt the importance of going against the tide of "upside downness" and finding a balance in life where my soul nature and human nature could live in harmony.

It really is quite beautiful and mysterious the many ways guidance can be given. Being open and receptive to these sometimes subtle, intuitive messages brings a whole new dimension to life.

After going through a relationship crisis in my early twenties, I found myself feeling quite disconnected and lost. As things came to an end, I spent a period living alone.

During that time, my eldest brother had just begun attending a group derived from the teachings of Gurdjieff. Gurdjieff famously said, "Mankind is asleep," and coined the phrase "the work" as a way in which an awakening from this sleep could happen. One night, after attending this group, he visited me.

I have always been fascinated by and sensitive to energy and although at times I struggle to accurately understand what I'm feeling, sometimes it's abundantly clear.

So, on this night, as I walked down the hallway of my apartment to open the door for my brother, I could already sense a change in the atmosphere. As he entered, I felt he was emanating what I can only describe as light. His face was radiant, and his overall calm and centred demeanour was awakening something deep within me.

As we talked and I made a cup of tea for us both I felt my energy changing, like I was being fed and nurtured on a very deep, soulful level.

It was during this subtle yet profound exchange that I just knew my life was about to change, and as I looked out my kitchen window onto a partial view of the Sydney Harbour Bridge, I felt whatever he had come in touch with was speaking to me, too. I felt I was aligned and tapping into something greater. I was standing the right way up after my life had fallen apart!

It's interesting to note that before this experience, I had been party to many interesting and robust discussions with a philosophical bent on the meaning of life, all of which, while interesting, I was beginning to tire of; good fodder for the mind, but not life-changing.

What I experienced that night was beyond words; it was a living experience, a change in consciousness, and hardly a word was said.

There is a saying that salvation is found in the physical and this brings me back to the body and how it can be an important guide on the spiritual path.

There have been many occasions where I haven't always listened to this guidance, but I've recalled a sensation or feeling in retrospect and realised my body already knew something my mind had overlooked or dismissed at the time.

This has been part of an important learning… learning to listen in a deeper way. Also, just as important is to see where I've ended up when I haven't acted on my body's signals.

Gut reactions that are red flags, feeling suddenly drained, a feeling of shrinking rather than expanding, and receiving guiding words that seem to come from nowhere have been sensations worthy of note.

The body holds a key and can be a powerful guide. If you find yourself kicking yourself for going down a rabbit hole after ignoring a guiding sensation, know there will be another opportunity at some point to tune in and listen more deeply. Some life lessons need repeating where you learn just that little bit more, even if your mind would tell you otherwise.

My middle brother, just 18 months older than myself, had tummy troubles from a baby, and this led to more serious problems as he got older. At the tender age of 37, he was diagnosed with bowel cancer, and sadly, after two major operations, he left this life at 50.

Even with his medical history, his passing was still unexpected and, like him, understated. Life irretrievably changed in what seemed like a split second. The next day, I woke up wondering if it had really happened. I was in shock, and my heart was breaking.

The grief I felt was so physical I literally felt frozen, like time had stopped, and the warmth of his energy field connected to me as his sister was moving on. At the time, I was living in a north facing apartment that got good sun all day long.

So, I remember going out onto my balcony that morning and sitting down to try and absorb what had happened. I closed my eyes as the sun began to warm me from the inside out in what felt like a growing embrace of not only sunlight but *light*. I was not alone but held in all my grief in loving warmth.

Nature, as it can in so many ways, reaches deep into the soul and supports you on your path of awakening, as it did me in this instance. Once again, I felt a friendly, mysterious intelligence with me, connecting me in a very personal way to something greater.

I often feel a sense of mystery, like some key ingredient to living life to its full potential is missing. At times, this has led to strong feelings of emptiness and despair. Yet it's been these very feelings that, while putting me way out of my comfort zone, have set me on a search to find that missing piece of the puzzle.

Being part of a school in Sydney for many years now, where "finding stillness" is at its core, continues to be a great support.

In a daily practice of coming to stillness, I've found something I can trust, a place of peace and connection that feels timeless, a state I welcome, and which feels like coming home. It's also a great practical support in navigating the twists and turns of everyday life as it provides an energy of calm and space.

It's interesting that even as I say this, there is often resistance to putting away time for this simple "meditation". It's like the tide of everyday life is going in a completely different direction and rhythm, and so, like the salmon, it can feel like swimming upstream in making a simple attempt to stop, slow down, and take a new breath!

I've come to understand that this is an important part of growing a "spiritual" muscle. The important thing is returning to a place of calm and presence. No matter what has happened, you can begin again. Don't let self-criticism or guilt have the final say!

In my late twenties, as I approached my Saturn return, I found myself going through a career crisis. Never really knowing what I wanted to do after leaving high school, I opted for a gap year before going on to university to study philosophy. I thought that would be where I could find some real answers to my search.

I started a job with a family-run typesetting and design business, just a ten-minute walk from home. After this gap year passed, I left. Then, after only three months at uni, feeling somewhat lost and disillusioned, I ended up returning to my previous place of employment to take up their offer of a four-year apprenticeship. It was here I got into a field I would never have expected: graphic design.

After finishing my apprenticeship, I got a role with an advertising agency. Over this time of around three years, I learned a lot about stress and its effects on the body. I became my own human guinea pig as I felt a level of tension in my body as never before, anxiety about meeting deadlines that carried on after work hours, the need for perfection before anything went to print, and the dynamics of working in a team of gifted, but often stressed colleagues.

Suddenly I knew, for my overall well-being and wish to nurture my spiritual search, I needed to move on. The more under pressure I felt, the more I was moving away from a subtle but important openness and receptivity in my overall being. It was okay for a while, but not indefinitely.

As I thought about what I wanted to do, once again, I felt unsure.

Then, seemingly out of the blue, these words floated into my consciousness, like someone had carefully crafted them just for me to hear right there and then: "You need to do something with your hands." And this soon became first-person as I said to myself, "I need to do something with my hands." Something finally felt right!

After this revelation, I studied Swedish and Remedial massage, Aromatherapy, and eventually Reiki. I continued to work part-time as a graphic designer and set up a room in my home devoted to these calming and relaxing practices.

This journey into healing has taken me on an evolving appreciation of the importance of times of simple but deep relaxation, not only so the body has a chance to kick in its natural healing intelligence but also for the mind to soften and be held in the wonder of a greater, more heart-based intelligence.

So once again, I found myself standing the right way up at a crucial crossroads in my life with so much good life experience to draw on!

♡ ♡ ♡

Jan Denham lives in Sydney, Australia, and is a graphic designer and digital artist, having exhibited in three art exhibitions: Quintessence – Five Artists Explore the Wonder of Nature and Being (2022), Connections ~ Birds, Blossoms & Fungi (2023), Magical Moments in Unpredictable Times (2024)

She designs year calendars with digitally enhanced imagery from her walks in nature.

"I find great joy in capturing images and creating visual moments that soothe the soul, celebrating the important place of nature as a source of reflection and renewal in a quickening world."

From many years of working with stillness and breath, Jan finds great support in blending the demands of everyday life with something deeper and greater. She practises Reiki, foot massage, and relaxation as an experience of letting go, healing, and beginning again.

Website: www.jandenham.com

Art: www.redbubble.com/people/jandenham/explore

Instagram: www.instagram.com/jan.denham

23

The Night I Found My True Self

By Angel Minuto
Kenmore, New York, USA

On a brisk spring night many years ago, filled with self-doubt, overwhelmed and exhausted from the immense emotions washing over me, I sat on my living room floor sobbing, pleading with the universe for a sign. Newly sober, I questioned why I stopped drinking and why I was doing this to myself.

Fear bubbled up around me. I worried I couldn't handle confronting everything I had buried with alcohol for so many years. I longed for something to tell me I was on the right path. To say to me not to have a drink to wash everything I was thinking and feeling away.

As I sobbed, I contemplated having a drink just to ease some of the pain I was feeling. Until I heard my internal voice cutting through all my sorrow. This voice came through clearly, reassuring me that I was on the right path, to have faith and that I would be guided.

As I listened to the voice, I felt this warmth wash over me. A sense of safety as I leaned into this warmth, this guiding light. A reminder that I was not alone on this journey, reinforcing what the voice was telling me. At that moment, I intuitively knew I would be okay.

Spiritual awakenings come when we need them the most. When we are far from our rightful path, unable to see how stuck and disconnected we've become. My spiritual awakening was no exception. At the time, I was overwhelmed with depression, anxiety, feelings of insecurity, and unworthiness from past programming, conditioning, and limiting beliefs that began in childhood. This all warped into perfectionism, people-pleasing, codependency, and self-criticism.

I felt so empty, lost, and hopeless. I lost sight of who I authentically was, and I began to drink, quickly spiraling into alcoholism. Drinking was how I tried to cope with the constant discomfort I felt, quelling the critical voice that was a mainstay in my mind. It was how I attempted to fill the emptiness inside.

My spiritual awakening began as subtle nudges well before that spring night. A small voice wanting me to reconnect with myself. Assuring me there was something greater out there. This voice reminded me of my hopes and dreams. Promised it could fill the emptiness inside.

I was so afraid of this voice that I attempted to drink that away, too. I didn't believe it. I didn't trust it. Even though I was so miserable, I was too afraid to change. I was too afraid of what else would change if I changed. But that voice persisted, becoming louder and louder. It was always there, not giving up on me.

When I finally stopped trying to quiet it with alcohol and began listening, something deep inside of me shifted. I realized that voice was my higher self, my true self, my intuition—that deeper part of me connected to the divine, the universe.

As I settled into the sense of peace and hopefulness that inner voice gave me, I began to believe it, trust it. My true self became a beacon, guiding me to pursue my goals and dreams. To do things I longed to do but was afraid of doing.

Through that voice, I was given the strength to return to college and become a therapist. When limiting beliefs flooded in, telling me I wasn't smart enough or focused enough, something I had heard since childhood, I was sent signs to see a professional regarding my undiagnosed ADHD.

My true self and intuition helped me through imposter syndrome, guiding me to trust that I am capable and good enough. I began dismantling my old belief systems that kept me stuck and disconnected. As I tuned in, listened, and took aligned action, my perceptions began to shift, and aspects of my life began to change. I felt more connected with myself.

My spiritual awakening didn't stop there. The universe had one more request. To be fully connected with my higher self, I had to stop drinking. Drinking was my armor, protecting me from everything I buried long ago. All the past programming, conditioning, and limiting beliefs brought on by past traumas, other people's judgments, expectations, and my own need to fit in and feel accepted dictated how I lived my life.

Even though I had already begun doing the work to dismantle these, I knew I wasn't going to get far if I didn't quit drinking. So, I quit. And everything I tried to drown out, run away from, came flooding back in. The things that affected every aspect of my life. Those limiting beliefs, difficult emotions, unhealthy patterns of perfectionism, people-pleasing, and codependency. Through this, my internal voice guided me to get to the root, to go deeper into the subconscious layers that held onto everything I tried to ignore for so long.

Experiencing a spiritual awakening Is like experiencing an earthquake. It shifts our perceptions and everything we've come to know. Erupting the belief system that has taken root, disconnecting us from our true selves.

Our spiritual awakening is also just the beginning. We must integrate what we've learned and experienced and what we've downloaded. This is uncomfortable but necessary work to become who we were meant to be.

After that night I sobbed on my living room floor, I got to work integrating my spiritual awakening. I began working with a therapist and devoured everything I could on inner child work, shadow work, and building self-worth from within. I also incorporated all of the skills, tools, and practices I learned as a therapist.

I built a spiritual practice based on self-compassion, forgiveness, and grace to feel safe to be my most authentic self. I leaned into yoga and meditation and learned how to use mindfulness techniques to ground and center myself. All of this helped me become fully present in the moment to tune into my intuition, that inner voice.

The more I dug, explored, healed, and set free inside of myself, the more I realized that I was co-creating the life I always wanted. As I became open to the possibilities, the more deserving and worthy I felt of those aligned actions that crossed my path. With each step forward and every aligned action I took, I began feeling more confident, able to stand in my authenticity and worth, connected and aligned with myself than ever before.

My spiritual awakening brought a deep sense of knowing, creating an unbreakable link between my intuition and the universe. When I tune into my gut and follow those intuitive hits, nudges, and signs, I make decisions in alignment with my true self. I know I am supported and guided throughout. This has helped me greatly, both personally and professionally. I have taken risks and leaps of faith, all with that innate knowing that I am supported throughout.

As I integrated my spiritual awakening, I noticed external and internal shifts. Some were positive, like feeling confident enough to leave a toxic work environment and build a business that aligns with my beliefs and values. Other shifts were difficult, including the erosion of some of my relationships, including my first marriage.

As I grew, expanded, healed, and became aligned with my authenticity, I shed those unhealthy patterns of perfectionism, people-pleasing, and codependency. As I did, my relationships became strained. The more I changed, the more my relationships pulled apart.

As we break out of unhealthy patterns, people who share those unhealthy patterns and rely on them as the glue to a relationship become upset. As we learn to set boundaries, have a voice, and live in alignment with who we are, some people struggle to understand. Through my experience, I learned people can feel betrayed as we go on this journey. The changes we experience can be scary and unsettling.

For my first marriage, a part of me hoped that maybe he would change and come on this journey with me. But I had to accept that he wasn't ready to change, and I couldn't force him to, either. It took time and deep reflection to understand and gain acceptance so I can move forward. Although I felt so hurt and heartbroken, I knew I couldn't stay. I leaned into the universe for strength, to guide me. And as I did, I was comforted knowing I did the right thing for both myself and my daughter. Throughout all this, my relationship with my daughter, now a young adult, only became stronger. Again, this shows me to trust in the universe.

After releasing my old relationships, I attracted wonderful new relationships full of support, kindness, and compassion. We celebrate each other's victories and successes, show up, and hold space during the dark times. We feel safe to be authentically and wholeheartedly ourselves. I am truly blessed to have the friends and a partner in my life that I do today.

There's a blind faith that comes after a spiritual awakening. A knowing that every difficult decision we make is in alignment with our true self. For instance, leaving toxic work environments, starting a business, shedding unhealthy relationships, or setting boundaries can be so scary but also very freeing. All aspects of our lives are interconnected. As we heal different parts of our lives, we become more open to receiving in other areas, not just the area we worked on. As we release what no longer serves us, we become fully open to what the universe has to offer.

Before my spiritual awakening, I allowed parts of me to take over and get sucked into the "noise," the fears, anxiety, and overwhelm from old wounds, past programming, conditioning, and limiting beliefs. Thus disconnecting me from my intuition, my true self, and from the guidance of the universe. Now, I make a conscious commitment every day to integrate a more spiritually aligned way of living.

Through this journey, I learned to trust and follow my intuition, align with my true self, and separate from those parts of me that get caught up in the "noise." This is what grants me the opportunity to be open to receive nudges, signs, feelings, knowings, and downloads from the universe. And it is better than I could ever imagine.

To integrate a more spiritually aligned way of living, I had to understand that our true self, what connects us to our intuition and the universe, and the aspects of our personality, or parts of us, that make us human and help us function in the world, are always within us. We cannot rid ourselves of these parts, including the ones in the shadows, but we can help them heal from the burdens they hold onto.

That "noise" brought on by old wounds and limiting beliefs disconnects us from our true selves and intuition. As I show compassion, curiosity, and openness to these parts holding onto these burdens, like my inner child, I help them let go and heal. Before my spiritual awakening, I would have ignored, dismissed, or invalidated these hurt parts.

Remember, we are spiritual beings having a human experience. We are not immune to what happens in the world. However, we can choose how it affects us by showing up compassionately for ourselves. This is one way I align with my true self. How I find peace, stay grounded, centered, and in touch with my intuition.

Excellent ways to align with your true self and your intuition are through meditation, mindfulness, being out in nature, or being creative. This helps me to feel connected, open, compassionate, curious, in a state of flow, and it's how I access my intuition.

The more I became familiar with how that energy felt inside of me and around me, the easier it became to evoke that energy at any time. Now, if I feel anxious, overwhelmed, or fearful, the same feelings often mistaken for intuition, I know a part of me has taken over. As I align with my true self, I can compassionately separate or "unblend" from the parts of me that are activated by my human experiences, blocking my intuition. This shifts my perception from how this fearful part of me sees things to the perception of my true self, free from the "noise."

It's important to note that these are protective parts, trying to help us. Even if it doesn't seem like it. Showing up compassionately for all parts of ourselves, even the parts of us in the shadows or our inner child parts, we build a trusting relationship between these parts and our true selves. Then, we can give them permission and reassurance that it's safe to take a step back and take a break. This is how to unblend your true self from a part; you ask the part if it would please step back. When the part unblends, we will notice the thoughts, feelings, and body sensations become less. Then, we can align with our true selves, follow our intuition, and become open to receiving what the universe is telling us.

By doing these simple practices daily, I have integrated a more spiritually aligned way of living after my spiritual awakening. I'll be honest; I'm not perfect at it. But when I slip, and finally notice a part has taken over, I show myself compassion and grace. Then I take a breath, recenter myself, realign, and find my intuition again to guide me.

Angel Minuto is an IFS-informed coach, Licensed Psychotherapist, and founder of True Self Manifestation. Angel empowers women to overcome limiting beliefs that have kept them feeling disconnected and reclaim their authenticity to manifest their most amazing lives. Trained in Internal Family Systems, EMDR, and many other therapy models, she uses her skill set intuitively, weaving together her expertise with her experience in manifestation and spirituality with a sprinkle of woo. Angel guides women through their internal worlds, releasing past programming, conditioning, and limiting beliefs that have kept them out of alignment with their True Self, unable to manifest the lives they were meant to have.

End the cycle of self-doubt and limiting beliefs. Reclaim the person you were put on this earth to be. Join me on a journey of alignment, connection, and empowerment, igniting your most magnetic self.

Website: www.trueselfmanifestation.com

Instagram: www.instagram.com/trueselfmanifestation

More Links: www.trueselfmanifestation.com/links

24

The Way Through is the Way In

By Carolina Arriagada Gonzalez
Santiago, Chile

I think many people can relate with the feeling of "not belonging". I lived with it most of my life; no matter how much I tried and cared, I didn't find a place or people where I felt like I belonged. It was a lonely experience, and although I love my own company, there was also a longing for empathy and companionship with another and equanimity within myself.

As I grew, I went through complicated experiences that ended up shaping my character and also my perceived limitations: bullying by classmates, teachers, and friends, my parents' divorce, being the older sibling, sexual abuse, and depression. As a sensitive person with an enormous capacity for empathy and a need to be loved, I was there for everyone when they needed support, but that meant that I was, unknowingly, the last on my list. Eventually, I realized that I was the last on the list of most of my loved ones, too.

These experiences kept piling up until, at one point, life rioted; I couldn't find a job, I was having conflicts with my parents, and I realized that the friends I cared for so much didn't care for me. That broke my heart, and I chose to distance myself from them. All of this happened after I had been backstabbed by older women who I thought of as friends and mentors. In that moment, I deeply understood that I deserved better, that as much as they deserved a kind and loyal friend at their side, so did I, and it was time I put myself first, so I made a choice that took me through a path I did not fully expect.

Although the reasons why we go through this awakening are all individual and unique to everyone, the root of it is very similar; we wish for growth, freedom, peace and to find ourselves and that which lies through the veil of the material and is at the center of who we are; our souls and our divinity. Life is complicated, and so is being human, which is why this path finds us, perhaps, when we are broken and need it the most, and therefore more open to truly see and change because of our pain, which on this path becomes an ally, and if we allow it, a loyal friend who will help us achieve our soul's desire, our wish for freedom from our life experiences, from our past, from society and everything else that holds us down.

As I said, we are all unique, and that is why every challenge and every lesson is catered by the universe specifically for us so we may progress and grow, despite how difficult it all may seem. Awakening is not a constant, and it's not a one-time thing, it is a path that you choose to walk day after day, but as with everything else in life, the efforts you put into it build up, and every new day the road becomes a bit easier than the day before. And although progress, like life, is not a linear path where everything always goes smoothly and easily, know that practice and constancy make progress, and know this: you will progress because that's the way the path goes, ever forward.

There were many lessons I learned that took me from being insecure, sad, and lonely to finally loving myself and feeling confident in my own knowing and skills. Still, there is one lesson, one teaching that to me has been the most valuable of all, one knowing that took me from pain to love, and it will take you safely through the woods, through the pain, through the insecurity, fear, and anxiety. Because to awaken, we need to heal first, we need to go through the forest, we need to go inside, integrate, love, and then come into the light as a whole.

This is a lesson about what we call the shadow, the ego, and our inner demons, as well as how and why we need to love them. Our wounds exist to remind us of the experiences we have gone through, the trials and challenges, and how we have overcome them and lived through the pain and with the pain. It is not failure or unsightly; it is part of who we are. Our wounds and the lessons we have learned have made us who we are, and I know I wouldn't be here without them, so I honor them because I honor myself, and I am proud and happy being who I am. I thank those wounds and my shadow for taking me on a journey that has made me more me than I have ever been, a journey where I have learned that being vulnerable is not a weakness but a strength, where confidence in oneself is not arrogance, and that age doesn't matter when it comes to wisdom. Even when sometimes I can be expressing all of my "bad qualities," I still honor them and thank them, for only I know the challenges I have gone through and the wounds I have sustained. I know where the light and shadow in me come from, and I honor them both equally, for my pain has been my teacher, my guide, and now, my friend.

Your shadow is the part of you that has suffered the most. It's where all your pain, your scars, and your traumas reside. It is, in a way, a deeply wounded child that needs nurturing and love. Let me ask you this: if you find a crying toddler in the streets at night all alone what would you do? Ignore them? Walk away, calling it "silly"? Or would you approach them, hold them, try to make them feel better, and find the ones who love them?

When I began this journey, I faced too many things that hadn't seen the light yet. The teachings I was following and the books I was reading dealt with the shadow as if it were a whiny child to be left alone, but the more I did that, the more my sense of self became fractured until I was not one, but three: ego, divinity and myself. I had to live and hear all three at once for more than a year without a clear sense of who of those three I was being. On the one hand, I was absolutely connected to source, to the divine. I felt myself existing inside every living thing and everyone in this world; from plants to insects, to the wind and the sky. I was aware, awake. I finally knew who I was. I floated through the void, the emptiness we all come from, and found peace. But on the other hand, my vessel, my body, and my brain were in extreme pain because the way I was learning wasn't focused on integrating, it was about awakening while growing apart. True awakening is not being apart from yourself. It is about being everything that you are; light and dark. Through my experience, I now believe that integrating first will allow you to go through this path in a gentler way as it will allow you to know yourself fully and heal.

To work with our shadows, we need to listen to them, listen to our pain, and not to collapse ourselves in it. We need to ask, "What do you need, my friend? Why do you cry? Why do you hurt?" And hold them. We spend an inordinate amount of time hoping other people will love all we are when we can't do that ourselves. Our shadow doesn't need another's love, but our own. And know, the more you are there for yourself with a compassionate stance, willing to listen, to be open, vulnerable and strong, and you can observe with kind neutrality and hold yourself, the easier the journey will become.

Being whole and wanting to be whole when you are ignoring a part of you is an impossibility. We were brought here to be both human and divine, and being human means living in both darkness and light. It means we feel sadness to know joy, we feel love to know hatred, we are brave even though we are afraid, and that is the beauty of it all. We are a bridge, a joining point between light and dark, human and divine, perfect and imperfect. We are a meeting of polarities, and that is our gift. We can be both light and dark. We can change and choose. Without this range of being, we can't grow, and we can't expand. Polarity is not bad—polarity is choice and choice is freedom. We are here to freely exist, to explore and fully know ourselves. We are God/Goddess knowing and experiencing itself through us and all the possibilities within that divinity and humanity.

Now, let's do a small exercise. I suggest you read all the instructions first and then calmly practice it. Remember that through facing and loving our shadow we need to keep ourselves steady. We need to feel. We need to acknowledge and listen to our darkness, but not to collapse ourselves in it. That pain comes from experiences that are past, even if it is a present experience, like grief, illness, and so on, but right now, in this moment, you are here with me, with all of us going through this experience, walking this path. Know that you are safe.

Please sit or lay down; just make sure that you are comfortable and focused, and if you fall asleep at any point, then allow it to happen. Our brains and bodies know what they need more than our conscious mind does. Now feel your body, your weight upon the place where you are sitting. Feel the contact of your back and the surface you're supporting your body on, your butt on the chair, your legs, your hands touching each other or lying on your lap or your feet on the floor. Ground yourself in these sensations, in the weight of your body; this is your root. Is it soft? Is it hard? Cold, warm, fluffy, smooth? When you find yourself grounded in these sensations, I want you to go inside.

Create a place within you that holds dark and light, like a forest with light shining through the leaves and comfortable shadows to rest under or a breezy beach on a cloudy day. Pick a place where you feel like you, a place you enjoy, a place that makes you feel safe. And from this place, call forth your pain, just one—think about something that has been bothering you, a recurring nightmare, a recurring hurtful feeling, or perhaps just an issue you have with yourself—any belief that casts a shadow within. Picture it, call it forth with kindness and compassion, and ask: "What do you need from me? Why do you suffer?" Treat it as you would a friend you love so much, or a relative, or even a furry friend. Talk to it with that same care and compassion, and you will find secrets that not even you knew about yourself. And if you can't speak to it, or you don't hear anything, just act on that same line of caring for a loved one—hug them, hold them, pat their head, tell them they are loved.

Let whatever needs to come through come. Follow your intuition. You know the best way.

You can finish this exercise whenever you want. If it's too difficult, just stop, breathe, take a walk, or eat something, and be present in those actions. If you are still upset, sit down and focus on your body again, without going within this time. Our bodies ground us; they let us know that we are safe despite what we may be feeling, so I suggest that you practice being in your body and feeling it as much as you can. Do not focus on your breath, for the breath can upset us more if we have endured difficult and traumatic experiences. Just allow yourself to be where you are, feel the sensations of your clothes on your skin or the touch of your hands, and if it's not enough, become aware of the sounds surrounding you or the sights of the room you are in. Listen and observe, and allow your body to have the response it needs to have. If you feel tired, sleep and rest. If you need to cry, then please do so. Follow your intuition and trust your inner knowing.

And last but not least, read, listen, learn, and adapt these lessons, for all of us are unique, and no teaching fits us all the same way—or even more so, not all teachings work for us. To awaken, you must have mastery over yourself, and that involves the responsibility for your own growth; you are your own mentor, not just a follower. This path is one of self-mastery, and so it is your own inner teacher that is the one with the last word. I encourage you to take what resonates within your heart and let go of what does not. We all have different timings; every teaching has its time and place, and whether that time arrives or not is not up to us to know, nor is it ours to force. We must be like a leaf in the wind and allow ourselves to be carried by life, spirit, the divine, for it is when we let go, when we accept, when we trust our own soul, that we find what we have lost: our people, our purpose, our worth, love and ourselves. And remember, the way through is the way in.

Carolina Arriagada Gonzalez is an illustrator from Chile, passionate about knowledge, nature, and art, whether it is writing, crafts, painting, and anything in between. She spent the last few years dealing with past traumas and an illness that resulted after facing herself through the awakening process, but she can safely say that it was worth it. She believes that the best way to carry through life is to know how to laugh at things, especially oneself, to accept life and challenges as they come, to be grateful even if you are struggling, and to allow spirit and creativity to take the lead, because art does heal and it is a wonderful ally.

Instagram: www.instagram.com/hellocarohere

25

The Art of Being Messy

By Amanda DeBernardi
Pinedale, Wyoming, USA

I was built from hemp and wildflowers, but I was raised in a climate where nothing grows.

"What's wrong with her?" I heard my Aunt say to my mom. "She never smiles."

When I see that little girl in my mind's eye, my heart aches for her.

"She doesn't want to be like you!" adult me wants to scream in defense of little me. Why does she have to please everyone around her? What does she have to be quiet, hold still, and stay small?

My adult frustration only compounded because I knew that even if I screamed, they wouldn't listen.

They would only tell me that I'm too sensitive and that I'm a drama queen. They would tease me about it later, playing it off like their admonishments were love, while I convinced myself to be grateful for their attention.

I desperately wanted to make them happy, but it was impossible to figure out their unwritten expectations. Navigating their landmines cost me more than a few limbs. At first "they" were my family, but later a mysterious mob of peers, teachers, diet culture propaganda, and vaguely determined standards of righteousness banded together to torment me.

I was determined to work my way through life, offending no one, making no waves, remaining pristine, and doing everything right.

I would run myself into the ground trying. Being messy was never an option.

How strange that awakening felt more disorienting than euphoric.

The realization that I would never be able to win and that the only way to be happy was to be myself was no comfort at all. The only way to win is to not play, but I didn't know how to remove myself from the field.

It turns out that my creativity was my lifeline back to my highest self.

I was always into making things. I loved to get lost in my thoughts and become one with my daydreams. Unfortunately, I reached the time in life where I was expected to get serious. Pick a career. Decide on my path.

There was a part of me that longed to be free and paint all day and be adored for my artistic abilities. That part was at war with the longing to fit in, make my parents proud, and execute the plan of the "perfect life."

When I was 18, I learned that I was pregnant, and it soon became clear that I would be raising my baby on my own. In order to combat the image of my perceived irresponsibility, I decided I would become the most responsible, educated, and productive member of society that has ever existed in the history of forever. Things got messy, and this was something that I couldn't hide.

Not only did I finish college, but I did it while working and taking care of a baby on my own. I showed them! I wasn't going to be a dismal statistic. I AM worthy. I AM capable. I AM valuable.

I did all of the things that checked all of the boxes, even if I did them slightly out of order. I got married. I got a good job. I had another baby. I got a master's degree. I was proud of myself for all of these accomplishments, but somehow I was never satisfied. I was exhausted, sick, and unhappy. I was still pretending to have it all together, while on the inside, I was dull and gray.

One day, I was scrolling through social media when I saw that a local yoga studio was holding a reiki class. I felt the strangest compulsion to click for more information. I had no idea what reiki was, but a deep resonance welled up inside of me. I knew that I had to see what energy healing was all about.

At my first reiki class, I sat down in a circle of perfectly arranged chairs and nervously took in the scene. I was definitely not a joiner. What was I doing here? Going to a class where I knew no one and didn't really understand what I would be learning was totally out of character for my tightly controlled type-A life.

When the instructor asked us to introduce ourselves and share what had brought us here, I cried. I said I didn't know why I was there, but I felt like I needed to be. For the first time, I was in a space where my sensitivity was valued. I learned about the chakra system and how to tune into my body and feel the subtle vibrations all around me. I learned that I had control over how I used my energy, and I had the ability to set boundaries around my field.

The more I tuned into my internal world, the more calm and centered I felt in my everyday life. I quickly developed a morning routine of meditation and journaling. I was coming to terms with my sensitivity and learning how to nourish my nervous system and care for the wounded parts of me with loving tenderness.

With my newfound self-compassion came the shocking realization that I had spent so much of my life creating things I didn't actually want. I abandoned my creative self because I thought that making art was a luxury for people who had gotten everything else done. There were always dishes to wash and laundry to fold. There was always a paper to write or a report that was due. Creativity was selfish and frivolous. I had no time for that.

Except that now I realized that my creative self was still a part of me and she was starving. I had joined "their" team. I became one of the voices who made the unwritten rules. I had allowed myself to be my own oppressor. I had dampened my spirit and ground my soul into dust.

Me. It was me. I did it to myself.

When I realized that being a highly sensitive human was not

something I needed to overcome but something that I needed to embrace and nurture, everything changed. When I realized that the rules are all made up and are, indeed, bullshit, I began to design my days to energize me instead of drain me. When I realized that I am never going to be happy when I don't care for my creativity, my relationships with the people I love the most improved drastically.

I wish I could say that awakening was like flipping a switch, and then everything became clear. In reality, awakening was flipping a switch, catching glimpses of truth, but being so disoriented by the unfamiliar landscape that I had to flip the switch back off to regain my bearings.

Returning to myself meant returning to creativity. I started to value the activities that made me feel alive. My husband gifted me an iPad with an Apple Pencil and I began to explore digital collage. I loved the process of taking design elements that didn't seem to belong together and making a surreal tableau that seemed to perfectly reflect how I felt inside. What I learned from my reiki training was that everything is energy. I began to view my creative endeavors as a way to transmute energy.

I would get lost in my own colorful, dreamlike landscapes until I looked up and realized the sun had gone down and my bladder was about to burst. The freedom to be creative was not something that I missed out on, it was just an urge that I had ignored for far too long. I felt the digital elements meld together and come alive. My digital works greeted me with enthusiasm as each layer of shape and color morphed into an unexpressed feeling that was living inside of me.

It felt good to explore my inner world instead of ignoring it in favor of being productive and perfect. It also felt strange and confrontational at times. Gradually, I began to gain the confidence to examine uncomfortable feelings and body sensations as they emerged through my art. The more I released, the more I healed.

I shared with my therapist how much I missed painting. She suggested that I paint a safe place as an art therapy prompt. I was immediately excited about the idea because if she assigned me "homework," then I had to do it. It was permission to indulge in a "frivolous" creative activity, and I jumped into the assignment with enthusiasm.

I began by painting a giant peach where I could safely hide away from the world. My peach was warm, and the colors soothed me. No one could find me there. Outside of my peach was a storm. The wind and rain were pelting the outside of my peach, but its flesh was not getting damaged or bruised. Toward the edge of the painting was a bear with glowing red, angry eyes and bared teeth. As ferocious as the bear was, it could not penetrate the walls of my sweet and juicy fortress.

This art therapy assignment helped me open the door to a sacred part of myself that had been hidden. I learned that my painting helped me acknowledge challenging feelings and experiences that I had buried deep in my body and my subconscious. I had not been able to look at these parts of myself, let alone put words to them.

I realized that if I truly had the power to make my life a work of art. I could design my own safe spaces. I understood that I could not rely on others to validate my experiences nor to keep me safe from harm. I am the creator. I validate myself, I heal myself, and I love myself.

Soon, I was making art as a part of my daily spiritual practice. I took what I loved about my digital collages, the process of combining layers and seemingly disconnected design elements, and combined them with the sensory delights of using paints, magazine clippings, oil pastels, and any other medium I could get my hands on.

I wrote down my most uncensored thoughts in my sketchbook and then painted over them to keep them safe. I took scrap pieces of cardboard and experimented with using different painting techniques to express emotions. I slathered on thick layers of acrylic paint and watched them blister under a heat gun, expressing deeply festering anger. I watched watercolors drip down and over the edges of my work, representing the messy and uncontrollable tears that couldn't yet escape my body. I splattered watered-down india ink in a carefree and spontaneous way because I never allowed myself to be carefree and spontaneous in life.

Finally, my sensitivity had an outlet. I wasn't judging myself for my feelings, and I was able to examine them from a safe distance.

Each time that I sat down and let myself make messy art, I healed the little girl inside a bit more. She was getting to have a voice. It didn't matter if anyone else was listening or approved. She got to be free.

Now, I look at my life through the lens of a creator. I create my own safety. I create my own health. I create beautifully supportive and nourishing relationships. I value my imagination, my ideas, and my intuition. I have a stronger connection to my higher self through the process of making messy art. I ask myself what colors are appealing to me today. What paint do I want to use? What image from a magazine or a piece of junk mail is saying what I want to say?

If I have a challenging situation, I paint it. If I am happy, I collage it. If I am sad, I scribble it. When I am faced with two sides of myself that seem to be at odds, I make a piece to express the conflict I feel inside. My creative practice grounds me.

When I share my processes, my techniques, and my journey toward making messy art, I make genuine connections with others. I feed my soul by being alongside others who are getting to know the creative part of themselves.

A highly sensitive person is a beautiful thing to be now that I know how to design my environment to nourish my roots and provide enough sunshine and space for my inner world to bloom. When I walked into that reiki class, I saw myself as something more than a harsh environment was allowing me to be. I never imagined the doors that would open from that one experience.

A highly curated and false sense of security never brought the safety and acceptance that I craved. Awakening to my own energy and creative power will be a lifelong process. I am learning to love and appreciate each new layer of myself as it is revealed.

There was never anything wrong with me. I am messy, wild, and free.

♡ ♡ ♡

Amanda DeBernardi (she/her) is a coach, messy artist, and blogger who is fascinated by our connection between the earth and the cosmos.

A cosmic creatrix masquerading as a mountain hippie, she uses the moon as an anchor in her self-care practice. She is passionate about sharing her tips, tricks, and rituals with other neurodivergent creative types who want to live in harmony with their natural energy cycles.

She is the creator of The Cosmic Playground Oracle, leads workshops and classes, and works 1:1 with women who are designing lives built on freedom, pleasure, and creativity.

When offline, she can be found on her favorite hiking trails with her furry best friend or basking in creative bliss with her iPad, watercolors, or sewing machine.

Blog: www.theartofbeingmessy.substack.com

More Links: www.linktr.ee/amanda.debernardi

26

Rebel with a Cause

By Rosa Maria Velasquez
Big Bear Lake, California, USA

Death. Death cracked me open. The deep sorrow and longing that grief holds is the flip side of absolute love and ecstatic joy. But it has been hard for me to trust, so with death, there is no chance of betrayal.

This is not how I expected to begin sharing my story, but this is what came when I turned on the voice recorder, deciding to let what needed to pour out of me flow freely.

Reflecting on what came through, I will share with you how Death has woven into my life in a way that only those who can go into the depths with another, into their caves and shadow and hold the lantern to illuminate the path out, will understand. So, I trust someone will find my story illuminating.

I have learned that many of us have similar beginnings. Feeling out of place, plopped into a family that is so foreign to us. Oftentimes, a deep wound and trauma has occurred. We already had to keep family secrets. It's this feeling of loneliness even when we're in a room full of people we are related to. So, kindred spirit, if this is you, I see you. We are like lights flickering around the globe, mirroring the stars.

When I was about 9 or 10 years old, I had a year of night terrors. Horrible dreams that always left me terrified to go to sleep. Faces floating around me, staring at me, the feeling of being watched when I hid my entire body under the covers, making sure not one inch of me was exposed, dreading the touch of whatever was staring over me.

During the day, premonitions came so suddenly, this tsunami-like wave of dread and fear would pummel me. Sometimes, it was excitement. I didn't know where the feelings came from, but it was like I was a radio, and these frequencies were playing through me. It made me a very nervous kid. It was hard for me to explain this to adults as I just knew it wasn't how everyone felt. A classmate a few rows away would get in trouble for something, and while being scolded, I would be hit with a feeling so powerful it made me cry hysterically.

Thinking back on this now, I see how this is what we empaths feel. We feel the trees, animals, people, and all their emotions that sometimes they don't know how to process, so we process it for them. This, unfortunately, can attract people who use us like their dumping station. With them feeling so light afterward, we can become depleted.

Like many of us, I didn't understand my gifts and wanted them to be shut off. I prayed for the monsters to leave me alone. To not "know" when things were going to happen. To be normal. I learned to become invisible. Maybe a bit too well.

Puberty hit, and I started to mask myself. I put up walls and drowned myself with alcohol. Wanting to not remember things that happened to me. To not have people stare at me. The invisibility no longer worked. I grew tall and stood out. So, I wore a mohawk and put up a really hard front.

I was angry. Angry at my past, angry at my parents, angry at God. I hurt myself, knowing that it would hurt God. I know that may sound odd, but I have always felt angels around me, a devotion to the Blessed Mother, and I can understand messages from the Divine.

I put myself in such compromising and dangerous situations. I can honestly say I should have died at least three times during that really violent time. I became promiscuous and careless because I felt unworthy and hated being me. It was like being in a life and body that wasn't the real me.

I was getting into so much trouble, and yet, somehow, there were adults who vouched for me. In incredible ways. They saw through the facade. I like to say that we try to hide our light, and we think we have a cloak over it, or even a lampshade, when it's more like a thimble—and we can't hide it, even if we tried!

I received a court-ordered drug and alcohol rehabilitation instead of being sent to a detention camp for two years. It felt like my last chance. There was an intern counselor, Sandra, who held me, and saw me, and pushed me out of my comfort zone emotionally. She told me to stop carrying the world on my shoulders.

By the time I turned 21, I was two years sober, stopped eating meat, didn't wear animal skin, shaved my hair, and was discerning to become a Carmelite Cloistered Nun. Yes, I know. The "eyes crying and laughing out loud" emoji belongs here for about two paragraphs. (This is a story for another time.)

Detoxed, I fell back in love with mysticism. My relationship to the Divine realm. Hearing the whispers of the angels and all the Creator's creations, even my own soul's song was echoing in my body. Yet, I heard a message I didn't want to hear. "You've done this many times before. This is too easy for you. This (leaving this world and entering a monastery) is escaping. You belong on the front lines." *You belong on the front lines.* I still hear that message today. I understand its profundity and claim it. Like Joan of Arc, "I was born to do this."

Three decades after this stamp on my heart, I am here to share with you that this is only the beginning.

You see, three amazingly empathic children were the exchange. So incredibly worth it. I knew I wanted children. I say I was born a grandmother (not yet in this present existence), and I can say now, at 51 years old, I have finally landed and feel completely comfortable as I am. It's a wonderful feeling. But it wasn't always.

Being a mother was daunting at times. I worried, I was short-tempered, I was stressed, AND I was completely in it with them when we'd sing and march and play. The way only a mother can understand that it is possible to feel scared, overwhelmed, jubilation, and pride all within 30 seconds, and this repeats throughout the day.

Women especially, should understand that this spontaneous creativity we devote to raising our children is the same creative energy we can offer to a business. This business doesn't have to look like anyone else's. It's how you offer your gifts to the world. Understand this: You being you is the gift—but you shining bright, because you love who you are, makes any place you are a bit sunnier. If people say that they feel better after they talk to you, offer coaching sessions. If people say they love your hugs, learn a hands-on healing modality like massage or hairdressing. Why? Because this gives you a container to share your gifts without just being the charging station.

I will now explain my opening words. Death cracked me open.

Almost 10 years ago, a sudden and unexpected death of my husband's nephew occurred. He was only 27 years old. Two weeks later, another death. This time, it was a niece's boyfriend, who was suffering from PTSD as a veteran of war. It was triggered by his girlfriend's cousin's death. I cannot easily explain how these deaths absolutely tore me apart. Especially the suicide. It was as if somehow I felt guilty. I felt like I understand how isolating and painful it can be to not know you are an empath, a soul who feels so lost when they don't understand that feeling everything so deeply is an extremely difficult gift.I remember crying and saying, "I get it. I will do this work." I didn't know why I was saying that. It was like I had to stop pretending I didn't know I was meant to lead others. So, I made a deal. "I will do this work, but you (God) must bring them to me. If there is someone who isn't meant to work with me, allow that to be shown quickly. I don't have time."

I have these conversations, perhaps with my Higher Self, who is still a part of the One, the All. The one who can access the Akashic field and tap into everything at any time. This feels like God to me. I don't get too hung up on the Mystery. I actually love the unknown aspect of this life. This Dream. It makes it more like Wonderland. This Fool's Journey is where we are the accidental heroes like Po from *Kung Fu Panda*.

Only when our story is told by others is it a Hero's Journey. This quest for knowledge and truth will be like a labyrinth if we need to know the answers before we begin. The answer is you. You are the light of the world. You will see that all these threads will weave into a tapestry of a life you choose to live.

I see that, my entire life, death has been the way I went into the underworld. I found my light again. My essence, my gift, my soul's calling. Over and over again, our soul or Higher Self calls back to us, showing us that, like Dorothy, we had the way home all along. But we had to travel with trusty companions who were all part of us. We think we don't have enough knowledge like the Scarecrow, and yet he was the one who always had a plan. Or we don't have enough compassion or heart and can't stop "rusting" ourselves. And, of course, the Cowardly Lion was the bravest of all, because you need to be scared to have bravery and do a courageous act with knees wobbling.

If you learn to trust yourself, you will see that the path is set before you. Sometimes, you need a machete to clear it, but it is always visible.

I now work as a hospice chaplain, offering friendly conversation and emotional support to the dying through listening to stories, singing songs, and welcome playing crystal singing bowls to the patients in their homes. We welcome the transition to the other side.

I see that we die every single day and are born again with the sun. These parts of us are like falling leaves whose decay nurtures the soil for new beginnings. We are alchemists, but of our own life. That is how we help others. We get really comfortable with ourselves, the quirks and all. "It is not what you do, but who you are while doing it," as one of my mentors shared with me.

The choice is not to be a healer or lightworker; this is our gift to humanity. To be the sentinels, to show and teach others how to lead with Love. Not to shy away from the shadow.

Be brave. Don't allow anyone to put you in a box. There is no box. Be a rebel WITH a cause.

This is all improv theatre. We have a set and setting, and we make decisions on the spot. We can plan, but we are not in control. Release it. This is what I can share with you. Things turn out differently than planned, and it can be painful. Death can be. Grieve it. Then, know you are in the birth canal and ready for your new, raw skin.

My life has not been easy, but I don't learn the easy way.

Today, I share that my 30-year marriage has ended; I can say, it is all worth the experiences and lessons. My husband was a schoolmate and his presence was what I needed to help me know I can work through difficult times and come out as two individuals again who respect each other for who we are. That's what I can offer on that. Because two years ago, that's not where I was. Time heals. You heal. We heal together.

I am creating a new life that I dare to create. I still stay away from animal products but am less strict about it. I can do better about honoring what I put into my body and how I move it. That is my next season that I'm reclaiming. I enjoy my substances that numb me more than I would like to. But I am in a transitional time and will always allow myself grace. That's how I love myself and not punish the parts of me that are not quite ready. It's a new way, and it's lovely to be in this space of gentleness with myself. The walls have come down, and I even let myself feel it all. Grieving this part of me while simultaneously calling in what is to be.

I see you as a fellow traveler. I know you as a fellow seeker. I feel you as a fellow lightworker.

Thank you for entering into my world for a few moments. Before this, I did not exist to you, and now our worlds have merged and gotten a little more expansive.

Keep finding yourself. Keep discovering and staying curious.

Be a lighthouse, not a tugboat.

Signing off.

♡ ♡ ♡

Rosa Maria "Rosie" Velasquez is a partera or midwife to souls. She is a highly-sensitive empath who was born with the ability to access multiple dimensions and lifetimes, seeing the potential of all things, places and peoples' paths. She is a guide, mentor, weaver and, most of all, a wisdom keeper who shares lessons through storytelling.

Born in Los Angeles, California of immigrant parents from Mexico, she is the second to youngest of 6 siblings. Rosie found solace and peace in a crowded home in the wonderful inner world of her imagination and dreams. She still speaks to the Angels, who are her protectors and companions. She is the creator of The Mystic Rose Studios, Weaving Dreams (a new coaching approach), and founder of Vigilio, a non-profit, in Big Bear Lake, California.

Websites: https://rosievelasquez.com
www.themysticrosestudios.com
Instagram: www.instagram.com/rosie.velasquez_
Facebook: www.facebook.com/themysticrosestudio

27

Unlearning the Art of Playing Small: A Path from Burnout to Inner Peace

By Charlotte Chipperfield
Portland, Oregon, USA

Have you ever kept an old phone *way* past its prime, watching the battery drain faster every day until charging it became your full-time job? Then you finally upgrade, and suddenly you can go a whole day without hunting for outlets. You find yourself apologizing to your old phone for all the times you cursed at it while waiting for your camera to load.

That's what my spiritual awakening felt like—a slow burn over time. I clung to that laggy old phone like my life depended on it. But when I finally opened myself to change, I realized I hadn't just been stuck with an old device—I'd been stuck in an old version of myself, missing all the updates life had been quietly offering me all along. Looking back now, I can see how clearly it started...

From a young age, I had a deep sense of who I was. My intuition was strong and my ability to read people has never failed me. I preferred staying home to write stories rather than playing video games. I loved swimming more than soccer, and my lack of coordination—especially around moving objects—was proven when I attempted to kick a soccer ball, only to fall backward and break my collarbone. The worst part? It delayed my "self-publishing" deadlines for crafting my hand-written books with cardboard covers and ribbon bindings. Before you judge, I did "sell" my first book to my former preschool teacher, which meant creating a second copy that she read to her current class. At the age of ten, I felt like I had made it!

But stories, like life, rarely follow our earliest drafts. Writing has always been a soul calling of mine. Unfortunately, my dream of being a published author peaked with my preschool teacher. At least, until my spiritual awakening took place. Life took me on a winding journey that detoured from what I loved as a child. I fell into the all-too-familiar trap of "shoulds." Somewhere along the way, I absorbed beliefs like "you can't make a living as a writer," and "go to college, get a job, and prepare for retirement."

In school, I found it challenging to show up as my full self. People often misunderstood me or mocked me because they thought it was funny. I still remember third grade in Miss Drake's class, where the new boy from California—with his perfectly curly blond hair—sitting next to me would repeatedly put his arm on my desk during a test. Magically, he seemed to remove it every time the teacher glanced in our direction. I became annoyed, flustered, and downright pissed he was getting away with this. I decided a firm boundary needed to be set. The next time he slammed his forearm on my desk, I raised my opposite hand and sent my nails diving into his skin, breaking the surface just enough that a pin drop of blood escaped.

Let's just say, he never put his arm on my desk again. He harassed me, yet I got detention. My teacher told me, "He probably likes you." While he never bothered me again, I was left wondering why I was punished and made to feel guilty for reacting to his behavior. That was my first lesson in how the world wanted me to behave as a woman: stay quiet, don't make a fuss, be agreeable. So that's what I did.

As I entered the professional world, I became a people-pleaser because it seemed to get me further than being my full self. I became reliable, dependable, and a "get things done immediately" kind of person who even won awards for this behavior. But this created an internal divide—I was myself behind closed doors, and in the "real world," I played small to make others comfortable.

This continued as my career grew into becoming a Director of Marketing for a start-up. At this peak of my career, I was firing on all people-pleasing cylinders. I was running an entire department with limited resources, and because everyone else had a full plate, I always took on more. Spoiler: I had a full plate, too, but I didn't know how to set boundaries to save my life. I lived in constant resentment. Even when I received public praise and awards, my one-on-one meetings with my manager were filled with comments like, "This isn't enough," or "You're not bringing in enough revenue to cover your salary." I'd wake up at 2 a.m., working in my sleep, my brain desperate to solve problems. My nervous system no longer felt safe at work, and this led to complete burnout.

Letting the world suck my confidence out like it was bone marrow on a dinner plate while trying to people-please my way into the c-suite was a recipe for disaster. Years of enduring this pattern left me hollow, tanked my confidence, and left me disconnected from who I was. I had always been a career woman, certain of my path, motherhood not in my plans.

As with most grand plans, they never go exactly as we wish. The universe didn't just tap me on the shoulder—she dismantled my entire life. Just like that time in a sailing class when the boom hit my head and sent a sharp crackle down into my entire skeletal system, my world had broken apart. Back-to-back layoffs. A relationship shattered. Friendships dissolved. Giving up my high-rise apartment. The foundation of my life was swallowed swiftly into a sinkhole. What had been certain vanished into thin air. That feeling of connection to myself I had when I was younger was now a dust pile of confusion. I had no idea what value I had to offer. I was unhappy. Any hopes I had for the future felt impossible.

I had two choices: grow or check out.

For the first time in my life, I had no plan. I've always been an action-taker, an idea-into-reality maker. But as I sat in my soon-to-be-vacant apartment, selling my things, I knew I couldn't keep pushing in the same direction. I needed to pivot and redirect. The time had come to stop and slow down. I had to take a hard look at my inner world and stop avoiding the truths I didn't want (or know I needed) to face. I needed to reconnect with that bright-eyed girl who wrote stories with cardboard covers. If I wanted real change, I was going to have to dig deep into my beliefs to reshape my identity, tap into my true essence, and rebuild trust in myself. It was time to wake up—spiritually.

When we're able to slow down, the facades start falling away. The key isn't to rush to rebuild them but to sit in the uncertainty and wait for what truly aligns. I thought this would be easy—after all, I was great at checking boxes and getting things done. But reframing beliefs isn't like redecorating a room. It's more like excavating an ancient city buried under years of sediment, carefully examining each artifact of thought, and deciding what to keep.

And if that sounds painful, it sure is!

Pop some Advil and let's go there.

The process of letting go: of what I thought life would be, of letting the past define the future, of thinking that crying for days about a problem meant I was processing it (spoiler: that's not feeling your emotions, it's rumination).

The hardest part wasn't the letting go—it was facing how much of myself I'd already let go of along the way. Every "yes" when I meant "no," every smile when I wanted to scream, every time I made myself smaller to make others comfortable—they were all stored in my body like tiny time bombs of discontentment. I had to learn that discomfort wasn't my enemy; it was merely the growing pains of my true self pushing through years of carefully constructed armor. Some days, I felt like I was excavating my own spirit with a teaspoon, carefully brushing away layers of other people's expectations to find the gems of my own truth buried underneath.

To get back to my essence, I had to learn to trust myself again. The mere thought sent me into panic—how could I not trust myself? I started small, tuning in to what my body needed, even with simple decisions like what to eat for dinner. Each tiny decision became a stepping stone back to myself. I began following what felt good.

That led me to obtain a life coaching certification and become a developmental editor—choices that didn't make logical sense at the time. But as I honored those pulls, momentum built. I started a new business, traveled, and began the delicate work of pruning away people, beliefs, and expectations that no longer served me.

But let me be clear—this letting go process was like performing surgery on yourself while running a marathon. For eighteen grueling months, I faced old hurts, forgave past colleagues, and retrained my nervous system to understand that peace wasn't just possible but it was safe to feel. Sometimes, the things we crave most—like thriving instead of surviving—feel threatening simply because they're unfamiliar.

Walking through the fire is the only way forward. It might feel like a never-ending nightmare, but eventually, you experience small shifts. The most surprising part of transformation isn't the big moments—it's the little glimmers that catch you off guard. Like the first time I declined a lunch invitation without making an excuse or feeling guilty. Or when I allowed myself not to be tied to my computer at 2 p.m. on a Wednesday. These weren't changes in behavior; they were signs of a deeper shift. Each small act of authenticity was like a vote of confidence in my own worth, a quiet rebellion against years of believing I had to earn the right to exist in my own life.

As a self-proclaimed "recovering people-pleaser," I learned to say, "That sounds interesting. I'd love to take 24 hours to consider this." That single phrase became my act of defiance against a lifetime of instant agreement. Taking a moment to tune into yourself before responding is the greatest thing you can do to build trust with yourself. This created a question that kept circling in my mind: are you contributing stress to the world—or art, peace, and joy?

We have a finite amount of time on this planet and if we lived forever, then I guess being stuck longer would be ok, but we don't live forever. If we *really* want our lives to look differently, we have to respond differently and allow our bodies and nervous systems to feel safe in doing so. Real change isn't an overnight transformation— it's continuing to walk through the fire until it becomes an expansive, lush field of possibilities.

At the end of my life coaching certification, eight of us gathered for an exercise where everyone shared words they associated with each other. During my two minutes, I couldn't believe what I was hearing. Truth after truth landed like petals from a cherry tree: you can't hide your essence, even when you've lost connection to it yourself. People-pleasing was just a cloak I'd worn, but my true essence was always there, waiting for me to reclaim it.

When I set out to learn to trust myself again, I didn't know the path would lead right back to where I started—only this time, without the masks. I don't believe there's an "end" to a spiritual awakening—just new chapters that build on the last. Now, as I write books and help other women do the same, my hope is that we can all move through life with intention, inner peace, and trust in our true essence.

Change is hard, but do you want to live by the "shoulds" or by who you truly are? Playing small only restricts those who need your gifts. I knew mine from a young age but ignored them due to external influences. The universe kept nudging me back toward my truth, even when I tried to run from it. Each setback, each crisis, each moment of clarity was leading me home to myself.

Now when I sit down to write, I feel that same spark I had as a child with my ribbon-bound books, only stronger. The difference is that I no longer need anyone's permission to create, to speak, to be. The little girl who knew exactly who she was? She never left. She was just waiting for me to be brave enough to write my way home and become her again, this time with the wisdom to protect her gifts and the strength to share them with the world. She was waiting for me to unlearn the art of playing small.

Thankfully, I've found my way back, and my wish is that you do too. Your essence is waiting.

♡ ♡ ♡

Charlotte Chipperfield is an author, developmental editor, and book coach who empowers women and underrepresented authors through her platform, Her Narrative. With years of experience in crafting compelling stories, she combines editorial expertise with compassion to help writers unapologetically develop their unique voices and narratives. As a recognized public speaker and book judge for book competitions, including the Independent Publishers of New England and the Women's Fiction Writers Association, Charlotte has established herself as a leader in the publishing industry. Through Her Narrative, she creates a space where authors can develop their writing skills through courses and community. Charlotte advocates for voices that have historically been overlooked or marginalized, believing that stories have the power to challenge perceptions, build empathy, and enrich our collective narrative—a mission that drives her coaching and editing work.

Website: www.hernarrative.com

Instagram: www.instagram.com/hernarrative_

TikTok: www.tiktok.com/@hernarrative

YouTube: www.youtube.com/@hernarrative

28

The Universe is Only Removing What Isn't for You

By Vanessa Grace
Vancouver, Washington, USA

I was having panic attacks during therapy. I'd never had one before, so I didn't know what was happening. I told my friend about my symptoms, which involved a lot of chest tightness and clenching, you know? She laughed, as only a person with anxiety could when it was so obvious to HER, and said, "Vanessa! That's a panic attack!" My reaction was, "Say What Now?" *I was having panic attacks? How could that be? I've never had panic attacks before.*

I should clarify, though. I wasn't the client in these therapy sessions. I was the therapist. Having a Panic Attack. In the middle of helping my clients. This confused me because I loved my private practice. So, what was happening that I was having panic attacks while therapisting?

At home, I had a husband who was an alcoholic, and I didn't know what to do about it. This felt pretty fucked up because he wasn't one when we got married. I would lay in bed, sleepless and fretting, imagining the worst-case scenarios. I ended up going to therapy.

It was this situation that led me to discovering a hard truth: I was codependent. Sure, I knew a little about codependency. But like many people, I knew a watered-down version that was incomplete. I felt appalled because I was a Perfectionist Good Girl who thought His choices reflected on Me.

The Gloves are Off, It's Spiritual Awakening Time!

Spiritual awakenings are like a gut punch. They fucking smack you in the face and MAKE you pay attention. Each person going through an awakening will have some sort of life disruption. What happens specifically to you in your life will depend on what area of growth you're most in need of and what soul contracts you made for this lifetime. The people in your life right now may have soul contracts to be part of this growth for you.

What is really happening is a hard lesson. Maybe you've been given hints before that you needed to work on this certain area through whispers from your guides or mentionings from friends, but the Universe has taken its gloves off now, and it's time to get tough to make you pay attention. They are going to make you learn this lesson if they have to hold you by the ankle and shake you upside down until everything falls out of your pockets. Yeah, it's like that.

Seeing the Reality of Myself Was Hard

I spent about two years in a therapy group that specialized in helping codependent people. Everyone loved someone who had addiction issues. I had so much shame about my situation. In the beginning, I could barely say, "My husband is an alcoholic," without crying. I learned a lot, though, and so many patterns left my energy field.

I figured out I was TOTALLY FUCKING CODEPENDENT. I unwound programming about obligation to others, self-sacrifice, and ignoring my own needs. I learned about enabling, overhelping, and letting go of the deep guilt I would experience if I said, "No," quieting my voice if I thought it would upset certain people.

No one had specifically taught me boundaries or how to listen to my own gut intuition. Every step felt like it was a mile, and all of them were scary.

I could go ON about what I learned. I began setting boundaries and using my voice in ways that were intimidating for me. Eventually, my husband did stop drinking. I knit all of this into myself and my therapeutic knowledge of people. (FYI, we just celebrated our 20th Anniversary. ;)

Looking back, I can see that changes in my spiritual growth have always influenced what I express through my business. This started when I added a business called Soul Amplified alongside my therapy practice. I invented my title: Codependency Coach. I started a podcast called *The Soul Amplified Podcast* where I went in-depth on codependency and psychology. Soul Amplified and I had just embarked on a wild ride.

Riding the Spiritual Gifts Wave

Spiritual Awakening is not just inner personal lessons. Parallel to this is the emergence of spiritual gifts. I was being exposed to spiritual ideas I'd never heard of before through a close friend. I was raised Christian (and still am), so ideas about Universal Energy, the concept of Vibration, or the Universe giving you circumstances to help you learn lessons were all totally foreign to me. I was staying open to them, though, even though they didn't make sense to my current worldview.

Several other experiences helped propel me in my awakening, too. I had a curiosity for tarot. I watched the movie *The Secret* and was blown away by the concept of manifestation. I started meditating, learning about chakras, and experiencing energy, and I bought myself my first tarot card deck.

There is a Reason This is Happening

Just like how the life disruption you experience in your Spiritual Awakening will be unique to you, so will the gifts and talents that start to come through. Honestly, I feel these are not new gifts to your Soul, just to your human experience. What's really happening is your human self is remembering what your Soul already knows. You may have vivid or lifelike dreams, hear voices, know information without knowing why, hear ringing in your ears, experience sensations in your body that are the flow of energy, or connect with energies, Spirit Guides, or those who have passed on.

This process can make you feel like you are losing your mind. And you are. You're losing everything that isn't for you anymore. Everything. It is quite the fucking roller coaster ride. When you don't know what is happening, this feels like a personal attack and a nightmare. This upending has a purpose. It took me a while to look back and realize my husband's alcoholism was a gift. Without it, I never would have purged from myself all of those destructive codependent patterns I couldn't see.

All of this is raising your vibration (that's a good thing), which can cause illness-like symptoms in the body; sweating, feeling nauseous, foggy-headed, off balance, or having no energy. My legs would jerk during energy work. This list could go ON and ON. This is your body releasing what is a lower vibration and trying to calibrate itself. It's also your body trying to 'turn on' the new spiritual skills, and it is trying to tune into the station. There is usually static in the process.

Spiritual Awakenings or Upgrades are like potato chips; once you start, you can't have just one. I've had many. All of the Awakenings will feel like a death. However, you will start to understand the process of it. To know how to handle being in the liminal space of shedding ego-based ideas about self, life, and control. To change from a mindset of lack and fear about what is happening, to a mindset of curiosity about how all this pain and change is going to transmute into something unimaginably good. Because that's what is on the other side.

You.

Will.

Feel.

Fucking.

Amazing.

Sliding into the D.F. (Divine Feminine, that is)

I connected with a couple who taught on a concept called Divine Masculine and Divine Feminine. It fascinated me. I worked with them for two years. This worldview again blew the lid off what I knew and expanded how I see things. I realized I had been pushing in my masculine for years (decades?), and my feminine was burnt out. I rapidly evolved as I incorporated the ways of life of the divine feminine into how I actually lived and ran my business. I needed to replenish myself. I created more time to go slow, and allowed more space for emotions and creativity. I tried to step back from how much I was controlling and allow flow.

During this time, I felt brave enough to add discussions of spirituality to my work and in my podcast. I told my very Christian parents I was a tarot card reader. Them not knowing was holding back the freedom of my voice to Uplevel. They had to know this part of me, or I was tethered to a lower vibration.

I have always wanted to be a mother but had inconsistent periods and ovulation. Sometimes, they just wouldn't show! I was working on understanding how to heal my menstruation but had no guide. Through community, I was introduced to exactly what I needed to learn. (Such synchronicities are common on a spiritual path.) My mind was blown. I learned of Pelvic Steaming and the Four Phases of the Menstrual Cycle. Most importantly, I discovered concepts that combined the Divine Feminine, periods, spirituality, and the sacredness of the womb. *Say what? Spirituality intersects all these things I'm super passionate about?*

I was so fucking excited, I dove down the rabbit hole of books by authors like Lisa Lister, Alisa Vitti, and the Bertrands. You best believe I was on that Pelvic Steaming, too. Please. Give. Me. More. I was so happy when, by utilizing mostly alternative health methods and being in my Divine Feminine, I was able to bring my menstrual cycle into a healthy state of monthly bleeding.

Divine Masculine and Feminine have become a lens I use to perceive life. I am aligning my life to the Four Phases of the Menstrual Cycle. Once I've incorporated an aspect of it, I learn & incorporate another aspect of it. This morphed into living my life with the seasons of the Earth and phases of the moon. I was feeling less passionate about being a therapist in private practice. During the summer of 2022, I closed my practice and went all in on Soul Amplified.

After the next winter, where I experienced deep contemplation, rest, and purging I realized I could release being a codependency coach, too. Again, I invented my title: Radiance Coach. I threw myself into it with glee, creating a new program, a retreat, and consistently sharing my new passion. The wild ride with Soul Amplified continued.

Spirit Baby Knows Best

My journey to motherhood has been very emotional and bumpy. I spent many years crying and wondering why it was not happening. Even though at this writing I have not become a mother, I no longer react this way. Through doing meditations and working with healers, I would get messages from my spirit baby. To be able to carry her pregnancy and parent the kind of person she will be, I needed to raise my vibration significantly, and my beliefs needed a total overhaul. Back then, I would get messages about how to become pregnant, and they didn't make sense to me. I didn't have the framework and beliefs to understand them. I understand better now. If she had come before, I would have missed out on all my lessons and how I have remade myself. It is better this way.

My Spirit Baby also needed to come when it was a certain vibration on earth. This vibration did not happen until I was already 40. I continue on my journey of expanded self-love and increasing my vibration to be able to hold her vibration when it is time for the pregnancy. I know there is more energy work for me to do, and I am linked with aspects of it now.

How I Have Changed

I am a completely different person than I was 12-ish years ago when my initial Spiritual Awakening happened. I have tried a multitude of spiritual practices. Some are still part of my spiritual life while some I have evolved past. Each of them has contributed to my growth. They are Reiki, tarot, manifestation, grounding, being an empath, The Emotion Code, The One Command, vibration/frequency awareness, energy healing, EFT Tapping, DNA Upgrades, the clairs, chakras, crystals, altars, moon stuff, working with my Spirit Guides, channeling, protections for auras and then home/land, living with the seasons, the four phases of the menstrual cycle, Womb Communication, and Womb Magic. I'm sure there are more I forgot. In your Spiritual Awakening, follow what lights you up—those are the practices that are for your growth.

These iterations of myself have come with much inner upheaval. Personal relationships have changed. No more murder mysteries for me (cry). Grocery stores? No thank you, I order and pick up. I love time to read, do spiritual shit, meditate, and go slow. And all I'm really interested in talking about is Spiritual Shit. This is how I now see the world and make decisions in my life. Vibration. Energy. Divine Masculine and Feminine. Connecting to and chatting with my Spirit Guides. I have conversations with Mary Magdalene, who is totally The Shit. My extroverted self is now an ambivert. I like alone time more than ever.

That said, I have frequently felt lonely over the last few years due to friendship changes, and I'm still seeking the depth of community I crave. I don't want to go to the game. I want to go in-depth on chakra chats, what your Guide said to you today, or what life lessons the Universe is throwing your way right now. Add a charcuterie board, and we're good!

Connecting with Me and Evolving

There are things I am discovering and practices I am engaging in right now that are not ready to be shared yet. This is always my way. Experiencing, growing, releasing. Often in very raw ways for myself. So. Much. Crying! Then, understanding them enough to share with others. Teach. Lead in the practices. Anyone interested in connecting with me and being a Soul Sister will observe this growth and benefit from it because it is a part of who I am. Also, Books. I will tell you about all the books. All the time.

Vanessa Grace, LICSW is a Radiance Coach. She combines psychology, spirituality, and the divine feminine to help people live their dream lives with an open heart. She loves to talk about epigenetics, chakras, and why your menstrual cycle is the secret to everything. Her diverse expertise, kind heart, and a dash of light humor help her clients heal the life moments or traumas that distance them from peace and happiness. Her clients experience a deepening of their spiritual gifts, trust in self, and connection to their feminine.

Website: www.soulamplified.org

Instagram: www.instagram.com/soulamplified

Podcast: www.soulamplified.buzzsprout.com

Membership: www.soulcirclealliance.com/checkout/vanessa-soulseekermembership

29

My Dance with Awakening

By Catherine Galardo
Kennesaw, Georgia, USA

What is an awakening? According to Webster's dictionary, it means "to arouse from sleep, rousing from inactivity or indifference, a revival of interest in something, or coming into awareness."

According to my journey, to awaken is to wake up and snap out of a programmed trance of beliefs, rules, and regulations that I was living under and coming into the awareness of my true authentic self.

Both definitions include a turning point moment. A pattern interrupts when one shifts from the of "sleep" to one of waking up. I believe that there's a moment in time in the cosmic calendar of all of our lives when we have this call to awaken. It's already planned and written.

When this pattern interruption arrives into one's life, it can cause massive chaos, confusion, disorientation and dysregulation.

And it never gives you a warning.

You just happen to find yourself in this season and you don't even realize it. It appears unannounced to disrupt your life in the most inopportune time, although with the best of intentions. It has come to shake you up and has one of the most important missions of your lifetime: to lead you to the authentic version of yourself and your mission.

This has also been called a "Dark Night of the Soul" by many, a midlife crisis, or a kundalini awakening. But nonetheless, it's the beginning of the end of an era.

My Journey into Awakening

The sleep and trance I was woken up from was a loveless marriage, a stressful job that wasn't aligned with my purpose, a tendency to put others' needs before mine, and wearing masks that I thought were required for a woman in our society today. I was living a life that wasn't mine. I was playing a role in a movie.

However, from the outside looking in, it looked like I had it all together. We had a big house, nice cars, happy children (one of my greatest and most authentic things that happened before my awakening), and I was always saying yes to what anyone asked of me. I was well-liked. In a nutshell, it looked as if I had it all.

I was good at performing and pretending to be happy, but in reality, I was so lost. Deep down, I was just existing. I didn't know how to care for myself and had lost my own sense of who I was, what I liked, what I wanted to do, and who I wanted to be. I lived for my family.

What I know today from all my studies and personal development is that what I was doing before my awakening was living a life of suppression. I was taught to suppress and repress my light, joy, and authentic self. And then I started to live from that repressed place.

But what is repressed and in the dark will eventually have to come to the light. So when my dark night of the soul began, I had to express all the years and heal from repression and suppression.

I turned to food to cope with all the stuck energy in my body that didn't have permission to be expressed. I ended up eating my emotions to numb and escape. There was a period of years when I didn't even cry, and I never felt elation or excitement. I was just frozen and stuck!

I want to tell you that there is purpose behind all the tears, all the pain, and all the hurt. Before we get taken to the next level of our lives in an awakened state, we have to empty and clean out all the old ways of being and programs that aren't ours to carry. There is a messy season before we have our breakthrough. Know that you are not alone. I have been there. It hurts like hell, but keep going, sweet soul, because the only way out is through.

The medicine that allowed me to release my past

It's in the death of the old and in the darkest nights where we are really being polished and pruned. People don't talk about the "stripping away" that we must go through during our awakenings. This opens the bridge to allow us to become the very best and most authentic version of ourselves. When we live for decades repressing the truth of who we are, we are full. There is no flow. Energy is stuck that needs to be moved to make more space for new things. Awakening involves the emptying of your vessel, which is painful but inevitable. To live a life of joy, truth, flow, ease, and purpose, we have to release all that isn't that.

This requires us to do very specific work on a mental, emotional, somatic (body), and spiritual level. Often, people work on all levels except the somatic level, which leaves out an important element where most of our past is stored.

When I talk about somatic work, what I am alluding to is working with and relating to the body through sensations, impulses, and movement. This is where trauma gets stored in the body. Have you ever heard the saying, "Your issues are in your tissues"? This is exactly what is meant by this. We can't just talk about our past, meditate, and process, we also must reset our nervous system to feel safe to let go of old issues! This can only happen using the body (not our heads). Too much repressed and suppressed emotions take space in the body and this creates a body that is "full" and can't receive anything new.

The biggest medicine that supported me in healing myself again was dance. Dance taught me how to start trusting my intuition again. I was a ballerina as a child and I performed with The Atlanta Ballet for many years. Looking back at my life as a child, it was only when I was dancing that I felt truly alive, it was the one place that I felt like my authentic self.

Because dancing allowed my body to express and release energy, emotional regulation happened. At the time, I did this instinctively, but today I know that through dance, our bodies can shift from activation, disconnection, stress, and being stuck in our heads to relaxation and regulation. Dancing brought me back into my body, where I felt good. It was my safe place. But outside of dance, my habit was to leave my body and live from a disconnected place in my head where I couldn't access my needs or feelings.

As I started to get older, I stopped dancing, and therefore, I stopped accessing my safe place. I remember one of the times I was at my lowest in my life in my late 20s. My husband and I had decided to start trying to have children again. I was happy and excited and very hopeful about having another child. Then the worst happened: I lost not one but two babies in a matter of 18 months. Having a miscarriage was devastating. I made up a story in my mind that I was a complete failure as a woman. It made me feel worthless, unfit, and undeserving of love. All lies, of course, but I took on those beliefs.

This was the first time I went into a deep depression. I remember thinking that I wasn't in a good place and I had to do something different. I asked myself for the first time in a long time, "When were you last happy, and what were you doing?" What came up for me was the times when I used to dance.

I looked into adult dance classes near me and signed up for a Hip Hop class. That class started to make me feel connected, grounded, and alive again. I looked forward to going every week.

Then, unexpectedly, a few months later, I became pregnant with my first daughter, and shortly after she was born, I was pregnant again with my second daughter. They were both truly a light that illuminated my life. I ran with the high, and I threw myself into being the best mother I could be, making my children the center of my life and I started to lose myself in my children all over again. The glimpse of finding myself was short lived but I got a taste of it.

I will never forget the morning when everything changed for me. I woke up and went to the bathroom and looked in the mirror and realized that I didn't even know the person that was looking back in the mirror.

I did not recognize her! I was overweight and unhappy. My body ached, I looked exhausted with circles under my eyes, and I was a hot mess.

I knew right then and there I had to make a change again! Us humans seem to do this in life, coming in and out of patterns as we hit many different rock bottoms. I refused to go on living the rest of my life looking and feeling the way I did. I was so angry with myself for allowing myself to get like that. Not only did I feel worthless, but I also felt numb. I hadn't felt loved, excited, or alive. I was existing and in survival mode.

In the shower, I just started crying. Today, I know this is a way for all of the suppression to move into expression, and it's a very good thing. It started small, then the floodgate came open, and I couldn't stop sobbing. It was a type of cry I hadn't felt before. A deep cry. It felt like I was letting go of many years held in. I couldn't stop yet I could feel this was a pivotal moment for me. I could feel this was a cry of letting go of deep pain, rage, and hurt.

That day changed the trajectory of my life, and I will be forever grateful for those dark years that led me to that bathroom moment where it broke me open. From there, my awakening journey started, and I learned how to express all that had been suppressed. It was a journey of liberation through expressing my emotions and finding safety in being in my body again through dance, somatic work, and learning how to own my power.

How do you find your authentic self?

Well, I will tell you what it looks like.... A BIG MESS!

And the key to the messy process is to surrender and accept the journey exactly as it is. Let the tender days be there. Allow the sadness to be there and breathe your way through it. Don't try to control or pick it away. This will only delay the process. This will be very tumultuous, but this is actually where I learned to be comfortable with discomfort and to trust in uncertainty. This is where I was forced to let go of control. This season of being in the mess is where I built a lot of character and where I learned a lot of skills to let life be life.

I learned that there was nothing wrong with expressing (which I wasn't allowed to do as a child). In fact, I learned that not expressing myself would eventually kill me from some illness. I had to allow myself to face what I feared. At the center of that was me not feeling worthy of love. I thought if someone actually saw all the yuckiness in me, I would be alone, exiled, and made fun of. And I had to get to the root of the limiting beliefs to be able to face it and heal it. This is what the awakening journey offers us. Deep healing.

I took baby steps, decided to date myself, and got to know myself. I had to take the time to learn who I was. I started saying yes to trying new foods, listening to different music, talking to different people, going to new places, and doing things I'd never done before.

I started asking myself what would make me happy each day and then went and did that. I started listening to my body and that was when I started to dance again! It's like that was what my body was asking for. I was rebuilding a relationship through dance. I allowed the music to move me and take over my senses, and my body responded.

By listening to what my body really needed and honoring what it told me, I regained my confidence in my feminine power, lost weight, got healthier, and had the energy to pursue things I never had before. For the first time, I was able to see, understand, acknowledge, and love the little girl inside. I became ME! In doing so, I fell in love with myself! This was when I came home to myself.

During this process of finding myself, I gained self-confidence. I regained my power. I came back into my body and felt vivacious and sexy. This gave me the courage to divorce my husband of 31 years, set boundaries with my children and family, leave jobs that no longer aligned with me as a person, travel the world, and start my own company teaching what most lights me up: Divine Flow Movement.

I created a brand new life from the ashes of the one I burned down. My new life is so full of love, laughter, joy, friendship, health, and wealth. I am embracing new opportunities, experiences, and people. In order to stay grounded, connected, and open to life, these are my top five practices that have supported me the most: meditation, dance, daily self-care that makes me feel grounded and nourished, training my mind to think differently, and practicing gratitude.

So, sweet soul, I lived a lot of my life numb and with suppressed emotions, not knowing who I was. Then, it was my time to awaken, and while it was not pretty, I wouldn't change it for the world. The amount of light I can hold in my body and the capacity to hold joy is something I never dreamed of. Dance was my bridge to my authentic life. And perhaps it can be the medicine for you as it was for me. The joy of dance is that one thing that will support you in your journey, and I know that reading a book like this with so many of our stories has filled you up with some love and light, too.

Catherine Galardo is an Embodiment Coach and the creator of Red Stiletto Era Programs and Divine Flow Movement. One of Catherine Galardo's gifts is her infectious zest for life and her passion to live to the fullest. It is her life's mission to help women understand their unique passions, find their inner radiance, and get their sexy back so they can shine their beautiful spark in the world. Through her CG Methodology, Red Stiletto Era Programs, and her proprietary "Divine Flow Movement" practice, she helps women come back to their bodies as they increase their capacity to learn how to love and accept their bodies thoroughly!

Catherine's clients usually come to her before or after big changes in their lives, whether it's from a divorce, becoming an empty nester, following a new career peri/post menopause, or starting a new chapter or rebirthing journey. She is known for helping women release the past that has been stored in their minds, bodies, and spirits so they can step into a new era of power, sovereignty, pleasure, and aliveness.

Website: www.catherinegalardo.com/red-stiletto-era

Facebook: www.facebook.com/redstilettoera

30

Finding the Will to Live Beneath the Draconic Wings of Chronic Illness

By Kristen Girard
Saratoga Springs, New York, USA

I felt the ragged talons of despair dragging me down into the lands of severe depression again. The nips and bites of chronic illness scarred my body and psyche more deeply every day. The heavy wings of grief reached farther and further into my life, separating me from the light of joy and hope more and more with each desert dry thirst causing high blood sugar spike, or life-threatening low blood glucose event.

The stinging pangs of loneliness and isolation burned as I had to pause the goings on of life for the painful pricking of my fingers until I bled enough to satisfy the blood glucose meter before each and every meal, any exercise, shower, driving, meeting, or anytime I felt more confused than usual. Basically, having to inflict sharp objects on my fingers every waking hour whether I wanted to or not. Does anyone want to? No.

The choking sensation of defeat that arose with each failed insulin pump site would then cascade into a struggle to live against the absence of my body's ability to make the life-giving hormone insulin, no matter how fast I recognized there was a problem. The endless spiked tail whips of frustration came with the onslaught of alarms from my continuous glucose monitor day and night as I fought for my life and a night of decent sleep, every hour of every day against a dragon so fierce the only escape was and still is... death.

Then, in moments when it hurt the most, the implication that type 1 diabetes was "no big deal". How hard can it be to replace the function of a critical organ like a pancreas? It's "just" a math problem of carbohydrates to insulin, right? NO! This type 1 diabetes dragon is much more endlessly demanding than that. And then the hideous dragon of char-inducing judgment and blame reared their head when called into being by anyone and everyone from doctors to family members because I must have "done something" to "deserve" this—and how dare I enjoy a cupcake?!?!

Also, there was the nausea-inducing flavor of shame that this incurable autoimmune chronic illness was something I had "done to myself" from spiritual circles because my energy wasn't all love and light enough, or I must have done something awful in this life, or truly horrific in a past life to be condemned as unworthy of freedom in my own body. It should be something I can heal if I could "just" align with the energy of being totally healthy... I wish.

It didn't help that, for many reasons, I felt worthless, like a burden, and that I didn't matter at all. Neither did my dreams or art. There were a lot of situations in my life coalescing to emphasize those horrible feelings. A big part of that was, of course, the inescapable daily churn of the type 1 diabetes dragon that often seemed like the only thing that mattered because of its invasive and all-consuming nature. The impact it was having on my life and ability to function in conjunction with the other chronic illnesses that had flown into my life uninvited was devastating.

Another challenge was my spiritual nature, it felt like another dragon—the dragon of persecution. I could feel energy and other's emotions, sense things just beyond sight and words, hear my guides, know things intuitively, and remember past lives. Energy healing was second nature, and I knew that animals, plants, and the Earth are alive and really no different than humans at all—and infinitely worthy of love, care, and respect. And yet, if I allowed this multi-faceted side of me to show, it didn't go well.

To be me, authentically me, was terrifying. It felt like I was waiting for a death blow at any moment. I was used to anything I cared about or needed or wanted being taken away, soured, dismissed, put down, treated as an inconvenience, mocked, abused, half-starved, never ever being good enough, and devalued. It didn't matter that I lovingly treasured those things. I had been so convinced over the years that I didn't matter that for me to value anything at all meant that nothing good could come of my light. My caring and love had been weaponized against me for so long that it was very hard to see that caring and love are strengths, not weaknesses that make you a target.

I lost my will to live.

For a long time.

One beautiful fall day, I found myself standing on a time-roughened dock, brokenly staring down into the lake water, wanting to die so the pain of being alive would finally stop. I tried to force myself to enter the water, to will myself to the peace I needed so terribly. I closed my eyes, silently crying as sunlight danced on the crystal-clear surface.

Then, as the sunlight sparkled through my eyelids, I was enveloped in warmth, light, and LOVE. I was safe. In those moments, I was protected tenderly and kindly in an incredible golden light that felt like the gentle fires of Divine Creation. It was LOVE itself.

My Higher Self appeared. I knew this being was me, but so much more. She lit up the dark shadows of my soul, highlighted my inner light in golden ripples, and infused everything in between with love. My Higher Self showed me that both my light and shadow are there for a good reason.

I don't remember the words my Higher Self spoke, but I do remember the feeling that somehow everything actually was going to be not just okay but good. She imparted the wisdom that I mattered, and so did my art and dreams. She helped me realize that I didn't want to die. The truth dawned on me that I actually wanted to live, but I had forgotten how to want to live. I was worthy of being ALIVE!

When that truth rose up, the light somehow deepened and expanded like a warm hug. The golden light of Divine Love remained a bit longer, enveloping me in peace as that new knowledge percolated through my being.

When I opened my eyes after this spiritual awakening, I was surprised to be back in the here and now of Earth. I stood on the dock feeling the warm fall breeze on my skin as the sunlight continued its dance on the placid lake waters, wondering how I could learn to want to live every day but trusting that, somehow, I would indeed learn step by step.

And that's when the hard work of healing myself, my life, and making peace with my dragons started.

A week later, early on in my healing journey, I was at a group art studio working on a pencil drawing based on a selfie I had taken just prior to my spiritual awakening. The goal wasn't to draw myself but instead to draw whatever felt right. I didn't know it then, but since that day on the dock I was channeling divine messages anytime I picked up a paintbrush or pencil and allowed myself to step out of the way so intuition could lead. At the time, I just thought my imagination was coming back online as part of the realization that I wanted to live. So I drew and drew, not at all focused on what I was drawing, simply enjoying the flow of art through my being. The studio session ended, so I packed the drawing away, not thinking of anything except that, at some point, I needed to finish it.

Some time passed as I explored what it is to *want* to live—and how to go about it. I learned about daily gratitude practices and affirmations. I bought myself a necklace from artist Megan Auman. To me, this necklace stood for hope. It was a simple black chain with a lovely dendritic opal, a black and white stone, that reminded me that even when all seems darkly lost, there is still light. It was my talisman for many years that I still bring out on occasion when I need to remind myself that I matter, and so does my art and dreams. It also reminded me that artists can do good in the world AND make a wonderful living doing it.

I started listening to podcasts that opened up my universe. Many aha moments ensued as I learned about gaslighting, narcissism, toxic positivity, and what self-care really is. Eventually, I would find a counselor who helped me understand foundational places where the grief was coming from in ways I needed an outside perspective to see. I also began to encounter wonderful people in daily life and online communities who also talked with their guides, remembered past lives, and felt the sacred earth energies, too.

At the same time, I was also starting to realize that I wasn't my dragons. I wasn't "type 1 diabetes" or any other chronic illness. I was Kristen, who happens to live with a dragon called diabetes, who is very fierce, but not actually me. I wasn't the different traumas I had lived through. I wasn't all the things others did to me or said about me or tried to force me to be or do. I was Kristen. That was beautifully enough.

Even more importantly, I started to realize that these dragons weren't there just to make me miserable; they were messages, wisdom givers, and even helpers who were asking for acknowledgement. Did they leave? No. Was everything rosy? Not at all. But I was learning to let go of who I thought I had to be and what I thought I had to do, releasing the cultural demands I had taken on about what a "healthy" person was.

Instead, I began working with my body, listening, and making peace with what it means to be an energetic being who chose a "hard" mode incarnation that requires more self-love and care than many people are asked to learn. I started realizing that choosing to engage with self-love and compassion on the level I am being asked to is actually a divine gift because love is what we are here to learn about and grow into, especially loving ourselves.

Then, one morning, I felt the urge to finish the drawing I had started a few weeks prior. As my eyes alighted on the artwork, I almost fell over in shock. Unknowingly, I had drawn my Higher Self! I was able to see who I was, including my human self, from a fresh perspective with clarity and love in a whole new way. It was like being reborn.

Something deep within me healed as I gazed in wonder at that drawing of my Higher Self. It became a talisman, something to show me on rough days that I am so much more than I can possibly imagine, that I matter, and am definitely NOT my dragons. And on good days, the portrait reminds me that my dreams can come true. It also helps me to remember that my spiritual gifts are a vital part of who I am.

Every time I went through an intense painting or drawing spree, my life and health would shift, sometimes in really good ways and sometimes through "breakdown to breakthrough" situations. Looking back, I can see what was happening as energetic upgrades or needing to learn a lesson—sometimes again—usually about self-worth, being the leader in my own life, and loving and accepting myself.

I also started to realize that even though my flock of chronic illness dragons was growing, this wasn't happening to me but *for* me. That idea is something that often feels dragon-fang sharp and biting when something awful or challenging is happening. However, looking back over how I have grown, those times were often gifts, not because I wanted any more shadow-winged experiences, but because of what I learned about what it means to be truly alive—and free to be me regardless of how many dragons keep me company.

At one point, I was facing a lot of convergent situations that seemed to demand that I give up the art that encouraged me to feel alive and vital—and instead settle into a more "acceptable" life with a "real" job. Despite the spiritual journey to learn how to want to live that I had been on, I started to backslide. Big time. Once again, the dragons were roaring.

At the same time, I kept experiencing visions of past lives where I had set aside what mattered to me to do what was "right". The reason why

I couldn't do what I "should have" was that the diabetes dragon, with a few of her best chronic illness buddies, threw so many temper tantrums that it became clear I had to do a few of the most difficult things a being can be asked to do: have faith in myself and love myself enough to have the courage to trust in myself, my abilities as an artist, a mystic, and an astrologer, and to trust that the path to a normal life had been repeatedly blocked because my soul came here to rise, not to conform, and to learn that you can live a wonderful life—and matter—despite and because of dragons.

For me, my spiritual awakening has been about learning to value, love, and trust myself. It's still unfolding; there is much yet to learn, especially with my dragons in the picture, but now, I can see my light as well as my shadows—so I can soar with wide-spread wings, too.

Kristen Girard is the founder of Radiance and Grit, an art and astrology studio. As an artist, astrologer, and writer, her work is about self-reclamation, resilience, and loving who you are. She specializes in creating Higher Self portraits and astrological portraits to help you see yourself from a fresh perspective with clarity and love. Her husband, Kirby, continually wonders why she needs so many books to read. She loves draft horses, especially her Clydesdale buddy, Big Mac. Cats have brought a lot of light and love into her life, particularly Little Dude while he reigned over the household, and now his heaven-sent inheritor, Maximus Caticus, supervises all of Kristen's creations.

Website: www.radianceandgrit.com

Art: www.radianceandgrit.com/portraits

Youtube: www.youtube.com/@radianceandgrit

Instagram: www.instagram.com/radianceandgrit

31

Stillness in the Storm

By Viviana Arbor
Queen Creek, Arizona, USA

I watched my grandmother sleeping alongside dozens of snoring bodies sprawled out on cots across the floor of the small storm shelter. Leaning back against the wall, I breathed a sigh of relief as I listened to the echoes of slumber, a welcome exchange from the tree-cracking, house-leveling winds of the days prior. We'd been traveling all day and into the wee hours of the night. The storm had downed all the cellphone and electrical towers, leaving us with no form of navigation aside from intuition. This hurricane was the second in just a few short weeks to drown and demolish the lands of my origin.

I allowed my thoughts to unfurl the course of events my mind had yet to assemble. The day before the first storm, my ex-husband stole custody of our son. Before that unimaginable reality could sink in, I was hastily evading a storm that took lives by the thousands. In a few short days, I had lost my son, my job, and my home and witnessed catastrophic failings of leadership, causing widespread death and destruction. The experience was numbing; it left me fragmented, directionless, and hollow.

I decided to journey alone a thousand miles away, into the mountains. Upon arriving, the open earthy views and quiet stillness swept away my sadness. I began to reflect upon why my life had been deconstructed. Had I not built it with tenacity, attention, and care?

As I deepened my questions, more relevant references came into focus. I hadn't chosen a path for growth, nor a path I co-created with Spirit or from my higher awareness. As I evaluated pivotal decisions of my past, I began to see the extent they were based on truths that were not my own. The beliefs, expectations, and limitations of my family, culture, and peers had formed a structure that I had unconsciously imprisoned myself within, and in doing so, surrendered my deepest truths, my heart's desires, and the path that beckoned me to follow.

Having this realization was like being a child who'd wandered into a maze of dead-ends and was suddenly lifted out and given a canvas to finger-paint with authority and unbridled imagination. The emerging image glimpsed me into the life I could be living, a daring and purposeful adventure. I made a vow to myself to honor this insight.

I commemorated this path with a memento, the words "nosce te ipsum" tattooed across my shoulder. I'd long loved the layered symbols within Greek myths. "Temet nosce" is the Greek inscription above the entrance to the cave of the Oracle at Delphi. Those visiting Mother Gaia's temple were urged to "know thyself" before beseeching the prophetess. I chose the Latin translation because it is the language known to ward off corruption. Many years later, I would discover the full translation to be "Know Thyself which is of the Soul."

As I began to rebuild my life, I created from my values, starting with what mattered most. I listened deeply for guidance from Spirit. I gave myself space, removed pressures, investigated my desires, and aligned myself with my heart's deepest yearnings. Instead of analyzing my way through life, I began feeling, sensing, listening, and responding. As I made the shift from discerning primarily from my mind into my heartspace, what I once viewed as life-upheaving disasters became divine blessings. I was finally free to pursue the questions held sacred in my own heart.

I took stock of my missteps and course-corrected, asking for forgiveness. Through one divinely guided choice after another, a new life full of purpose was built for me. I was invited to be on a frontline disaster relief project.

The people surrounding me and the lives I touched constructed a new reality, one that allowed me to be myself and be incredibly valued while making an impact extending much further than I'd imagined. Recalling it fills me with joy even now, twenty years later. When I trace my life backward, I can connect every significant aspect to the choices I made then, guided by Spirit, after being stripped of arrogance and all illusion of control. When my previous life was taken, the one I felt entitled to, there was finally space for the wisdom of my soul to shine through.

The practices I learned then still guide me today. I invite you to use the following exercises on your own journey of spiritual awakening. They allow me to decipher when I am on my path and when I have wandered off course. Each day I earnestly tend my relationship with Spirit, that is where my deepest joy and most profoundly alive experiences of love arise.

Calm Within the Storm

Hurricanes, though chaotic and destructive, have an eye, a calm center of low pressure. When you have been triggered by events, whether positive or negative, practice locating calm within you. You may have to pass through a more intense zone (similar to the eyewall of the storm) in order to find it.

In this exercise, we will be taking note of sensations within the body. This is distinctly different from thoughts or emotions or even sensations on the skin. We will be tracking the internal space of the body. We will practice noticing lightness, heaviness, coolness, warmth, expansion, contraction, movement, and stillness.

Gather pen and paper. Begin by sitting or lying in a comfortable position. Notice every point on your body that is resting against the surface beneath you, whether that be a chair, a bed, or simply the ground. How does it feel internally when you focus on the way your body is being supported? Name aloud the sensations as you notice them.

For example, you might feel warmth, softening, and expansion. Another person may feel lightness, coolness, and tingling. Whatever sensations you find, practice speaking them. Also, name *where* you are feeling that sensation, and if it travels or shifts when you place your attention on it.

As you begin to map your internal landscape, notice which areas of the body feel pleasant, unpleasant, or neutral. There's no need to linger in unpleasant areas—you will simply categorize it and scan over to the next area. Take some time now to move through the entire body.

Next, you will narrow your focus to an area that feels pleasant. In the event that nowhere currently feels pleasant, instead locate neutral. Speak out loud what you sense while focusing on this area of your body. Speaking aloud helps the mind to integrate the intelligence of the body. Give all of your focus to that area, no matter how small it is. It might only be a sliver of your pinky fingernail, but focus on it with as much awareness as you are able.

Now you will write down the sensations your body has in an area you've categorized as pleasant (or neutral, if unable to locate any pleasant areas). Add to the list each time you practice. If you get repeat sensations, just write them down again.

You've now created your unique somatic map of calm within. Revisit this exercise when you wish to feel more centered, collected, or relaxed.

Hearing Spirit

To receive messages from Spirit, I was taught to first shift from thinking into knowing. Peruvian mystics have an ancient wisdom teaching that states, "The mind seeks to learn in reference to what it already knows; true wisdom can only be learned through the heart." Thankfully, researchers are now scientifically validating what shamans and wisdom keepers have known for centuries.

According to the HeartMath Institute, the heart's electrical field is

60 times greater than the brain's, and the heart's magnetic field is more than 100 times greater than the brain's. Although many of us were taught to believe the mind to be superior, the heart actually sends more signals to the brain than the brain sends to the heart.

We will now practice moving from the headspace into the heartspace. Rest comfortably in a seated position. Imagine a light within your forehead, representing your awareness, currently residing within your mental energy space.

Now picture an elevator extending from your mind down into your heart. Guide the light from your forehead area down to your heart at whatever pace feels best for you. You can also use a staircase or playground slide to move from the head to the heart if you prefer. When the light arrives comfortably in your chest, allow it to explore your heartspace and stay there as long as it feels comfortable. If you find discomfort in your heartspace (which is common with grief and betrayal), revisit the previous exercise of finding calm.

While holding the light of your awareness in your heartspace, practice speaking from your heart. Speak aloud to hear the vibration of your words. This will help you to sense if they are conveying the energy of your intent. Start with speaking about how it feels to hold your awareness in your heart and also how it feels to speak from your heart (versus the head or lower energy centers).

Next, we will invite Spirit to speak with us. Because many spiritual beings respect our freedom and personal will by practicing non-interference, they therefore must be invited. Now ask from your heart to connect or speak with a particular being. It is best to start with one you already feel a connection with, whether that be a deity, a spiritual teacher who once walked Earth, spirit guides, or angels. There are many options. Typically, there will be a few that have made contact or attempted to communicate with you before.

Request in earnest that they speak with you. Notice your internal sensations. Typically you will feel a shift when they connect with you.

If it doesn't happen right away, keep notes for the next three days of any dreams, visions, synchronicities, or events that stand out. Often Spirit speaks when we are not expecting it, because it is then that our resistance is lower, allowing us to more easily receive spiritual guidance.

Once we have invited Spirit in, begin asking questions. Ask like you are five years old, with no limit on the amount of questions or the bounds of your curiosity and imagination. If one particular problem is weighing on you, ask about it from as many angles as you possibly can view the situation. This will open you up to the bigger picture, and it will also create more receptivity to guidance from Spirit. Often, people ask from a place of fear, not truly wanting to know the truth, hoping instead for validation. *This is a form of spiritual self-entrapment.* I would instead advise spending more time speaking aloud or writing from your heartspace, to uncover more of what has been hidden there.

Whether you can sense Spirit immediately or not, express how you feel knowing that Spirit is listening and finding a way to reach you. You might feel relief, encouragement, hope, gratitude, or vulnerability. Just speak whatever it is that's true for you. Also let Spirit know how important it is to you that you are able to hear from them. You are not only building a relationship with Spirit, but also the higher consciousness of yourself, and this process is most fruitful when you are as genuine as possible. Pretense has no place in the sacred.

If you are struggling to be present vulnerably or see the truth of a situation, express those feelings to Spirit. Ask for help removing all resistance to receiving support and guidance. Ask to feel the version of yourself that has already integrated these truths into your life. Keep asking questions until the energy shifts. If you persist, it will.

I recommend closing by letting Spirit know when you will reach out again, and practice holding those commitments to Spirit and yourself. Make note of any insights, feelings, and sensations. Throughout your day, continue to practice moving into the heartspace and receiving information via the heart (versus the mind). This will help you develop spiritual understanding and also open your receptivity to messages directly from Spirit.

Trusting Spiritual Guidance

Most of us grow up assimilating the truth of authority figures and our culture whether it resonates with us or not. We are quite vulnerable as children, and it is a temporary survival strategy. As adults, we have often habituated to suppressing our own truth. We will now reverse that process.

Gather pen and paper. Begin by writing your goal or intent. Keep it concise, as you may need to break it down into smaller goals. After each intention, write down your thoughts, feelings, sensations, and messages from Spirit. When you are finished, read each statement aloud and ask, "What is the energetic source of this information? Does it align with my intent?"

Notice the vibrational quality of your words and the sensations in your body. Often, if we are speaking from a truth we hold in our energy field that did not originate from ourselves or our spiritual guidance, speaking it aloud will sound "off". You might also notice contraction in your body, unpleasant sensations, or other signals your body gives when it feels unsafe.

Write down the sensations you notice when speaking your statements and asking the questions. You are decoding how your body signals to you when something is not right for you. When information is in alignment with your truth and your intent, you will feel cohesiveness internally. These sensations will be similar to those you felt when mapping calm.

If you are empathic, I recommend practicing alone behind a closed door. This creates some separation from others' energy. Additionally, if you live with people who project their energy toward you, I would encourage you to practice away from home initially. Once you've flexed this muscle and built up confidence, you can use these processes anywhere.

♡ ♡ ♡

Viviana Arbor is a somatic coach and intuition activator. Prior to her spiritual awakening, she was chronically over-committed, grinding, and strategizing her way through life. She's since had the great blessing of making extraordinary journeys and studying healing traditions from around the world. She loves teaching ancient wisdom practices, building spiritual communities, and researching the technology of energetic transformation. She offers her deepest gratitude to the indigenous healers who shared the beauty and power of their lineages. She is honored to be a spiritual vessel for a waking planet.

Website: www.vivianaarbor.coach

32

The Great Awakening Within is HERE!

By Emily Moon
California, USA

What a legendary time you have chosen to incarnate on Earth! The collective consciousness on our planet is rising at lightning speed as the remembrance of the divine beings we are is awakening on a grand scale!

Perhaps you have been feeling this remembrance for some time or are in the beginning stages of an expansive unfolding within. The rise in consciousness and awakening to our true essence is a divinely timed and orchestrated inner unfolding, unique for each of us. And for my journey, a sudden, unexpected, and fast-paced awakening in 2016 was the divine orchestration!

My Inner Awakening

By age 32, I was married, living in the same beach town in Virginia where I was born and raised, had a good career in the medical device industry, and owned a house. I had followed society's formula to success and happiness, yet I was nowhere close to being happy.

Following college and a series of events including a near-death experience, I struggled with bouts of severe depression and was on and off antidepressant medications for almost a decade. I was far from truly loving myself or knowing who I was—my Soul—my true essence. Something big always felt missing and I knew deep down I was here for something greater, but I didn't know what that meant.

Then summer of 2016 arrived. My life was about to do a 180 and fast!

I empowered myself to get off the antidepressants once and for all which was against my doctor's orders. That first step I took was an initial gateway into reclaiming my power and was a powerful inspired action of self-love. My Soul knew I was ready. Our inspired actions are communication to our Soul that we are listening to the inner "nudges" which allows expanded pathways of communication.

Big questions began to rise within me that I couldn't shake away, igniting a grand awakening to ME.

"Who am I?! What is my purpose?! Why am I here?!" Nothing else mattered to me at this time than coming into these truths.

For days and weeks, I would spend hours in nature by myself asking these questions of my existence—a lot of it late at night on the beach under the stars. It was all very bizarre and unusual behavior for me at that time.

I began hearing messages from deep within. I felt the presence of angels and loved ones with me, and a profound love for our precious Earth unlike anything I had felt before. The Earth began talking to me, kind of like Grandmother Willow Tree from the movie *Pocahontas*. Crystals began sharing messages with me through showing me images.

I had no idea what was happening to me, but it was magical, and I felt alive!

Being an empath my entire life, I knew what it felt like to feel things deeply, and I began to understand that feeling energy was one of my superpowers! Instead of trying to not feel too much, I was now using it to my advantage to guide me. This was all part of communication from my Soul, helping me to activate more parts of myself that I had denied before.

When we can appreciate parts of ourselves that we may have "run" or "hidden" from before, it allows a coming home to Self and a greater love within that is able to blossom.

My depression had fully healed and a higher power was coming through me as the answers to my big questions were pouring in.

I was connecting with my Higher Self/my Soul and falling madly in love with me for the first time since I was a child. From where I had been operating in my life for so long before, I would've thought this to be an impossible dream—but it was now my dream being realized!

I began journaling, which was like having a friend beside me who understood with a loving heart everything I was going through. Journaling is truly one of the greatest support tools on our journey and something I encourage clients and others to embrace!

Through my expanded level of consciousness, I questioned everything—from religion to society systems, relationships, my marriage, inner programs, and ways of operating in all areas of my life...literally shattering illusions of ways of living and being that I once knew to be true and safe. My inner reality was shifting rapidly; I was stepping into my power like never before, and I felt liberated. Yet at the same time, I still didn't know what was happening!

At this point, I was summoning someone to talk to. Through magical synchronicities, I was led to a holistic practitioner named Pamela, who I soon discovered was an intuitive—an angel sent to support me!

Within the first few minutes of talking, she explained that I was going through a spiritual awakening. I started to cry. There was finally an explanation for what I was experiencing!

I left her office still in tears that day with a deeper remembrance. This new me all made sense, but nothing in my life I had lived for so long made sense anymore. I saw the illusion for what it was: a dimensional reality I had chosen to live in for so long was now making way for an entirely new one to emerge within.

Intuitive information, including hearing messages, seeing visions, and downloading higher wisdom, was coming in frequently, and I had been guided to take a month off from work in December and go on a solo trip to Peru. This trip would expand my consciousness in ways I didn't know were possible—an entire chapter on its own!

From the moment I landed in Peru, I felt like I was receiving and unlocking dormant codes deep within my being—my heart and intuition were expanding at a quickening rate. Sometimes, we are called to certain places, not knowing why until we are physically there to receive the codes, the divinely led connections, and for a new you to emerge.

The human language became limiting for describing these profound experiences I was having at this time in my life, so I began drawing. I discovered that expressing myself freely without words was incredibly liberating!

Shortly after I returned home from Peru, my husband and I had one of the most raw and heartfelt conversations we'd ever had. I never would have initiated this conversation before, but I was now living from a place of empowered authenticity and I was ready. There were major aspects of our relationship that were not in alignment and hadn't been for quite some time. We wanted very different things in life, and we were going in two different directions. We cried as we both loved and respected each other so much, but we knew it was time. I felt a deep liberation, which I hadn't expected to feel. And it was important for me to realize that relationships don't have to end in such dramatic, painful ways.

After this, things sped up even faster. I felt a strong calling to move to Peru. I hired and trained a support team for my medical device business in Virginia so I could run it remotely. I sold the condo I had bought in my 20s and prepared to move to Peru! I felt freer than ever before!

Many people thought I had lost my mind, which was an accurate reflection! This time on the journey required even greater love for myself, incredible courage in listening to inner guidance, and confidence in my inner knowing. Challenging conversations were coming up with family, friends, colleagues, and my soon-to-be former husband. I didn't let the opinions of others sway me from living my truth. My great LOVE within was ever-present. And I was eternally grateful for Pamela, who was an incredible support as so much of this was new territory for me. I can't emphasize enough how important support is on our journeys, whether it be a loving friend, community, teacher, guide, your journal!

By 2017, I had moved to Cusco, Peru, and was living in a completely different dimensional reality—a total REBIRTH had occurred during my awakening! A love and confidence in myself I didn't know could exist radiated out from my heart! I was living in a way I never thought possible—where my behaviors, choices, and way of living were reflective of this great love within, empowerment, and pure magic.

This was what I came here for. And it was all just the beginning...

Love is the Master KEY to it all!

The greatest gift I learned from my awakening is that loving oneself is the master key to everything! This is foundational on the journey and leads to so much magic effortlessly unfolding for us. It's not just the greatest gift to you but also to humanity because when we truly love ourselves, appreciate who we are, and rise above former versions of self, we are embodying higher vibrational states of consciousness, and THIS is what contributes to raising the vibration on our planet!

Insights to Support Your Own Awakening

What if I had listened to those around me who didn't support my evolution? What if I never listened to my heart guiding me forward? Through behaviors, actions, and ways of living, we are either supporting the former self we have outgrown (old paradigm), or we are supporting the NEW self (new paradigm). When you consciously choose to live life aligned with the NEW you, the more the up-leveled dimensional reality will be part of your human experience!

I hope that by offering some insights below, you will feel even more support and encouragement on your own journey of inner awakening into the new you:

- Great transformation, healing, and shifts will take place throughout your awakening. Remember to be gentle with yourself. Your Soul is never rushing you or putting pressure on you—that is the mind, my friend. If you feel overwhelmed, tune into the things you know will help you come back to more peace and joy. Maybe this is spending an afternoon in nature by yourself, drawing, laughing with a friend, or reaching out to someone who can support you.

- Loving SUPPORT is huge! Even if it's just one person. For some time, Pamela was the only person who I could really talk to and I am eternally grateful!

- During stages of the ascension process, clearings and upgrades will be experienced, and prioritizing the relationship with your body and listening to its needs will help tremendously! Maybe the foods you eat will change, maybe you drink more water, rest more, spend more time out in nature, etc.

- Your Soul knows what experiences are most beneficial and expansive to serve you for greater realization and up-leveling of your consciousness. This can sometimes feel like challenging situations and circumstances. But try to honor them and also not judge them as much as you can—it's all happening FOR you.

- We all have our own soul journeys to experience, so try not to get caught up in wanting others to be where you are. They are exactly where they are meant to be in the divine unfolding

THE GREAT AWAKENING WITHIN IS HERE!

just as you are. Perhaps you're no longer sharing as much time and energy with those you don't feel good around, but you are honoring their path and letting go of needing to change or "fight" their soul's journey.

- Create a nourishing morning or nightly ritual.

- Journaling is one of the greatest supportive tools! Or perhaps it resonates to record voice notes or draw what you are experiencing to support and inspire you!

- Become more aware of distractions so you can lessen outside "noise" and stay focused on YOUR beautiful journey! For example, not showing interest in gossip conversations or lessening time on social media.

- Express yourself to help move the energy—sing, dance, move!

- Through listening to your inner guidance and taking inspired action, more confidence and trust will rise within.

- Keep listening to your heart no matter what others may say! Stay true to you, your inner voice, and be committed to magnificent YOU!

Soul Evolutionary Journey

It's truly all a continuous soul evolutionary journey into higher states of consciousness and dimensional realities. Everything I experienced from my awakening has impacted where I am today, including awakening to my Soul gifts and my service of "work."

By choosing to live life connected with my Higher Self, I bridge my

Heaven onto Earth and contribute greatly to the collective consciousness through my Soul embodied vibration. And this consciously chosen space to live from has created a life of magic, fun, and a freedom I didn't know could exist in the human experience!

From my own journey, I know what is possible. And I find great fulfillment in supporting and guiding others on their own path while also helping others connect with their Higher Self to experience life with more clarity, ease, and FREEDOM! And I hold this vision for all!

YOU/WE are the Great Awakening!

To have incarnated at this time during the greatest shift in human consciousness—the Great Awakening—is beyond a celebration! And all of our own inner awakenings are contributing in inconceivable ways to this shift.

We all have our divine Soul-chosen timing for our own awakening and unfolding. Each is unique yet equal to one another as we open to the truth and realization of who we are and it's huge!

The awakening to your Soul on Earth, to your inner divinity in physical form is just the beginning as the journey continuously unfolds and you come into even deeper remembrance of YOU.

And I know it isn't always easy and oh, the courage it requires! I see you and honor you deeply. We are all on this grand adventure together, holding hands, inspiring, and lifting one another up as we RISE on our own journeys and together as ONE!

Emily is a New Earth visionary, intuitive, channel, and Higher Self embodiment guide.

She weaves intuitive guidance, channeled messages, light language, and sound energy, among other modalities, into her offerings to help support others on their spiritual journey and empower a deepening connection with their Higher Self and their own inner channel!

She's passionate about helping others to move beyond "outgrown" versions of self and step more fully into their power, connect more sustainably with their Higher Self, and experience life with more trust, ease, playfulness, and ultimately more FREEDOM! She offers 1:1 sessions as well as in-person/online events, workshops, and retreats.

Website: www.higherdimensionswithin.com

Sessions: www.higherdimensionswithin.com/sessions

Newsletter: www.higherdimensionswithin.com/newsletter

Instagram: www.instagram.com/higherdimensionswithin

33

Ready for Takeoff: A Soul's Journey to New Heights

By Gina Hansen
Kaneʻohe, Hawaiʻi, USA

One moment, my life was gliding effortlessly through a sky of dreams, and the next, it came crashing down into an unrecognizable wreckage. What followed was a journey I never expected but one that changed me forever.

I was living the dream—married, healthy, and jet-setting weekly as an international flight attendant. The glamour, excitement, and freedom all felt invincible.

But life had other plans.

Within six months' time, my whole world unraveled.

I was diagnosed with cancer, separated from my husband, and walked away from my 28-year career.

Brace for Impact: Finding Peace in Being Grounded

Have you ever felt completely shocked, devastated, and paralyzed with fear?

It had taken years to build the courage to tell my husband I wanted a divorce. When I finally did, I felt a huge weight lift. I could breathe again.

But just four days later, everything screeched to a halt.

I sat in stunned silence as the doctor said, "You have papillary thyroid cancer. We'll send you to a surgeon to cut it out, and you'll be on medication for the rest of your life."

Panic, despair, and anger raged inside of me.

In that moment, it hit me—this wasn't just about the offensive, uncaring way the doctor announced my diagnosis. It was about *handing over my body to a system focused solely on the illness,* ignoring my humanity, my strength, and my potential to not just survive but to truly thrive.

Overwhelmed, I fled to Mexico in search of holistic treatments.

In Mexico, I discovered integrative therapies and bioresonance frequency technology. Each night, I attended lectures that expanded my understanding, and I immersed myself in a vast library of books. As I delved into topics like energy medicine and heart coherence, my mind opened to new possibilities and profound insights.

Stepping away from everything I knew, I discovered an amazing holistic world that was previously unknown to me.

After three weeks, I returned home—the tumors were shrinking.

Despite progress, my life felt hollow.

Separated from my husband, my teenage son alternated between homes, leaving me alone in a quiet house when he wasn't there. The silence was unbearable, and loneliness seeped into every corner. I cried almost daily.

Then came another blow: the pandemic's financial impact led my airline to offer early retirement incentives. My fun, fast-paced life came to an abrupt end.

I didn't recognize myself.

Depressed, lying on the couch, I noticed a shift: I craved solitude, peace, and introspection. Feeling stuck and frightened in the still, shadowy depths of a cocoon, I felt the loss of my wings and the freedom to fly.

Rising to the Light Within

My life was in chaos, and I needed help rediscovering who I was. Thankfully, an online coaching program threw me a lifeline, helping me get off the couch and back into life.

Bizarre things started to happen.

I felt light touches on my legs like whispers of energy brushing past. My friend, Hawaiian healer Kahu Láhela, explained these were spirits drawn to my light—a moment that revealed my clairsentience, the ability to feel energy.

In the group coaching program, participants could join a waitlist to work with a Shaman. Some even claimed he visited them in their dreams.

Curious, one evening, as I lay in bed, I invited him to visit me. Suddenly, I felt a ball of energy rise from the bed, travel up my spine, and reach my brain, where his laughing face appeared—then slowly faded away.

WTF? Did that really just happen? Freaky!

Over a year later, while texting the Shaman about our upcoming trip to the Mayan ruins of Chichen Itza, Mexico, his advice resonated deeply: spend time in solitude and reflection.

I couldn't have imagined how transformative this journey would become. In a quiet moment, an iguana appeared, its presence stirring something profound within me. As I connected with its soul, healing tears streamed down my face, opening my heart in a way I'd never experienced before. The encounter left me forever changed.

During my spiritual awakening, I was presented with profound lessons.

One Sunday morning at the beach, I spotted a struggling seabird crashing into the rocks. Without hesitation, I waded into the water, rescued the exhausted creature, and cradled him in my sarong.

Holding him close to my heart, I gently ran my hand along his Governing Meridian—a technique I had just begun learning in my energy healing training. To my amazement, within minutes, his strength returned. He climbed onto my shoulder, paused briefly, and then flew back to the ocean.

Exhaustion swept over me as I realized I had absorbed the bird's trapped emotions—grief, despair, abandonment, and depression. After clearing them from my body, I felt restored.

In that moment, I witnessed the miraculous power of Heart energy—pure love and compassion—and awakened to the truth: we are all interconnected beings of light, capable of deep healing through the energy we carry.

As my consciousness evolved, I began to trust the unspoken truths my heart revealed. One night, under the full moon's light, I woke with a knowing: my husband had been unfaithful. It wasn't a suspicion—I had a strong feeling. Grief, betrayal, and anger overwhelmed me, and I couldn't go back to sleep.

He admitted it when I confronted him. At that moment, I chose forgiveness—not for him, but for me. I released him and set us both free, finding peace.

My intuition and claircognizance (clear knowing), now fully awake, began guiding me toward life's wonders.

On my morning walk, I noticed a Mynah bird standing motionless in the road—oddly still as I passed. I kept walking, but after some distance, an unexplainable urge made me stop in the middle of the crosswalk and turn back.

Carefully stepping into the street, I shielded the bird from traffic and gently scooped it up. To my surprise, the wild bird stayed calm in my hands. Finding no visible injuries, I placed it on a nearby wall, safe from harm. Walking away, I felt a deep sense of connection and purpose, my heart full from the simple act of helping.

One evening in Hawaii, I wandered to a blooming yellow ginger plant after picking up the mail. As I leaned in to smell the sweet flowers, a tiny creature with a long, needle-like beak startled me—it hovered mid-air, staring right at me. I jumped back in fear. Frightened yet curious, I watched as it scanned me, darting high and low, sizing me up.

Hummingbirds don't exist in Hawaii, so I was mystified. Later, I learned it was a hummingbird moth, a creature I'd never seen before. The encounter felt magical, leaving me in awe of discovering a creature I had never seen in my entire life—a reminder of how much wonder still exists in the world around me.

One of my most cherished memories from my spiritual awakening was the moment of pure bliss I experienced waking up in a dream.

In the dream, a radiant being of light—an exquisite woman with long golden hair—placed her hands gently on my heart and forehead. My gaze was fixed on her hand over my heart when she softly guided my eyes upward to meet hers. Her face glowed so brilliantly that she appeared angelic.

Whoa! I felt like I was in Heaven when I awoke, feeling so much peace and joy.

Breaking Through the Clouds

Slowly, what had fallen apart began to come together in ways I could never have imagined.

Serendipitously, an email led me to *The Emotion Code*, a book by Dr. Bradley Nelson. It explained why my marriage felt so disconnected: we had a Heart Wall between us—layers of trapped emotions blocking love. Determined to heal, I worked with a certified practitioner to clear my Life Heart Wall. Each session lightened my soul.

Unemployed, I felt called to get my certification and help others release emotional burdens. Equipped with an amazing tool, I used *The*

Emotion Code to heal my relationship with my ex-husband. He used to trigger me just by saying my name, but as I released the trapped emotions tied to our past, I noticed an amazing shift. We are now able to speak respectfully and co-parent with ease—a transformation I never thought possible. During the challenging times of COVID, I also turned to energy healing to support my son as he transitioned to college. It not only helped him navigate the anxiety and uncertainty of those times but also allowed him to heal from the emotional impact of our divorce. Witnessing these changes reaffirmed my purpose and the power of this work.

In the past, I made decisions based on logic, but now I follow my heart—and it feels good.

Emerging from the darkness of despair, I am filled with gratitude for the unusual and timely experiences (I wish I could share more amazing stories!) that have propelled me forward to this beautiful soul I am becoming.

After leaving the airline four years ago, I thought my life would never be as exciting. Now, as an Energy Intuitive and Coach, I'm still able to travel and work from anywhere. The best part? Witnessing the incredible transformations my clients experience.

Ascending to Higher Frequencies: My Roadmap to Spiritual Awakening

Let's stick with the aviation theme—because, honestly, life is a lot like flying. It's exhilarating, unpredictable, and occasionally leaves you clutching the armrest. But here's the secret: even turbulence can lead to smoother skies if you learn how to navigate it.

To help you on your spiritual journey, I've created a flight plan called the 3 C's—Control, Communication, and Conditions. Think of it as your trusty in-flight manual for ascending to higher frequencies.

1. Control: Maintaining Stability

Picture yourself in the pilot's seat, hands steady on the controls. Stability comes when you're grounded in self-awareness, calm in the chaos, and deliberate in your actions. Sometimes, it's not about knowing the whole flight plan—it's about quieting the noise in your head and letting your inner compass guide you. I've been through some storms, too. Letting go of my 30-year marriage felt like I was spiraling mid-flight. But releasing that weight was the exact act that allowed me to regain control. Letting go—whether it's people, beliefs, or emotional baggage—might feel like free-falling, but it's really making room for your wings to spread. Think of trapped emotions and outdated beliefs as extra luggage. When you drop that baggage, you ascend to a lighter, freer version of yourself. A high vibration isn't just transformative—it's magnetic. You'll attract health, joy, and the life you've been waiting for. Friend, you cannot fly if your wings are heavy.

2. Communication: Collaborating with Your Team

Flying isn't a solo act; you've got a whole crew on this journey! Your inner team is always ready to guide you—you just have to learn how to listen. Here's your roster:

- **Your Intuition**: Your loyal co-pilot, giving you nudges when it's time to change course.
- **Your Higher Self**: The air traffic controller, with a bird's-eye view of your soul's path.
- **Your Inner Child**: The curious passenger, reminding you to laugh, wonder, and heal old wounds.
- **Your Spirit Guides or Ancestors**: The ground crew, offering quiet wisdom and keeping you safe.
- **Your Conscious Mind**: The navigator, plotting goals and keeping you aligned.

Learning to trust and communicate with your inner team makes you more resilient and helps you rise above life's challenges. They're always on call—so don't be afraid to check in with them!

I didn't realize I was clairsentient or claircognizant until I slowed down and started paying attention to my body. As a flight attendant, I was always on the go, constantly surrounded by people and chaos. It wasn't until I allowed myself moments of solitude in nature that I began to reconnect with my soul essence. Those quiet moments helped me tune in to my inner knowing and rediscover the wisdom I had been carrying all along.

3. Conditions Changing: Adapting to the Weather

No flight is turbulence-free, and the same goes for spiritual growth. Awakening can feel like flying through dense fog—confusing and disorienting. But even the clouds serve a purpose. They teach us to rely on our instruments—our faith, intuition, and inner team—when the path ahead isn't clear. When life throws unexpected storms your way, remember: love and trust are the wind beneath your wings. Surrendering to uncertainty isn't easy (I'll be the first to admit that), but it's where the magic happens. Here's what I've learned: Everything—yes, everything— is working out for your highest good. It may not feel like it at the moment, but trust me, the universe knows how to guide you.

Final Flight Insight:

Life's journey isn't just about reaching a destination; it's about evolving into the truest version of yourself. So, buckle up, my friend. This flight is about transformation, freedom, and endless possibilities. Take a deep breath, spread your wings, and get ready to soar.

Remember: The sky isn't just the limit—it's your infinite runway.

Wishing you blue skies and smooth landings. Let's fly high together!

♡ ♡ ♡

Gina Hansen, a globally recognized Energy Intuitive and Emotional Frequency Specialist, empowers clients to release emotional baggage, rebuild connections, and thrive in every aspect of their relationships. Drawing from certifications in NLP and the Emotion, Body, and Belief Code modalities, Gina blends conscious coaching, energy healing, and bioresonance technology to uncover and release the root causes of stress and suffering.

Born and raised in Hawai'i, Gina finds deep inspiration in the spirit of 'ohana (family) and her island roots. Her journey of personal growth and healing fuels her passion to guide others toward living more harmonious, heart-centered lives. Gina also leads courses on vibrational frequency, helping individuals unlock their potential to elevate their consciousness and create transformative changes in well-being.

With a vision to inspire meaningful change, Gina offers private sessions, group programs, and retreats designed to foster empowerment and emotional freedom. Her mission is simple yet meaningful: to raise the vibration of the planet, one soul at a time, by helping others heal, align with their authentic selves, and cultivate a life of love, balance, and peace.

Website: www.reinventmidlife.com

Instagram: www.instagram.com/reinventmidlife

Facebook: www.facebook.com/GinaHansen808

Youtube: www.youtube.com/@GinaHansen

Thank You

We hope you have enjoyed this compilation of spiritual awakening stories from around the world! Now it's time to spread *your* light far and wide.

Please take a quick moment to rate and review our book on Amazon, Goodreads, or wherever you purchased the book to help us spread our movement to more people!

Share the book with your friends, and when you do, be sure to sit down with a cup of tea and share about your own awakening experiences.

If you haven't already, also be sure to reach out to the authors of your favorite chapters to show them some love and share what you resonated with most from their stories.

Open more conversations on the subject of spiritual awakenings to both share and receive, so that we can normalize a phenomenon that is so widespread and unstoppable that no one else will ever have to feel weird or crazy when, actually, we are evolved and spiritually mature.

Thank you for spending your precious time with us! ♡

For more books like this, visit www.divineflow.co

Soul Rising
SUMMIT

Join the authors of this book for a free online virtual summit designed to celebrate you, our dear reader, as you move through and navigate your spiritual awakening.

Because no one should have to feel alone when you have found an entire spiritual community from a book!

Receive access to talks, presentations, and spiritual practices from our authors, exclusively for you as our reader, by signing up at
www.divineflow.co/soulrisingsummit

Publish your Book
with Divine Flow

We publish beautifully designed books written
by spiritual entrepreneurs who are raising the
vibration of the planet.